YOUR Health

Consulting Authors

Charlie Gibbons, Ed.D.
Associate Professor
Alabama State University
Health, Physical Education
  and Dance Department
Montgomery, Alabama; and
School Age Coordinator
Maxwell Air Force Base, Alabama

Jan Marie Ozias, Ph.D., R.N.
Director, Texas Diabetes Council; and
Consultant, School Health Programs
Austin, Texas

Carl Anthony Stockton, Ph.D.
Professor of Health Education and
  Department Chair
Department of Health, Physical
  Education and Recreation
The University of North Carolina
  at Wilmington
Wilmington, North Carolina

Orlando • Austin • Chicago • New York • Toronto • London • San Diego

Visit *The Learning Site!*
www.harcourtschool.com

Copyright © 2003 by Harcourt, Inc.

All rights reserved. No part of this publication may be reproduced or transmitted in any form or by any means, electronic or mechanical, including photocopy, recording, or any information storage and retrieval system, without permission in writing from the publisher.

Requests for permission to make copies of any part of the work should be addressed to School Permissions and Copyrights, Harcourt, Inc., 6277 Sea Harbor Drive, Orlando, Florida 32887-6777. Fax: 407-345-2418.

HARCOURT and the Harcourt Logo are trademarks of Harcourt, Inc., registered in the United States of America and/or other jurisdictions.

Printed in the United States of America

For permission to reprint copyrighted material, grateful acknowledgment is made to the following sources:

Advocacy Press: "Nell & Jack Horner" from *Father Gander Nursery Rhymes: The Equal Rhymes Amendment* by Father Gander. Text copyright © 1985 by Dr. Douglas W. Larche.

The Giles Anderson Literary Agency, on behalf of Maxine Kumin: "Sneeze" by Maxine W. Kumin. Text copyright © 1962 by Maxine W. Kumin. Originally appeared in *No One Writes a Letter to the Snail*, published by Putnam.

Bantam Books, a division of Bantam Doubleday Dell Publishing Group, Inc.: "Best Friends" from *The Other Side of the Door* by Jeff Moss. Text copyright © 1991 by Jeff Moss. "Jellybeans Up Your Nose" from *The Butterfly Jar* by Jeff Moss. Text copyright © 1989 by Jeff Moss.

Boy Scouts of America: "One Finger, One Thumb" from *Boy Scout Songbook*. Lyrics and music © 1970 by Boy Scouts of America.

Curtis Brown, Ltd.: "This Tooth" by Lee Bennett Hopkins. Text copyright © 1970 by Lee Bennett Hopkins. Originally published in *Me!* "Rainy Day" from *All On a Summer's Day* by William Wise. Text copyright © 1971 by William Wise. Published by Pantheon Books.

HarperCollins Publishers: "Momma Drives" from *Greens* by Arnold Adoff. Text copyright © 1988 by Arnold Adoff. Music from "The Mulberry Bush" in *Singing Bee!* by Jane Hart. Music copyright © 1982 by Jane Hart. "I Did a Nutty Somersault" from *A Pizza the Size of the Sun* by Jack Prelutsky. Text copyright © 1994, 1996 by Jack Prelutsky. "Oh my goodness, oh my dear" from *Father Fox's Pennyrhymes* by Clyde Watson. Text copyright © 1971 by Clyde Watson.

Florence Parry Heide: Lyrics by Florence Parry Heide from "Wheels" in *Songs to Sing About Things You Think About*. Lyrics © 1971 by Florence Parry Heide.

Irene Keller: *Benjamin Rabbit and Stranger Danger* by Dick Keller. Text copyright © 1985 by Irene Keller.

Margaret K. McElderry Books, an imprint of Simon & Schuster Children's Publishing Division: "Ruth Luce and Bruce Booth" from *Snowman Sniffles & Other Verse* by N. M. Bodecker. Text copyright © 1983 by N. M. Bodecker.

McIntosh and Otis, Inc.: "Rhinos Purple, Hippos Green" from *Breakfast, Books & Dreams* by Michael Patrick Hearn. Text copyright © 1981 by Michael Patrick Hearn. Published by Frederick Warne and Company, Inc.

Esther Nelson: "Head and Shoulders, Knees and Toes" in *Musical Games for Children of All Ages* by Esther Nelson. Lyrics and music © 1976 by Sterling Publishing Co., Inc.

Marian Reiner, on behalf of Aileen Fisher: "Good Night" and "New Neighbors" from *In One Door and Out the Other* by Aileen Fisher. Text copyright © 1969 by Aileen Fisher; text copyright renewed © 1997 by Aileen Fisher. Published by Thomas Y. Crowell Company.

Scholastic Inc.: "Exercises" by Bette Killion from *Poetry Place Anthology*. Text copyright © 1983 by Edgell Communications, Inc. Published by Instructor Books, an imprint of Scholastic Professional Books, a division of Scholastic Inc.

Michael Seeger: "Clap Your Hands" from *American Folk Songs for Children* by Ruth Crawford Seeger. Lyrics and music © 1948 by Ruth Crawford Seeger.

William Van Clief, Trustee: Music by Sylvia Worth Van Clief from "Wheels" in *Songs to Sing About Things You Think About*. Music © 1971 by Sylvia Worth Van Clief.

ISBN 0-15-334306-0

1 2 3 4 5 6 7 8 9 10 073 10 09 08 07 06 05 04 03 02

Teacher Edition Contents

About This Program

Program Components 3
Consulting Authors 4
Dear Educator 5
Reviewers/Field Test Teachers 6
Consulting Health Specialists 7
National Health Education Standards 8
Curriculum Integration and Assessment 9

The Chapters

Chapter 1 All About Me 10
   Lesson 1 I Am Special 16
   Lesson 2 I Have Feelings 18
   Lesson 3 Changing My Feelings 20
   Lesson 4 Helping Out 22
   Lesson 5 Getting Along 24

Chapter 2 Growing and Learning 26
   Lesson 1 I'm Growing 32
   Lesson 2 I'm Growing on the Inside 34
   Lesson 3 My Senses 36
   Lesson 4 My Senses Keep Me Safe 38
   Lesson 5 I'm Responsible 40

Chapter 3 Caring for My Teeth 42
   Lesson 1 My Teeth 48
   Lesson 2 Cleaning My Teeth 50
   Lesson 3 Keeping My Teeth Safe 52

Chapter 4 Staying Fit and Healthy 54
   Lesson 1 I Take Care of My Skin 60
   Lesson 2 Sit Tall 62
   Lesson 3 I Exercise Safely 64
   Lesson 4 Deal With Stress 66
   Lesson 5 Time for Bed 68

Chapter 5 Food for Health 70
   Lesson 1 Food Gives Me Energy 76
   Lesson 2 The Food Guide Pyramid 78
   Lesson 3 Choose Healthful Snacks 80
   Lesson 4 Food Safety Hints 82

Chapter 6 Staying Well 84
   Lesson 1 I'm Ill 90
   Lesson 2 Wash Away Germs 92
   Lesson 3 Staying Well 94

Chapter 7 Medicines Help—Drugs Hurt 96
   Lesson 1 What are Medicines? 102
   Lesson 2 Take Medicines Safely 104
   Lesson 3 Say NO to Drugs 106
   Lesson 4 Tobacco Harms the Body 108

Chapter 8 Keeping Safe 110
   Lesson 1 Stop, Look, and Listen 116
   Lesson 2 Staying Safe 118
   Lesson 3 Stay Away from Poisons 120
   Lesson 4 Know How Fires Start 122
   Lesson 5 Stop, Drop, and Roll 124
   Lesson 6 Water Safety 126
   Lesson 7 Dangerous Things 128
   Lesson 8 Car and Bus Safety 130

Chapter 9 A Healthy Community 132
   Lesson 1 Community Workers 138
   Lesson 2 Regular Checkups 140
   Lesson 3 Reuse It! 142

Glossary 144
Index 151

Read-Aloud Anthology RA-1

Teacher Reference Section TR-1

Program Components

Your Health provides components that meet a variety of instructional needs.

For Kindergarten
- colorful Teaching Charts in poster format
- comprehensive Teacher's Edition
- Activity Book
- Teaching Resources book (includes School-Home Connection letters, Take-Home Booklets, Assessment Options, and Patterns)
- Teaching Transparencies with Accompanying Copying Masters

For Grades 1 and 2
- Pupil's Editions
- comprehensive Teacher's Edition
- colorful Big Book
- Activity Book
- Assessment Guide
- Teaching Resources book (includes School-Home Connection letters, Take-Home Booklets and reproducible copies of the student Health Handbook)
- Teaching Transparencies with Accompanying Copying Masters

For Grades 3 through 6
- Pupil's Editions
- comprehensive Teacher's Edition
- Activity Book
- Assessment Guide
- Teaching Resources book (includes School-Home Connection letters, Computer Graphing Activities, and reproducible copies of the student Health Handbook)
- Teaching Transparencies with Accompanying Copying Masters
- Health Video Series
- Growth, Development, and Reproduction (an optional resource)

Technology
Visit Harcourt's growing Learning Site for a variety of teacher resources and student activities, including:
- The Health Webliography for Teachers (carefully chosen links to health background and teaching resources)
- Student Games and Activities
- Newsbreaks

www.harcourtschool.com

CONSULTING AUTHORS

Charlie Gibbons

Charlie Gibbons, Ed.D., has over 25 years of university teaching experience and is presently teaching at Alabama State University in the Department of Health, Physical Education and Dance in Montgomery, Alabama. He is also Coordinator of the Maxwell Air Force Base School Age Program. Dr. Gibbons is a past president of the Alabama State Association of Health, Physical Education, Recreation and Dance and a past vice president of the Southern District American Alliance of Health, Physical Education, Recreation and Dance (AAHPERD). He is presently serving on both state and district committees. He has served on numerous public service committees providing inservice workshops and presentations on various areas of school health curricula including such topics as HIV/AIDS prevention and physical fitness for children.

Dr. Gibbons has been the recipient of both the Alabama State Association and Southern District AAHPERD Honor (1990 & 1998) and Ethnic Minority Awards (1999 & 2001).

Jan Marie Ozias

Jan Ozias, Ph.D., R.N., has extensive experience in school health services and health education from a nursing perspective. She worked as Nursing Supervisor and Administrator of Health Services in the Austin Independent School District, Austin, Texas. Dr. Ozias holds adjunct faculty appointments in both the School of Nursing and the College of Education at the University of Texas at Austin from which she also earned an M.A. in Special Education and a Ph.D. in Health Education.

Dr. Ozias has worked as Director of Medical Underwriting, Texas Healthy Kids Corporation and presently serves as Director, Texas Diabetes Council/Program at the Texas Department of Health. She is co-chief editor of School Health Alert. She writes and presents on child health for school nurses and educators. Her other activities include leadership positions in the American School Health Association, such as the Task Force on Injury Prevention and the U.S. Pharmacopoeia's ad hoc Panel on Children and Medicine (education).

Carl Anthony Stockton

Carl Anthony Stockton, Ph.D., is department Chair and Professor of Health Education in the Department of Health, Physical Education and Recreation at the University of North Carolina in Wilmington. Throughout his professional career, Dr. Stockton has taught health education classes focusing on a wide variety of health topics. His curricula have included such diverse health topics as health programs in the elementary schools, nutrition, national and international health, accident and safety education, public health administration, and the use of technology in health promotion.

Dr. Stockton is a recipient of the College Health Professional of the Year Award by the Virginia Alliance of AAHPERD. In addition, Dr. Stockton has received the 1997 Outstanding Teaching Award and the 1999 Outstanding Service Award from Radford University. In 2001 Dr. Stockton was inducted into the American Association for Health Education's (AAHE) Fellows Honorary organization. The Fellows award is given for long-term dedication to the profession of health education. Dr. Stockton is currently a director for the national board of the American Association for Health Education.

Dear Educator,

Your Health is a comprehensive program designed to provide your students with the knowledge, life skills, consumer skills, and thinking skills they need in order to achieve good health.

Knowledge includes current information, facts, and concepts in the following content areas:

- human body systems
- emotional, intellectual, and social health
- family life, growth, and development
- personal health and physical fitness
- nutrition
- disease prevention and control
- drug use prevention
- injury prevention
- community and environmental health

Life Skills are health-enhancing behaviors that help children reduce risks to their health. ***Your Health*** provides opportunities for children to learn and practice life skills through lessons that use real-life situations. These important skills are:

- make decisions
- manage stress
- set goals
- resolve conflicts
- communicate
- refuse risky behaviors

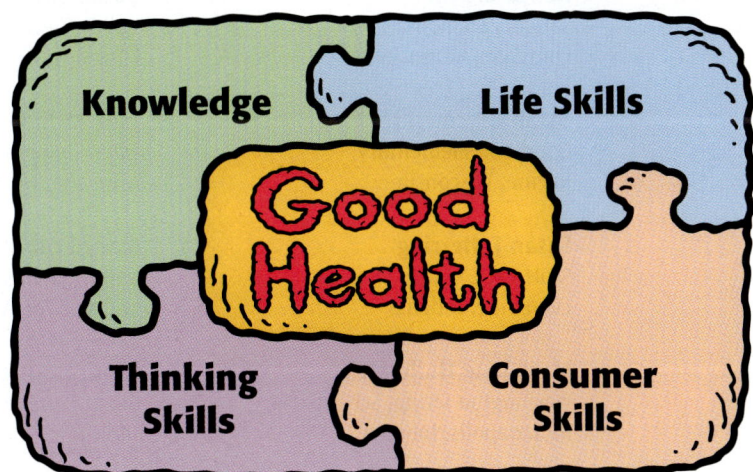

Thinking Skills connect to all subject areas in the school curriculum. They are essential for enabling children to use knowledge and life skills appropriately. Thinking skills include:

- critical thinking
- using facts
- problem solving

Consumer Skills are important for helping children evaluate the enormous amount of information that is transmitted to them via the media. These skills include:

- analyze advertisements and media messages
- make buying decisions
- access valid health information

We are confident that ***Your Health*** provides you with the tools you need to motivate your students to take an active role in maintaining and improving their health.

Sincerely,
The Authors

SENIOR EDITORIAL ADVISORS

Kathleen Middleton, MS, CHES
Health Education Consultant
Santa Cruz, California

Larry K. Olsen, Dr. P.H., CHES
Professor and Chair, Department of Health Science
Towson University
Towson, Maryland

CHILDREN'S LITERATURE CONSULTANTS

Anthony L. Manna, Ph.D.
College of Education
Kent State University
Kent, Ohio

Janet S. Hill, M.A.
College of Education
Kent State University
Kent, Ohio

Brenda Dales, Ph.D.
Department of Teacher Education
Miami University
Oxford, Ohio

REVIEWERS AND FIELD TEST TEACHERS

Carol P. Anderson
Mandarin Oaks Elementary
Jacksonville, Florida

Kenya Griffin
Sanders Elementary
Louisville, Kentucky

Susan Lomanto
Valley View Elementary
Longview, Texas

Linda Ashby
A.D. Harvey Elementary
Kingsville, Texas

Sarah Grycowski
Goodland Elementary
Racine, Wisconsin

Jane Milner
Estes Elementary
Asheville, North Carolina

Kristen Bullis
Centennial Elementary
Fargo, North Dakota

Susan J. Herring
Scott EVSC
Evansville, Indiana

Mary Lynn Powell
Milton Elementary
Milton, West Virginia

Ada Cuadrado
PS 112 Elementary
New York, New York

Mary Jane Hollcraft
Washington Irving, School #14
Indianapolis, Indiana

Sandra Gutierrez
Garza-Pena Primary School
San Juan, Texas

Cynthia Gadson
CC Spaulding Elementary
Durham, North Carolina

Carolyn R. Jones
Johnston Elementary
Asheville, North Carolina

Beverly Sanney
Lakewood Elementary
St. Albans, West Virginia

Kimberly Gay
Mango Elementary
Seffner, Florida

Rhonda Kelley
Middletown Elementary
Louisville, Kentucky

John Torres
PS 41 Elementary
Staten Island, New York

CONSULTING HEALTH SPECIALISTS

Harriet Hylton Barr, B.A., M.P.H., CHES
Clinical Associate Professor Emeritus
Department of Health Behavior and Health Education
School of Public Health
University of North Carolina at Chapel Hill
Durham, North Carolina

David A. Birch, Ph.D., CHES
Associate Professor
Department of Applied Health Science
Indiana University
Bloomington, Indiana

Glen Ceresa, D.D.S.
Clinical Instructor
Las Vegas Institute for Advanced Dental Studies
Las Vegas, Nevada

Michael J. Cleary, Ed.D., CHES
Professor
Department of Allied Health
Slippery Rock University
Slippery Rock, Pennsylvania

Lisa C. Cohn, M.M.Sc., M.Ed., R.D.
Nutrition Educator and Research Consultant
New York, New York

Mary Steckiewicz Garzino, M.Ed.
Director, Nutrition Education
National Dairy Council
Chicago, Illinois

Mark L. Giese, Ed.D., FACSM
Professor
Northeastern Oklahoma State University
Tahlequah, Oklahoma

Michael J. Hammes, Ph.D.
Associate Professor
University of New Mexico
Albuquerque, New Mexico

Betty M. Hubbard, Ed.D., CHES
Professor of Health Education
Department of Health Sciences
University of Central Arkansas
Conway, Arkansas

Rama K. Khalsa, Ph.D.
Director of Mental Health
Santa Cruz County
Soquel, California

Darrel Lang, Ed.D.
Health and Physical Education Consultant
Kansas State Department of Education
Emporia, Kansas

Gerald J. Maburn
National Vice President for Planning and Evaluation
American Cancer Society
Atlanta, Georgia

Cheryl Miller-Haymowicz, B.S., CHES
Health Educator
Salem-Keizer Public Schools
Salem, Oregon

John A. Morris, M.S.W.
Professor of Neuropsychiatry and Behavioral Science
University of South Carolina School of Medicine
Director of Interdisciplinary Affairs
South Carolina Department of Mental Health
Columbia, South Carolina

Patricia Poindexter, M.P.H., CHES
Health Education Specialist
Tucker, Georgia

Janine Robinette
Health Program Administrator
Monterey, California

Spencer Sartorius, M.S.
Administrator
Health Enhancement and Safety Division
Montana Office of Public Instruction
Helena, Montana

Jeanne Marie Scott, M.D.
Staff Physician
San Jose State University
San Jose, California

David A. Sleet, Ph.D.
Centers for Disease Control and Prevention
Atlanta, Georgia

Becky J. Smith, Ph.D., CHES
Reston, Virginia

Howard Taras, M.D.
Associate Professor
(Specialist in Medical Consultation to Schools)
University of California at San Diego
San Diego, California

Pamela M. Tollefsen, R.N., M.Ed.
Program Supervisor, Health Education
Office of Superintendent of Public Instruction
State of Washington
Olympia, Washington

Mae Waters, Ph.D., CHES
Executive Director of Comprehensive Health Training
Florida State University
Tallahassee, Florida

Your Health and The National Health Education Standards

The National Health Education Standards were developed by representatives of various health organizations, including the American School Health Association, the Association for the Advancement of Health Education, and the American Cancer Society. The standards describe what students should know and be able to do in order to be health literate. A health-literate person obtains, interprets, and understands basic health information and services and uses that information and those services in ways that are health-enhancing.

Your Health promotes health literacy in the following ways:

- provides students with the **knowledge** they need to make informed decisions about their health.
- provides students with opportunities to learn and practice **life skills** and **consumer skills** for positive health behaviors.
- encourages the use of **thinking skills** in order to solve problems and think critically.

Every lesson in *Your Health* was developed to help students meet the Standards. A correlation to the Standards is provided on each Chapter Organizer in this Teacher's Edition.

National Health Education Standards

1. Students will comprehend concepts related to health promotion and disease prevention.

2. Students will demonstrate the ability to access valid health information and health-promoting products and services.

3. Students will demonstrate the ability to practice health-enhancing behaviors and reduce health risks.

4. Students will analyze the influence of culture, media, technology, and other factors on health.

5. Students will demonstrate the ability to use interpersonal communication skills to enhance health.

6. Students will demonstrate the ability to use goal-setting and decision-making skills to enhance health.

7. Students will demonstrate the ability to advocate for personal, family, and community health.

Curriculum Integration

Your Health is designed to allow you to integrate health into your daily planning through the use of connections to all curriculum areas. Look for Curriculum Integration in the teacher planning section at the beginning of each chapter.

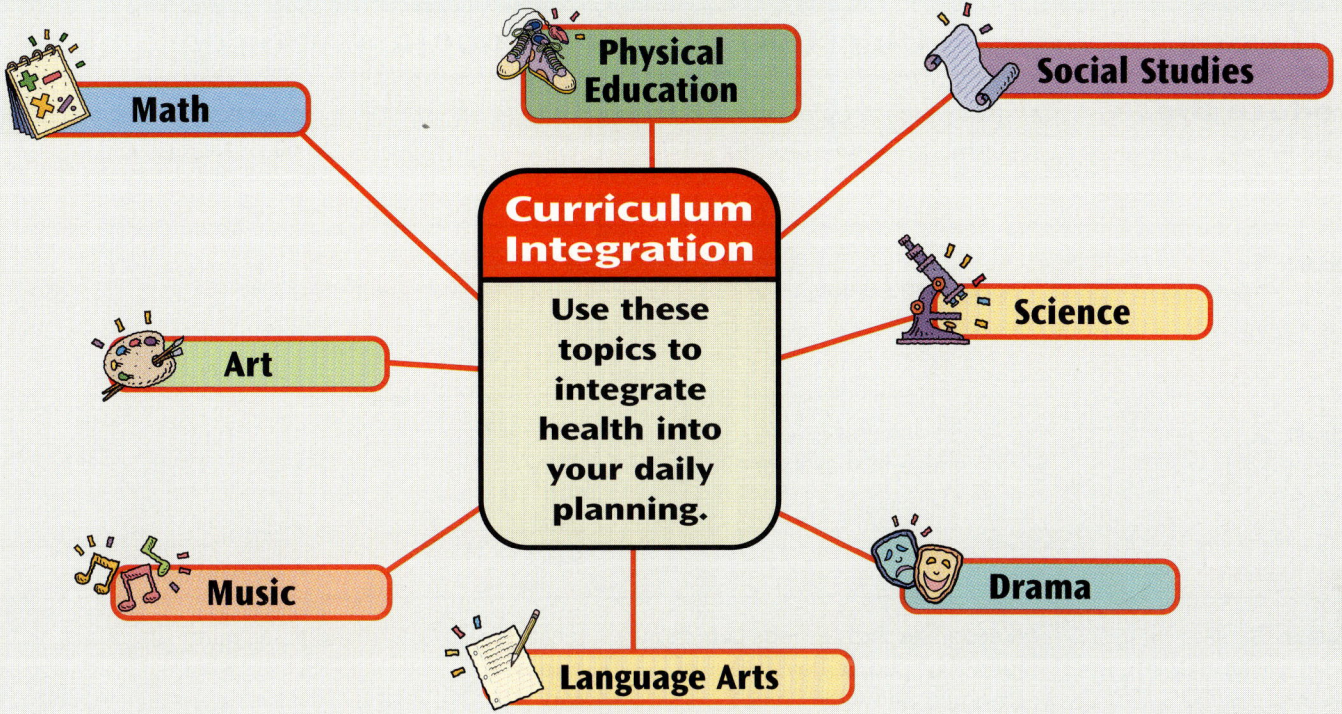

Program Assessment

Your Health provides a variety of assessment strategies and tools for assessing student health literacy. The assessment is based on the following model:

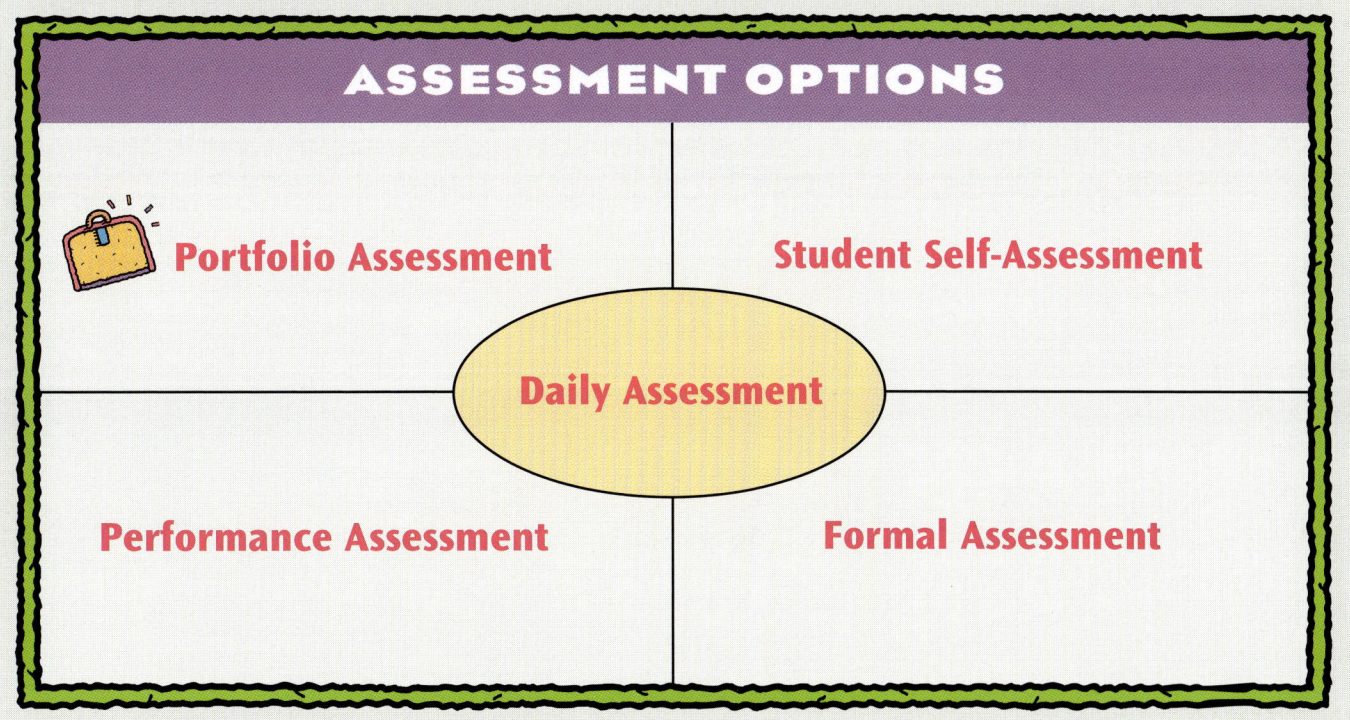

For more information, please refer to pages 32–33 in *Teaching Resources*.

CHAPTER 1  All *About* Me

Chapter Organizer

Lesson	Objectives	Vocabulary	Program Resources
Introduce the Chapter pp. 14–15	• Preview the chapter. • Introduce chapter activity center.		• School-Home Connection, TR p. 55 • Take-Home Booklet, TR pp. 73–74
Lesson 1 **I Am Special** pp. 16–17 *Pacing: 1 class period* ✓ 1•5	• Identify what makes each child special and unique.	special	• Teaching Chart 1 • Poem: "Best Friends," p. RA-2 • Pattern 1, TR p. 91 • Activity Book, p. 1
Lesson 2 **I Have Feelings** pp. 18–19 *Pacing: 1 class period* ✓ 1•5	• Identify feelings. • Recognize that everyone has feelings.	feelings happy sad mad scared	• Teaching Chart 2 • Pattern 1, TR p. 91 • Performance Assessment Summary Sheet, TR p. 46 • Activity Book, p. 2
Lesson 3 **Changing My Feelings** pp. 20–21 *Pacing: 1 class period* ✓ 1•3•5	• Recognize that feelings can change and that people have ways of changing how they feel.	feelings happy sad mad scared	• Teaching Chart 3 • Poem: "New Neighbors," p. RA-2 • Activity Book, p. 3
Lesson 4 **Helping Out** pp. 22–23 *Pacing: 1 class period* ✓ 1•2•7	• Demonstrate ways to cooperate with and respect each other.	cooperate (cooperation) respect	• Teaching Chart 4 • Story: "The Enormous Turnip," p. RA-5 • Activity Book, p. 4
Lesson 5 **Getting Along** pp. 24–25 *Pacing: 1 class period* ✓ 3•5•6	• Explain how to resolve and avoid conflicts.	conflict I-messages	• Teaching Chart 5 • Activity Book, p. 5

✓ National Health Education Standards
A complete list of the Standards is provided on the next page.

Key: TR = Teaching Resources

National Health Education Standards

1. Comprehend concepts related to health promotion and disease prevention.
2. Access valid health information and health-promoting products and services.
3. Practice health-enhancing behaviors and reduce health risks.
4. Analyze the influence of culture, media, technology, and other factors on health.
5. Use interpersonal communication skills to enhance health.
6. Use goal-setting and decision-making skills to enhance health.
7. Advocate for personal, family, and community health.

Curriculum Integration

Use these topics to integrate health into your daily planning.

Math
- Cooperation Numbers, p. 12
- Eye-Color Pictograph, p. 17
- Feelings Faces Patterns, p. 19

Drama
- What Am I Feeling? p. 12
- Puppets Help Out, p. 23
- Role-Play Conflict Resolution, p. 25

Music
- Sing It with Feeling, p. 19
- Feelings Change Song, p. 21

Art
- I Am Special Portraits, p. 12

Language Arts
- Rhyming Words, p. 23
- Rhinos Purple, Hippos Green, p. 25

ASSESSMENT OPTIONS

Portfolio Assessment
Have students select their best work from the following suggestions:
- **Feelings Collages,** p. 19
- **Feelings Change Books,** p. 21
- **Rhyming Words,** p. 23
- **My Best Work Portfolio Summary Sheet,** TR p. 42
- **Portfolio Summary Sheet,** TR p. 43

Student Self-Assessment
- **Student Self-Assessment Checklist,** TR p. 38
- **Healthy Habits Checklist,** TR p. 39

Classroom Observation
- **Observation Checklist,** TR p. 36

Performance Assessment
- **Wrap Up,** p. 19
- **Performance Assessment Summary Sheet,** TR p. 46

Daily Assessment
- **Assessment Tips,** pp. 17, 19, 21, 23, 25
- **Activity Book,** pp. 1–5

Cross-Curricular Activities

 **Art**

I Am Special Portraits

These portraits can be given to parents to commemorate the beginning of a new school year.

- Have children use their school pictures or other photos as references to draw color portraits of their faces on white paper.
- Have them carefully color in the background to make a rectangular shape similar to the school picture.
- Have students glue the finished picture to the center of a piece of black construction paper, so that the picture looks framed.
- Write childrens' names and the date on small rectangles that can be glued to the bottom of the frame to simulate a placard.

 **Drama**

What Am I Feeling?

This activity helps children recognize body language as an important cue about how a person is feeling.

- Have each child act out a feeling without using words. After each child finishes, allow the class to guess what feeling was being portrayed.
- If children need help, supply some of the following prompts.

Mad	stomp feet, put hands on hips
Happy	smile, dance, skip
Scared	put hands over eyes, huddle in a corner, hide under a table
Sad	hang arms, wipe eyes, put head in hands

 **Math**

Cooperation Numbers

This activity helps emphasize the importance of cooperation. Prepare several sets of cards numbered one to ten before beginning the activity. Then divide the class into groups of ten. If you have groups with fewer than ten children, remove the higher-numbered cards from that group's card pack.

- Give each child in a group a numbered card. Explain that the children in each group need to cooperate in order to line up so that all the numbers are in the right order. Only one person can change place at a time.
- As an easier variation, have children work in pairs and give numbers one through five to each group.

 **Bulletin Board**

Divide the bulletin board in half. Label one half *At School* and the other half *At Home*.

- Work with children to brainstorm a list of ways they help at home and at school.
- Have children pick an item from the list to illustrate. Help each child write his or her name on the picture.
- Display the pictures on the appropriate side of the bulletin board.

Resources

Books for Students

Read Alouds

Intrater, Roberta Grobel. *Two Eyes, a Nose, and a Mouth.* Cartwheel Books, 2000. Picture book of faces with a rhymed poem illustrates the beauty of the three elements listed in the title. **EASY**

Penn, Audrey. *The Kissing Hand.* Child Welfare League of America, 1993. Chester Raccoon doesn't want to go to kindergarten. Mother shares a hand-kiss to remind him of her love. **AVERAGE**

Langreuter, Jutta. *Little Bear Goes to Kindergarten.* Millbrook Press, 1997. Although Little Bear likes the teacher, other bears, and activities on his first day at kindergarten, he doesn't want his mother to leave. **ADVANCED**

Books for Teachers and Families

Bloch, Douglas and Jon Merritt. *Positive Self-Talk for Children: Teaching Self-Esteem Through Affirmations: A Guide for Parents, Teachers, and Counselors.* Bantam Doubleday Dell Publishers, 1993. This book provides ways of giving children positive messages and promoting good self-concept.

Hart, Dr. Louise. *The Winning Family: Increasing Self-Esteem in Your Children and Yourself.* Celestial Arts, 1993. A helpful manual for choosing positive words and supporting positive growth.

Video

Being Safe—Kindergarten, AGC Educational Media, 1990. (12 minutes) In a puppet play about feelings, communication, and self-respect, children are encouraged to know they are valuable.

Don't Pop Your Cork on Mondays, AGC Educational Media, 1993. (12 minutes) In an animated video for young students, stress and stress management skills are taught in simple terms.

Staying Out of Trouble, AGC Educational Media, 1993 (7 minutes) Animal puppets teach children the steps for staying out of trouble. Comprehensive leader's guide is included.

Your Health Webliography

The **Webliography** provides links to the Health Background and teaching resources that will support you as you teach the topics in *Your Health.* Simply choose a keyword and you will be taken to a page of links with descriptions of the content you can obtain at each site. The **Webliography** is located on the Teacher Resources page at www.harcourtschool.com/health. Please review websites before referring your students to them.

Organizations and Agencies

American Academy of Pediatrics
National Headquarters
141 Northwest Point Boulevard
Elk Grove Village, IL 60007–1098
847-228-5005
Provides information on emotional development and a variety of other health concerns for children.

American Family Society
5013 Russett Road
Rockville, MD 20853
Distributes materials that encourage parents to spend quality time with their families.

National PTA
330 N. Wabash Ave.
Suite 2100
Chicago, IL 60611
800-307-4782
The PTA provides programs and information on conflict resolution in schools, as well as on helping children build positive self-concept.

For more information about health organizations and agencies, please see the *Teaching Resources* book.

Community Health

Child Psychologist
Invite a child psychologist to discuss emotions. Have the visitor talk about how emotions can impact people's lives. Also have the visitor emphasize ways of dealing with uncomfortable feelings.

Note that information, while correct at time of publication, is subject to change.

Visit **The Harcourt Learning Site** for related links, activities, resources, and the health **Webliography**.
www.harcourtschool.com

CHAPTER 1
Pages 10–25

"A person raised in a loving family environment has experiences that help develop social skills needed to form healthful and responsible relationships."

—Comprehensive School Health Education

CHAPTER SUMMARY

In this chapter children
- examine ways in which they are the same and different from others.
- identify feelings that everyone has and learn how to handle unpleasant feelings such as anger and sadness.
- describe how respect and cooperation can help people get along.

LIFE SKILLS Children learn to use I-messages and other strategies to help *resolve conflicts*.

All About Me

Health Activity Center

The activities suggested for this chapter's Health Activity Center help reinforce the idea that we are all special, yet we share the same feelings and needs.

Our Book of Emotions

This activity allows groups of children to cooperate to make a class booklet.

Materials Needed (per group)
- construction paper
- magazines to cut up
- scissors
- glue
- markers
- Pattern 1, TR p. 91

What to Do Divide the class into four groups. Assign each group an emotion (happy, sad, mad, scared). Have the children in each group work together to make at least two pages that express their assigned emotion. They may find examples in magazines to cut and paste or draw their own pictures. Have each group make a cover sheet for their pages, using Pattern 1. Combine the group work to make one booklet entitled "Our Book of Emotions."

Macaroni Feelings Faces

In this activity children work alone to express their interpretation of feelings through art.

Materials Needed (per child)
- drawing paper
- assorted macaroni (different shapes and colors)
- glue

What to Do Have children use the assorted shapes of macaroni in the Activity Center to make faces that show different feelings.

Happy/Sad Sticks

In this activity students review ways of turning sad emotions into happy ones.

Materials Needed (per group)
- Pattern 2, TR p. 92
- craft stick or straw
- glue
- crayons or markers

What to Do Have children find a happy face and a sad face on the Feelings Faces Pattern to cut out. Have them color the faces and then glue the faces back-to-back with a craft stick or straw between them to serve as a handle. Suggest different situations that the students may have experienced, such as a trip to the zoo or an illness, and have the children hold up the face to show how they felt (or would feel) in that situation. Select volunteers to elaborate on why they felt that way and, in the case of sad experiences, how they were able to feel better.

Mad Sack

This activity will help children learn that, no matter how angry you are, the anger usually subsides over time.

Materials Needed (per child)
- a small paper bag (sack)
- markers or crayons
- cards that say *mad*
- labels that say *My Mad Sack*
- poem sheet (see below)
- glue
- scissors

What to Do Have children glue the label *My Mad Sack* across the top of their bags. Advanced children may be able to copy these words on small index cards as a challenge. Have children cut out and glue this poem onto their bags.

> Put your mad feelings
>
> In the sack.
>
> Look at them tomorrow.
>
> Do you want them back?

When a child gets angry, he or she should put a MAD card in his or her sack. When the angry feeling has passed, he or she should remove the card.

Take-Home Booklet

Distribute copies of Take-Home Booklet, TR pages 73–74. Have children fold the pages to make booklets to share with their families.

School-Home Connection

Distribute copies of the School-Home Connection (in English or Spanish), TR page 55. Have children take the page home to share with their families.

Alternative: Use the page for enrichment.

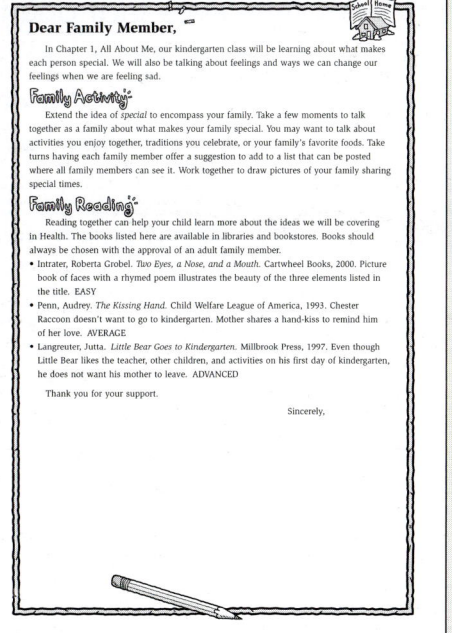

LESSON 1

OBJECTIVE
- Identify what makes each child special and unique.

VOCABULARY
- special

PROGRAM RESOURCES
- Teaching Chart 1
- Poem: "Best Friends," p. RA-2
- Pattern 1, TR p. 91
- Activity Book, p. 1

MATERIALS
- yarn in colors appropriate for hair
- multicultural crayons

I Am Special

Teaching Chart 1

Daily Safety Tip

Now would be a good time to emphasize common hygiene rules for the classroom, including washing hands after using the bathroom. Stress that these rules help keep everyone healthy.

1 Motivate

Finger Play Teach children the following finger play. Have children talk about the characteristics all people share. Then explain that even though people are similar, each person is also special.

> Two little eyes that open and close
> (Children open and close eyes.)
>
> Two little ears
> (Children point to ears.)
>
> One little nose
> (Children point to nose.)
>
> Two little cheeks
> (Children point to cheeks.)
>
> One little chin
> (Children point to chin.)
>
> Two little lips with the teeth closed in.
> (Children should smile with their teeth together.)

2 Teach

Learn from Pictures

Show children Teaching Chart 1. Ask a volunteer to describe the picture. a group of children

- **How are these children the same?** Possible answer: all the children have two eyes, two ears, and hair.

- Have children look at each other. **How are you like the children in the photo? How are you like each other?** Possible answer: most people have the same general physical characteristics—two eyes, two ears, and hair.

Discuss

Point to the word *special* as you pronounce the word. **What does *special* mean?** Possible answers: different, important. Explain that everyone is special; each person looks, acts, and feels different from everyone else.

- Redirect attention to the Teaching Chart 1. **What makes these children different from each other?** They have different color hair, eyes, skin; some are boys and some are girls. **What makes each of us special?** Answers will vary. Be sure children include personality traits such as sense of humor, shares well, friendly, and smiles a lot.

- Read the poem "Best Friends" on page RA-2. Talk about why a best, best friend might not feel special.

Activity

My Face Is Special Provide each child with a copy of Pattern 1. Have children decorate the pattern to look like themselves, using yarn and multicultural crayons. When finished, have each child take a turn holding his or her face in the "blank" spot on Teaching Chart 1 and describing what makes him or her special. Encourage children to describe both the physical and emotional characteristics that make them special.

3 Wrap Up

Have each child tell a partner one thing they have in common and one thing that makes each of them special.

ASSESSMENT TIP Look for responses such as we both have red shirts, you have short hair, you have long hair, you always share, you are a good friend, you jump rope well, and you color well.

TEACHER TIP

As an option, record on sentence strips each child's description of himself or herself. Display completed faces and sentence strips around the following poem.

I am special.
I am me.
There's no one else
I'd rather be.

TEACHER TIP

My Fingerprints Are Special Have children look closely at the tips of their fingers and thumbs for the small ridges that make up their fingerprints. Explain that everyone's ridges grow in a different pattern, so everyone's fingerprints are special.

Have children trace around one of their hands. Then have them paint the tips of the thumbs they traced around with a darker-colored washable marker. They should quickly press their thumbs onto the proper places on the tracings to record their thumbprints. Repeat with all the fingers of the traced hand.

Other things to do!

Math Activity

Eye-Color Pictograph Children can make a pictograph of eye color using class data. Have children count the number of people in the class with each eye color. (If class demographics are such that eye color won't result in much variety, have children count shirt colors or shoe styles.) Help children make a pictograph using eye color pictures.

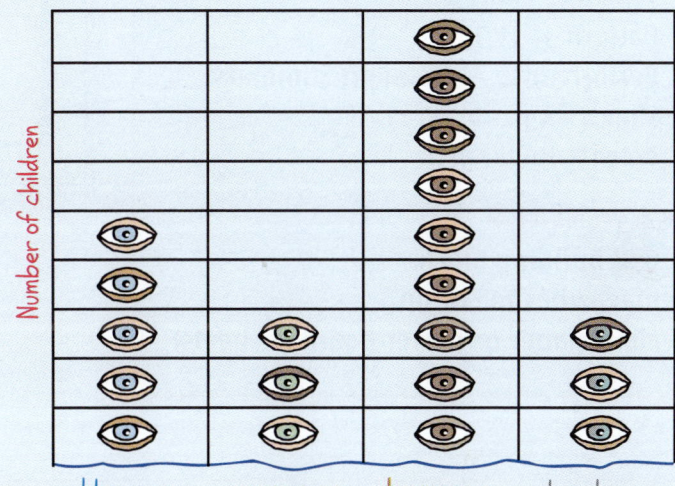

Eye Colors in Our Class

Using the Activity Book, page 1

This activity reinforces the idea that everyone is special. Children draw self-portraits and pictures of two special friends.

Special Friends

17

LESSON 2

OBJECTIVES
- Identify feelings.
- Recognize that everyone has feelings.

VOCABULARY
- feelings
- happy
- sad
- mad
- scared

PROGRAM RESOURCES
- Teaching Chart 2
- Pattern 1, TR p. 91
- Performance Assessment Summary Sheet, TR p. 46
- Activity Book, p. 2

MATERIALS
- 6–8 building blocks
- magazines to cut up
- chart paper or poster board (4 sheets)

Teaching Chart 2

Daily Safety Tip

Help children recognize that it is good to share feelings with friends and family. Smile and laugh if you are happy. Talk if you are feeling sad, angry, or scared. Then your family and friends will know how to celebrate with you or help you.

1 Motivate

Choose a child to build something using the blocks. Have another child knock down the blocks.

- **How do you think the child who built the block structure feels?** Possible answers: mad, sad.

2 Teach

Discuss

Have children list different feelings they have. Possible answers: happy, sad, mad, scared. After the list is made, ask children to think of times when they might feel each emotion. Possible answers: happy—birthday party, rainbow, amusement park; sad—feeling sick, broken toy; angry—friend not sharing a toy, having to go someplace they don't want to go; scared—loud noises at night, bad dreams.

Life Skills

 Communicate How do you know how other people are feeling? Possible answers: the way they act, the looks on their faces, the things they say, by asking them how they feel.

- Have several children act out being happy, sad, mad, and scared. Explain that children can tell what others are feeling because everyone feels happy, sad, mad, and scared at times.

Learn from Pictures

Show children Teaching Chart 2. Explain that the pictures show children who have different feelings. Point to each picture. **How do you think this child feels? How do you know?** The children's faces show how they feel (happy, sad, mad, scared).

- Read the four feelings words listed on Teaching Chart 2. Have one child point to the proper picture as you read each feelings word. Have the child explain how he or she chooses the picture that goes with the word. Then have another child point to the proper word and say it as you point to different pictures. Go back and forth between the words and pictures until everyone has had a turn.

Activity

Feelings Faces Provide each child with a copy of Pattern 1. Have children choose feelings to draw. When finished, allow each child to hold up his or her face. Have the rest of the class tell what feeling is being shown. Help the artist write the feeling portrayed under the face he or she has drawn.

3 Wrap Up

Divide the class into four work groups, one for each feeling. Have each group cut and paste magazine pictures onto chart paper or poster board to create a collage for that feeling. Display the Feelings Collages in the classroom for use throughout the chapter.

ASSESSMENT TIP The above activity can be used to evaluate children's performance. See TR page 46.

TEACHER TIP

A Memory Game Make several copies of Pattern 2: Feelings Faces. Cut apart the faces and laminate (if desired). Have children use the feelings face cards to play a memory matching game. All the cards are laid out face down in a square. The first child picks two cards and describes the feelings shown. If the cards match, the child keeps them; if not, they are placed back in the same positions in the layout. The next child then tries to match two cards. The game continues until children have matched all the pairs.

HEALTH BACKGROUND

Sadness and Depression It was once thought that only adults became depressed. Now depression, profound sadness lasting a long time, is being recognized in some young children. Depression affects mood, thought, body, and behaviors. The warning signs of depression include

- persistent sad, anxious, or empty feelings.
- loss of interest or pleasure in activities.
- restlessness, irritability, or excessive crying.
- feeling guilty, worthless, helpless, hopeless, or pessimistic.
- sleeping too much or too little, early-morning awakening.
- loss of appetite and weight loss, or overeating and weight gain.
- decreased energy, fatigue.
- thoughts of death or suicide; suicide attempts.
- difficulty concentrating, remembering, or making decisions.
- physical symptoms, such as headaches, digestive problems, or chronic pain, that don't respond to treatment.

Other things to do!

Music Activity

Sing It with Feeling Use the song "If You're Happy and You Know It, Clap Your Hands" to reinforce feelings. Substitute different feelings and appropriate actions for happy/clap your hands. For example: angry/stamp your feet; sad/wipe your eyes, scared/cover your eyes. Have children show with facial expressions and body language how they would look.

Math Activity

Feelings Faces Patterns Place the laminated Feelings Faces cards (from the Memory Game) in a basket in the Math Center. Have groups of two go to the center. One of each pair makes a pattern for the other to copy. When the pattern is complete, have the partner describe the pattern using feelings words. Have children start with a low number of faces and increase in complexity as time and ability allow.

Using the Activity Book, page 2

This activity reinforces the idea that everyone has feelings. Children match feelings words to pictures of the feelings.

Feelings Match

LESSON 3

OBJECTIVE
- Recognize that feelings can change and that people have ways of changing how they feel.

VOCABULARY
- feelings
- happy
- sad
- mad
- scared

PROGRAM RESOURCES
- Teaching Chart 3
- Poem: "New Neighbors," p. RA-2
- Activity Book, p. 3

MATERIALS
- Feelings Collages (from Lesson 2 Wrap Up)
- drawing paper

Teaching Chart 3

Daily Safety Tip

Remind children that we all have feelings. Sometimes our feelings change because of things or people around us. Encourage children to talk to an adult they trust if they feel scared or sad about something someone is doing around them.

1 Motivate

Direct children to study the Feelings Collages they made in the Lesson 2 Wrap Up. As an alternative, show Teaching Chart 2 again. **Which collages show uncomfortable feelings?** angry, sad, scared

Discuss each collage individually.

- **Why do you think these people are feeling this way?** Answers will be specific to the pictures.
- **What could they do to change how they feel?** Possible answers: talk to someone, play, do something they enjoy.

2 Teach

Learn from Pictures

Show children Teaching Chart 3. Discuss how the boy on the left-hand side of the page feels and how children know. Sad; he has a sad expression.

- Look at the same boy on the right-hand side of the page. **How does he feel now? How do you know?** Happy; he is smiling.
- **Why do you think he is happy now?** Discussion should elicit realization that his feelings changed because of something he did.

Discuss

Refer to the pictures in the center of the page. Have students identify what is shown in each.

- **How might these things make a person who is sad feel better?** Possible answers: They take your mind off the sad thing, they help you understand your feelings, they make you feel loved.

Life Skills

Manage Stress Emphasize to children that exercise is a good way to reduce stress and change feelings. With the class, brainstorm a list of physical activities children can do when they are feeling angry or sad.

Activity

Handling Angry Feelings Learning how to handle feelings of anger is an important skill. Provide each child with a sheet of drawing paper. Have children fold the paper in half. Work with each child to finish this sentence, and record it on the left side of the paper: I get angry when _____. If children have trouble coming up with ideas, remind them of how they might have felt if they had built the block structure that was knocked down in the Motivate portion of Lesson 2. Then have children draw activities or actions they could do to help relieve the angry feelings. Bring the class together to discuss ways of handling anger. Stress ideas such as talking about your feelings, taking time to cool off, and doing physical activities, such as taking a walk or riding a bike, that can help people deal with their angry feelings.

3 Wrap Up

Read the poem, "New Neighbors," page RA-2. Have partners discuss why the child was sad and what happened to change her feelings.

ASSESSMENT TIP Look for indications that children recognize that feelings can change over time or when a person does something to take his or her mind off the uncomfortable feeling.

MEET INDIVIDUAL NEEDS

Kinesthetic/Visual Learners Have children take a "feelings" walk around the classroom, looking at all the pictures of people on posters or in other displays. Challenge children to identify a feeling for each face, and tell what a person could do to change an uncomfortable feeling into a happy feeling. If resources are available, photograph children during class and recess. Then post the photos and have children take another "feelings" walk.

TEACHER TIP

Feelings Change Books Have children create Feelings Change Books to take home and share with their families. Have children draw pictures to answer these questions:

1. When I feel sad, I _____.
2. When I feel mad, I _____.
3. When I feel scared, I _____.

They may wish to label their drawings with the feelings each shows.

Other things to do!

Music Activity

Feelings Change Song Review "If You're Happy and You Know It, Clap Your Hands" from Lesson 2. This time, have children sing lyrics that reinforce the ways they can change their feelings. An example is shown below.

If you're scared and you know it,
tell your mom.

If you're scared and you know it,
tell your mom.

If you're scared and you know it,
then you really can control it.

If you're scared and you know it,
tell your mom.

Other verses could be:

If you're sad and you know it,
pet your dog.

If you're mad and you know it,
paint or draw.

Using the Activity Book, page 3

This activity provides an opportunity for students to show how they change their own uncomfortable feelings into more comfortable ones.

Feelings Change

LESSON 4

OBJECTIVE
- Demonstrate ways to cooperate with and respect each other.

VOCABULARY
- cooperate (cooperation)
- respect

PROGRAM RESOURCES
- Teaching Chart 4
- Story: "The Enormous Turnip," p. RA-5
- Activity Book, p. 4

MATERIALS
- common classroom object such as a board eraser or pencil cup

Helping Out

Teaching Chart 4

Daily Safety Tip

By learning to respect other people's property, children can avoid many day-to-day conflicts that can make classroom life less than pleasant. Encourage children to ask before playing with other children's toys.

1 Motivate

Hide an object the class uses every day. Tell children it is missing and you would like them to help you find it. Ask for suggestions about how to search for it. Guide children to make an organized search, such as a group searching a specific area of the classroom. After children find the object, gather them together and thank them for their hard work.

- Explain that as they worked, they were cooperating to find the object. Write *cooperation* on the board, and explain that it means to work together on a common task.

- **Why was it important to cooperate to find the object?** Possible answers: Everyone worked together to make a plan; we were able to look in a lot of places quickly.

2 Teach

Learn from Pictures

Show children Teaching Chart 4. **What is happening in the picture?** Children are getting ready to paint, helping each other, cooperating.

- **What other ways will the children need to cooperate?** take turns; hang up wet paintings; clean up

Discuss

Explain that a part of cooperating is having respect for one another. Write *respect* on the board, and explain that having respect for others means being polite and thinking how your actions will affect the other person.

- **How will the children need to respect each other?** Don't get paint on other children; paint only on your paper; say only nice things about other people's paintings.

Discuss

Read the story "The Enormous Turnip," page RA-5. Discuss how the characters in the story cooperated to remove the turnip from the ground.

3 Wrap Up

Have children take a walking tour of the classroom areas, such as the blocks area, the reading area, the dress-up area, and the different centers. Ask children how they can show respect and cooperation in each area.

ASSESSMENT TIP Look for answers indicating that children understand that respect and cooperation involve working together and being polite to each other.

TEACHER TIP

Review Emotions Use the sad and mad collages made in Lesson 2. Using one of the photos on the collage, have a volunteer make up a story telling why the person is sad. Then have the volunteer revise his or her story, telling how respect and cooperation could help the person feel better.

MEET INDIVIDUAL NEEDS

Kinesthetic Learners Play a cooperation game based on "Musical Chairs." Count out enough sheets of paper for half of the class. Arrange the papers in a circle. Have two children sit on or by each sheet of paper. When the music starts, have children walk around the circle; when the music stops, they sit on the nearest sheet of paper, in pairs. You may want to sing *The Sharing Song,* page RA-8, as students walk. Explain that the next time the music starts, you will remove one sheet of paper, but everyone will still need to find a place to sit. Start the music again. While the children walk, remove one sheet of paper, then stop the music. Two children will be left standing. Ask the class, "What should these children do?" *Guide answers so other children invite the two who are standing to share their paper.* Continue the game, removing one sheet of paper each round, until the entire class is sitting together in one group. Point out to children that this was fun because everyone cooperated and shared.

Other things to do!

Drama Activity

Puppets Help Out Use two hand puppets (Pattern 3, TR p. 93) or make two sock puppets and label them *Respect* and *Cooperation.* Explain that Respect and Cooperation don't know how they can help in the classroom. Have children take turns telling the puppets different ways respect and cooperation are important in the classroom. Accept reasonable answers. Possible answers: Respect—following classroom rules, being polite, being a good friend, sharing, not hurting someone else's feelings; Cooperation—working together to take care of the classroom and each other, monitor jobs, cleaning up and putting away materials, following classroom rules.

Keep the Respect and Cooperation puppets on display and use them to point out and commend children who exhibit these behaviors.

Language Arts Activity

Rhyming Words Point out that the words *mad* and *sad* rhyme. Work with children to make a list of other words that rhyme with *mad* and *sad*. Help children make up poems that tell about turning *sad* feelings into *glad* feelings.

Using the Activity Book, page 4

This activity reinforces ways that children can help out in the classroom.

Helping Out

LESSON 5

OBJECTIVE
- Explain how to resolve and avoid conflicts.

VOCABULARY
- conflict
- I-messages

PROGRAM RESOURCES
- Teaching Chart 5
- Activity Book, p. 5

MATERIALS
- Book: *The Berenstain Bears Get in a Fight* by Stan and Jan Berenstain (Random House, 1982.)

Teaching Chart 5

Daily Safety Tip

Help children recognize that when you are playing with friends, you both want to be happy. Encourage them to talk about conflicts if they are feeling angry. Remind them to use the words "I feel" when talking about conflict.

1 Motivate

Gather children together. Read the Berenstain Bear book up to page 5, where the conflict begins; stop after reading "Sister!" he shouted. "Get your dopey feet out of my face!"

- **What just happened?** Possible answers: Brother and Sister got into a fight, had an argument.
- As an alternative, have students describe a conflict that may have happened in the classroom or between children at home.

2 Teach

Learn from Pictures

Have children look at Teaching Chart 5. **What is happening in the small picture?** Two children at the dress-up center are fighting or arguing over a hat.

- **Why did the conflict happen?** Both girls wanted to play with the hat at the same time.

Life Skills

Resolve Conflicts and Communicate Explain that when people disagree, it is good to talk about the problem. When they talk to each other, they should talk about how they feel and not about the other person. It helps to use sentences that begin with "I," such as "I am angry. I want the hat," or "I feel bad. I need you to listen to me." These are called I-messages.

- **What I-messages could the girls use to help them solve this conflict?** Possible answers: I want to use the hat. I had the hat first. I have an idea—I will use the hat for a little bit, and you use the scarf; then we can switch.

- **How could these girls keep a conflict like this from happening again?** Accept reasonable answers. Possible answers: They could pull out a lot of clothing and make two outfits together, then take turns; they could take turns choosing one piece of clothing at a time.

Discuss

Point out the yellow bird on Teaching Chart 5. Explain that this bird will appear periodically on different pages. He often reinforces the important idea of the lesson.

- Choose a child who is able to read what the bird is saying (Let's work it out!), and have him or her read it aloud. Emphasize that maintaining a friendship is more important than who plays with what toy or getting your own way.

3 Wrap Up

Continue reading the Berenstain Bear story. Each time a conflict arises, ask children to suggest appropriate I-messages. As an alternative, have children resolve the following conflict using I-messages: One child on the playground has a ball; another wants it.

ASSESSMENT TIP Look for I-messages that clearly state how the speaker feels.

TEACHER TIP

Use Respect and Cooperation to Get Along Use the two hand puppets labeled *Respect* and *Cooperation* from Lesson 4. Explain that Respect and Cooperation are very helpful in resolving conflicts at school and with friends. Have children take turns telling how Respect and Cooperation would avoid conflicts as they clean up and put away materials each day, line up for recess and other activities, move to the story rug, and play in the different classroom areas.

HEALTH BACKGROUND

Dealing with Bullies Children of all ages sometimes find themselves the target of bullies. Bullies not only frighten children, but they are often the center of conflicts that may lead to violence. Here are some strategies children can use to deal with bullies.

- Ignore the bully. A bully tries to intimidate others and tries to make his or her victim upset. Crying or other responses reinforce this behavior. Encourage children to try to keep their composure and walk away.

- If a child is unsuccessful at ignoring the bully, he or she should be assertive in standing up for his or her rights. Encourage children to stand tall, look the bully in the eye, and say things like "Stop that now. I don't like what you are doing." Bullies like weak targets and will often move on if the victim can't be intimidated.

- Encourage children to play in groups with their friends. Children with strong friendships are less likely to be singled out as targets than are those who play alone.

Other things to do!

Drama Activity

Role-Play Conflict Resolution Describe the situations similar to the ones that follow. Have children role-play how they would resolve each conflict using I-messages.

- Two children are coloring together. One child colors on the other's paper.
- Two children are running toward the swings. They both reach the only open swing at the same time.

Language Arts Activity

Rhinos Purple, Hippos Green Read the poem, "Rhinos Purple, Hippos Green," page RA-2. Have pairs role-play the parts of the brother and the sister, making up likely dialogue for each part. Encourage children to include the conflict that occurs between the brother and the sister as well as different ways of resolving the conflict in their role-plays.

Using the Activity Book, page 5

In this activity children color happy faces yellow where the children are getting along, and color the sad faces blue where children are not getting along.

Getting Along

CHAPTER 2
Growing and Learning

Chapter Organizer

Lesson	Objectives	Vocabulary	Program Resources
Introduce the Chapter pp. 30–31	• Preview the chapter. • Introduce chapter activity center.		• School-Home Connection, TR p. 57 • Take-Home Booklet, TR pp. 75–76
Lesson 1 **I'm Growing** pp. 32–33 ✓ 1·3·6 *Pacing: 2 class periods*	• Describe how the body changes as you grow. • Identify major external body parts.	growing head arms trunk (torso) legs body	• Teaching Chart 6 • Pattern 4, TR p. 94 • Song: "Clap Your Hands," p. RA-9 • Activity Book, p. 6
Lesson 2 **I'm Growing on the Inside** pp. 34–35 ✓ 1·3·6 *Pacing: 2 class periods*	• Identify spine, lungs, stomach, brain, heart, and bones, and tell what each organ does.	heart lungs brain stomach bones skin spine	• Teaching Chart 7 Teaching Transparencies 3, 4, 5, 6, 7 • Pattern 5, TR p. 95 • Performance Assessment Summary Sheet, TR p. 47 • Activity Book, p. 7
Lesson 3 **My Senses** pp. 36–37 ✓ 1·3·5 *Pacing: 2 class periods*	• Identify the five senses and tell what they do. • Identify ways to keep the senses safe.	hear see smell touch taste senses	• Teaching Chart 8 Teaching Transparencies 1 and 2 • Activity Book, p. 8
Lesson 4 **My Senses Keep Me Safe** pp. 38–39 ✓ 1·2·5 *Pacing: 2 class periods*	• Identify how the senses help keep people safe.	safe dangerous smoke detector siren	• Teaching Chart 9 • Activity Book, p. 9
Lesson 5 **I'm Responsible** pp. 40–41 ✓ 1·6·7 *Pacing: 1 class period*	• Describe what it means to be responsible. • Identify ways to be responsible.	responsible	• Teaching Chart 10 • Story: "The Bundle of Sticks," p. RA-5 • Activity Book, p. 10

✓ National Health Education Standards
A complete list of the Standards is provided on the next page.

Key: TR = Teaching Resources

National Health Education Standards

1. Comprehend concepts related to health promotion and disease prevention.
2. Access valid health information and health-promoting products and services.
3. Practice health-enhancing behaviors and reduce health risks.
4. Analyze the influence of culture, media, technology, and other factors on health.
5. Use interpersonal communication skills to enhance health.
6. Use goal-setting and decision-making skills to enhance health.
7. Advocate for personal, family, and community health.

Curriculum Integration
Use these topics to integrate health into your daily planning.

Math
- Height Yarn Graphs, p. 33
- Food Graph, p. 37

Science
- What Is it? p. 28
- Make a Stethoscope, p. 35

Drama
- My, How I Have Grown, p. 28

Art
- Responsibility Collage, p. 41
- Understanding Age, p. 35

Music
- Body Parts Song, p. 33

Language Arts
- My Touch Book, p. 37
- Hearing Rhyme, p. 39
- Our Senses Keep Us Safe Book, p. 39
- Action Poem, p. 41
- *The Berenstain Bears and the Messy Room*, p. 41

ASSESSMENT OPTIONS

Portfolio Assessment
Have students select their best work from the following suggestions:
- **My Touch Book**, p. 37
- **Our Senses Keep Us Safe Book**, p. 39
- **Responsibility Collage**, p. 41
- **My Best Work Portfolio Summary Sheet**, TR p. 42
- **Portfolio Summary Sheet**, TR p. 43

Student Self-Assessment
- **Student Self-Assessment Checklist**, TR p. 38
- **Healthy Habits Checklist**, TR p. 39

Classroom Observation
- **Observation Checklist**, TR p. 36

Performance Assessment
- **Wrap Up**, p. 35
- **Performance Assessment Summary Sheet**, TR p. 47

Daily Assessment
- **Assessment Tips**, pp. 33, 35, 37, 39, 41
- **Activity Book**, pp. 6–10

Cross-Curricular Activities

Science
What Is It?
Scientists use the senses to investigate the world around them. Explain to children that they will be like scientists and use their senses to investigate some common objects.

- Have children use hand lenses to examine leaves, shells, rocks, flowers, their hair, and their own hands. Have children describe what they saw using the lens that they could not see with the unaided eye.

- Blindfold children and allow them to taste some common foods, such as apples, carrots, bananas, and saltine crackers. NOTE: Check for food allergies before allowing children to taste any foods.

- Have children try tasting the foods while holding their noses. Was it easier or harder to identify a food when you couldn't smell it?

Drama
My, How I Have Grown
Talk with children about how they are growing and changing. Discuss how their growth allows them to do more difficult tasks, such as riding a bicycle.

- Have children act out how a baby (who can't walk yet) gets across the room. Then have them act out how a small child (just learning to walk) might get across the room.

- Finally, have children act out things they can do now that they have grown. Examples are running, hopping, cartwheels and somersaults.

- Another thing that children do as they grow is become more responsible. One way in which to demonstrate this new responsibility is to show support for each member of your family. It is also important to show that each family member has value. Ask children to act out how they could show support to a family member.

Art
Drawing Your Family
Families change. A new sibling may be born, an older sibling may go away to school, a grandparent may die, parents may get divorced. Many children have already had to deal with a change in their family. The activities will help children identify feelings related to changes within their family and provide a way to express them.

- Have children draw one way in which their family has changed. Beneath the drawing, have them write at least two words that describe how they felt about the change.

- Have children make another drawing that shows how they handled the emotions caused by the change in their family. Emphasize that talking to a parent about feelings is one good way to handle change in the family.

Bulletin Board

Divide the bulletin board in half. Label one side *When I Was a Baby* and the other side *Now I Can*.

- Have children bring in baby pictures of themselves, draw pictures of themselves as babies, or cut pictures from magazines for the *When I Was a Baby* side of the bulletin board.

- For the *Now I Can* side, children can bring pictures from home, cut out magazine pictures, or draw pictures of themselves engaged in activities they enjoy doing. If equipment is available, take photographs of children at school to augment this side of the display.

Books for Students

Read Alouds

McMillan, Bruce. *Sense Suspense.* Scholastic Inc., 1994. A guessing game in this colorful, bilingual book. **EASY**

Leedy, Loreen. *Who's Who in My Family?* Holiday House, 1995. All family trees share one common feature—love. A delightful tribute to all families. **AVERAGE**

Munsch, Robert. *Love You Forever.* Golden Books, 1992. Classic picture book offers love across generations. **ADVANCED**

Books for Teachers and Families

Clark, Silvana. *150 Ways to Raise Creative, Confident Kids.* Soho Press, 1998. This book is full of resources for bringing fun and joy back to family life. Includes recipes, projects, and many other fresh ideas.

Covey, Steven R. *The Seven Habits of Highly Effective Families.* Saint Martin's Press, 1998. A motivational manual in support of families.

Videos

The Princess and the Rooster. TMW Media Group, 2000. (43 minutes) Teaches young children proper manners and behavior.

Barney's Sense-Sational Day. Lyrick Studios, 1996. (25 minutes) Barney shows how the five senses help children experience their world.

A New Baby in My House. Sony Music Entertainment, 1996. (30 minutes) The arrival of a new baby can be an upsetting time for older siblings. This video tells children it is natural to be confused and excited and that all children have special places in the family.

Sesame Street Kids' Guide to Life: Learning to Share. Sony Music Entertainment, 1996. (30 minutes) Elmo discovers that sharing can make playtime twice as fun.

Sesame Street Kids' Guide to Life: Telling the Truth. Sony Music Entertainment, 1997. (30 minutes) A fun way to teach young students that not telling the truth can cause big problems.

GO ONLINE — Your Health Webliography

The **Webliography** provides links to the Health Background and teaching resources that will support you as you teach the topics in *Your Health*. Simply choose a keyword and you will be taken to a page of links with descriptions of the content you can obtain at each site. The **Webliography** is located on the Teacher Resources page at **www.harcourtschool.com/health** Please review websites before referring your students to them.

Community Health

Bones Grow

Invite an orthopedist to visit the class and talk about how bones grow and develop. If possible, have the doctor bring X rays to show the class the bones of people of different ages. Children can then compare the bones to see how they grow.

Organizations and Agencies

Jack and Jill of America Foundation, Inc.
P.O. Box 468
Pickerington, OH 43147-8976
614-864-7085
This organization seeks to improve educational, cultural, and civic opportunities, to stimulate growth and development, and to help parents learn more about their children.

U.S. Dept. of Health and Human Services
Maternal and Child Health Bureau
5600 Fishers Lane
Rockville, MD 20857
301-443-2170
Provides background and statistical information.

For more information about health organizations and agencies, please see the **Teaching Resources** book.

Note that information, while correct at time of publication, is subject to change.

Visit **The Harcourt Learning Site** for related links, activities, resources, and the health **Webliography**.
www.harcourtschool.com

CHAPTER
Pages 26–41

"Growth is exciting; growth is dynamic and alarming."

—Vita Sackville-West

CHAPTER SUMMARY
In this chapter children
- describe ways the body changes as it grows.
- identify the five senses and their functions, including helping to keep people safe.
- describe what it means to be responsible.

LIFE SKILLS Children *communicate* what their senses tell them to help keep them safe. Children discuss how being responsible can help *resolve conflicts* at home.

HUMAN BODY Children identify major internal and external body parts.

Growing and Learning

Health Activity Center

The activities suggested for this chapter's Health Activity Center help reinforce the location and names of body parts. They also provide experiences for using the senses.

Listen to Your Heart

This activity helps children understand where the heart is located and its function.

Materials Needed
- stethoscope

What to Do Let children use the stethoscope to listen to their hearts. Then have them perform some activity, such as running in place or doing jumping jacks. After exercising for a minute or two, have them again use the stethoscope to listen to their hearts. Can they hear a difference? Point out that exercise makes the heart beat faster and helps the heart stay strong.

Shake and Match

In this activity children use the sense of hearing to identify matching sounds.

Materials Needed
- 8 margarine tubs, each numbered
- sand
- birdseed or rice
- pennies
- buttons

What to Do Make pairs of shakers with matching materials so that they make the same sound. Have children work in pairs to find the matching sounds. Have them guess what is inside each set.

Touch and Feel

This activity helps children understand the importance of touch and what touch tells us about the world.

Materials Needed
- several cloth bags with numbers written on the outside
- materials of different textures, a different material for each bag (Examples include fake fur, buttons, marbles, feathers, blocks, and yarn.)

What to Do Put a different material inside each bag. Have children work in pairs. The first child puts his or her hand in a bag, feels the object inside, and describes it for the second child. The children guess what is in the bag, and check their guesses by looking in the bag. Partners then switch roles.

What's That Smell?

This activity helps children understand the importance of the sense of smell.

Materials Needed
- several margarine tubs with numbered lids
- cotton balls
- various extracts or other materials to make distinctive smells, such as vanilla, peppermint, crushed garlic, and crushed onion

What to Do Soak a different cotton ball in each scent. Place each cotton ball in a different margarine tub. Ask children to work in pairs. Each child should pick a tub, open the lid slightly, and inhale the odor. Have pairs talk over what they have smelled and see if they can agree on what the odor is.

Take-Home Booklet

Distribute copies of the Take-Home Booklet, TR pages 75–76. Have children fold the pages to make booklets to share with their families.

School-Home Connection

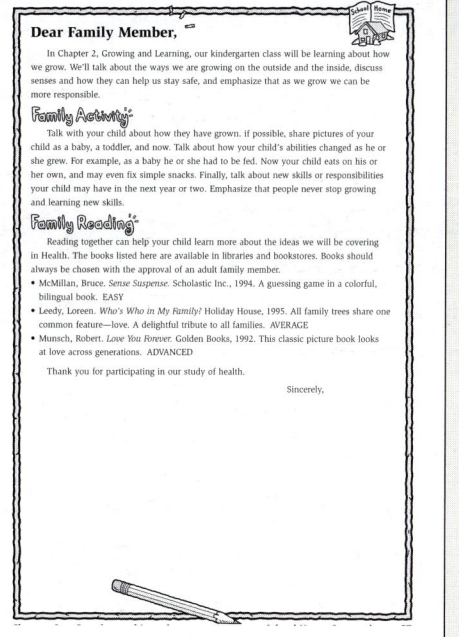

Distribute copies of the School-Home Connection (in English or Spanish), TR page 57. Have children take the page home to share with their families.

Alternative Use the page for enrichment.

OBJECTIVES

- Describe how the body changes as you grow.
- Identify major external body parts.

VOCABULARY

- growing
- trunk (torso)
- head
- legs
- arms
- body

PROGRAM RESOURCES

- Teaching Chart 6
- Pattern 4, TR p. 94
- Song: "Clap Your Hands," p. RA-9
- Activity Book, p. 6

MATERIALS

- 4 shirts in obviously different sizes, such as adult, 12-year-old, kindergartner, baby

Teaching Chart 6

Daily Safety Tip

Exercise helps young bodies grow and become stronger. Encourage children to use proper safety equipment, especially helmets, when they ride bikes, skateboard, and skate.

1 Motivate

Layer the four shirts on the floor with the largest on the bottom and the smallest on top.

- **What do you see? Who do you think these shirts would fit?** Children should describe the pile and probably suggest that the shirts will fit people of different ages.

- Hold up the baby shirt. **Will this shirt fit anybody in the classroom?** no **Did it ever fit anyone in this classroom?** yes, when we were babies

- **Why doesn't it fit you now?** We grew. Explain that as they grew, more than just their body size changed.

2 Teach

Learn from Pictures

Direct attention to Teaching Chart 6. Have children describe what they see. a child as a baby, then a toddler, then a kindergartner

How are the pictures different? They show how the child has grown—he has gotten bigger and is able to do more things.

- Make a class list of things children can do now that they couldn't do as a baby or two or three years ago. Children might suggest eating on their own, dressing themselves and choosing their own clothes each day, riding a bike, and swinging themselves on a swing. Encourage students to include cognitive activities, such as writing their names, counting to ten or more, and identifying shapes. Some students may also suggest that they can now share and work with others, which they couldn't do as well when they were younger.

 **Activity**

Identify Body Parts Reinforce the following body parts: *head, arms, legs,* and *trunk*. Either point to the parts of the body on Teaching Chart 6, or use colored felt or flannel cut into body part shapes. (Use Pattern 4: External Body Parts as a cutting guide.)

- After children are familiar with the vocabulary, play a game of "Simon Says" to review.

3 Wrap Up

To wrap up, sing the song "Clap Your Hands," page RA-9.

- Use verses such as these to review body parts:

    Nod, nod, nod your head, . . .
    Whirl, whirl, whirl your arms, . . .
    Stretch, stretch, stretch your torso, . . .
    Bend, bend, bend your legs, . . .

- Use verses such as these to review how children have grown, reinforcing what they can do now that they could not do when they were younger.

    Write, write, write your name, . . .
    Sing, sing, sing a song, . . .
    Ride, ride, ride a bike, . . .
    Count, count, count to ten, . . .

ASSESSMENT TIP Individually, ask students to name three things they can do now that they could not do when they were younger.

TEACHER TIP

Flannel Board Alternative If a flannel board is not available for the activity, enlarge, cut out, and laminate the external body parts on Pattern 4, TR page 94. Using hook-and-loop tape, attach the body parts to a body outline drawn on chart or butcher paper as you discuss them.

HEALTH BACKGROUND

Human Growth The first five years of human growth are filled with rapid spurts of physical and intellectual development. The first year is full of milestones. Babies go from being infants who do little more than cry, eat, and sleep, to one-year-olds who can smile, say simple words, and often walk. By age two, children have grown considerably in their ability to understand language. Between the ages of two and three, children begin to communicate verbally. They love to imitate behaviors, playing with toy lawnmowers, rakes, and brooms as a parent uses the same tools. By age three, a child's coordination improves. He or she is able to climb stairs with alternating feet and stand on one foot. By age four imagination takes off, and the line between what is real and what is imaginary may be indistinct. By the time children reach kindergarten, most are ready to begin to learn to write and read.

Other things to do!

Math Activity

Height Yarn Graphs Have each child lie down with his or her feet against the wall. Cut a length of yarn to accurately record each child's height. Find a place in the classroom to tape the yarn lengths, marking them with the date and the child's name. Several times during the year measure each child, each time using a different color yarn.

Music Activity

Body Parts Song Sing and act out the song *Head and Shoulders, Knees and Toes* (p. RA-8). Leave out singing one body part on each successive verse, while still doing all the motions. For example:

Verse 1 Sing as shown on page RA–8.

Verse 2 Sing: ____, shoulders, knees, and toes, knees and toes . . .

Verse 3 Sing: ____, ____, knees, and toes, knees and toes . . .

Verse 4 Sing: ____, ____, ____, and toes, ____ and toes . . .

Verse 5 Sing: ____, ____, ____, and ____, ____ and ____ . . .

Using the Activity Book, page 6

This activity helps reinforce external body part names as children draw lines from the word to the proper body part.

My Body on the Outside

LESSON 2

OBJECTIVE
- Identify spine, lungs, stomach, brain, heart, and bones, and tell what each does.

VOCABULARY
- heart
- stomach
- spine
- lungs
- bones
- brain
- skin

PROGRAM RESOURCES
- Teaching Chart 7
- Teaching Transparencies 3, 4, 5, 6, 7
- Pattern 5, TR p. 95
- Performance Assessment Summary Sheet, TR p. 47
- Activity Book, p. 7

MATERIALS
- flannel board and external body parts from Lesson 1 (or laminated external body parts)
- internal body parts (Pattern 5) cut from flannel or laminated as in Lesson 1
- box and wrapping paper
- bicycle helmet

Daily Safety Tip
One important internal body part is the brain. Emphasize the importance of protecting the brain by wearing appropriate safety gear (helmets, mouth guards) when playing active sports or riding bikes.

1 Motivate

Before class, prepare the internal body parts, place in a box, and wrap as a gift. (See Teaching Tip on p. 35.)

- Show children the gift. Let them pass it around, shake it, and so on.
- Explain that the body can be compared to the box a present is wrapped in. The body has a wrapping, just like the present. There are also things inside the body, just as there are things inside the box.

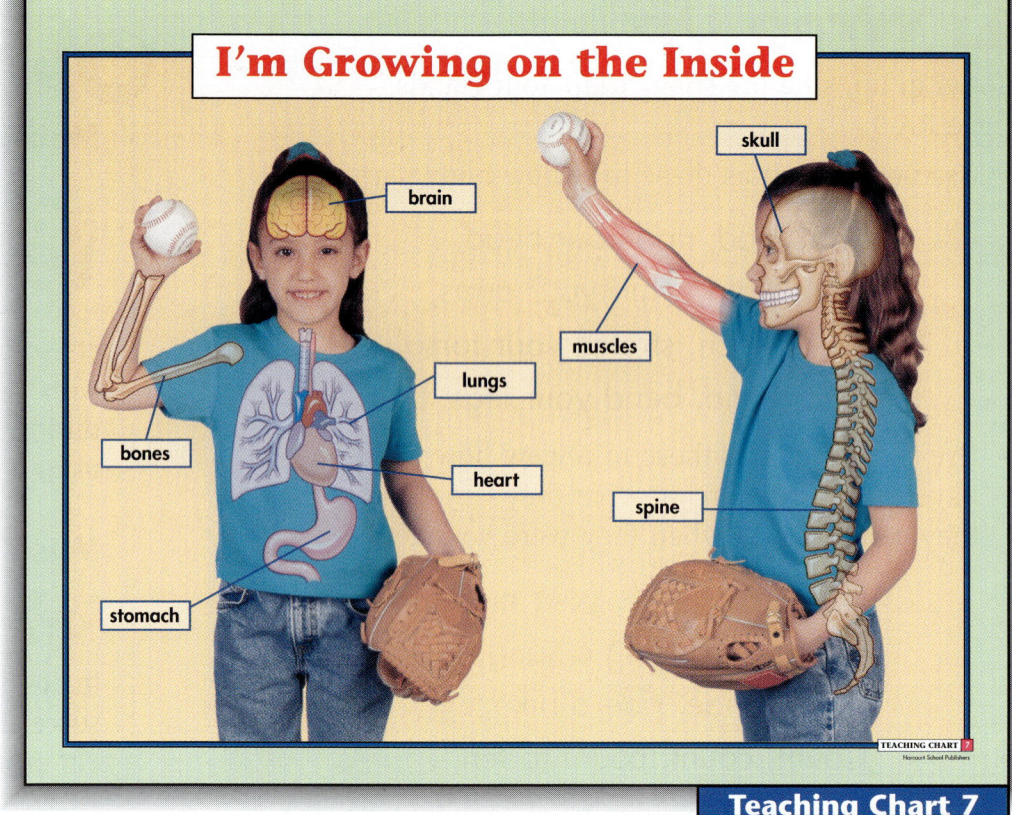

Teaching Chart 7

2 Teach

Discuss

Have children identify the wrapping on their bodies. Children may suggest clothes, but lead them to understand that the skin "wraps" the body.

- Have children feel their hands. **Do you think there is something inside your skin?** Possible answers: something hard, bones, blood, muscles.

Learn from Pictures

Show children Teaching Chart 7. Point to identifying words and ask children if they can tell you what the words are (by looking at the body part and the body outline).

- Have children locate each body part in their own bodies (feel heart beating; feel bones, skull, and spine; flex muscles in arms; breathe in and out.)
- Explain that you cannot feel your brain because it is protected by the skull. Compare the way the skull protects the brain to the way a bike helmet protects the head. If available, show the parts of a bike helmet.
- Discuss what each body part does. For example, the heart pumps blood around the body; the lungs move air in and out of the body.

Activity

Work with Body Parts Open the package to show children what is inside. As you take out each internal body part, hold it up for children to identify. Have volunteers place the body parts on the body outline that already contains the external body parts.

Use Teaching Transparencies

Use Teaching Transparencies 3, 4, 5, 6, and 7 to reinforce how the internal body parts are related to one another.

3 Wrap Up

Remove the internal organs (felt or laminated) from the body outline. Have children take turns putting them back on the outline. As each child places a body part, have other children point to it on their own bodies and name the part. Have a volunteer tell what the part does.

ASSESSMENT TIP Use this activity for performance assessment. See Performance Assessment Summary Sheet, TR page 47.

TEACHER TIP

Prepare Internal Body Parts Using Pattern 5, cut the internal body parts from felt or flannel for use on the flannel board with the external parts from Lesson 1. Or enlarge, cut out, and laminate the internal body parts and use hook-and-loop tape to attach them to the external body parts already displayed on butcher paper from Lesson 1.

MEET INDIVIDUAL NEEDS

Kinesthetic Learners Teach the following poem to the class. Use hand motions to point to body parts.

> Inside of me are many things,
> and I can say them all.
> A brain that thinks,
> A heart that beats,
> Two lungs that breathe,
> A stomach to eat,
> A spine in a line,
> Blood that's red,
> And lots of bones from my toes to my head!

Other things to do!

Science Activity

Make a Stethoscope Have children cut the bottom of a paper cup to form a funnel-like shape. Children can place the funnel on each other's chest, back, and stomach to hear heartbeats, breathing sounds, and stomach sounds.

Art Activity

Understanding Aging Have children complete the following art activity to demonstrate their understanding of the aging process.

Have children draw a baby, a toddler, an elementary school child, a high school student, a parent, and a grandparent. Below each drawing have children write one or two words that describe the needs of each of the type of person shown. For example, below the baby they might write "bottle" or "diaper." Below the parent they might write "job" or "home." Have volunteers share their drawings. Emphasize to children that as we age our needs change.

Using the Activity Book, page 7

Children identify various internal body parts.

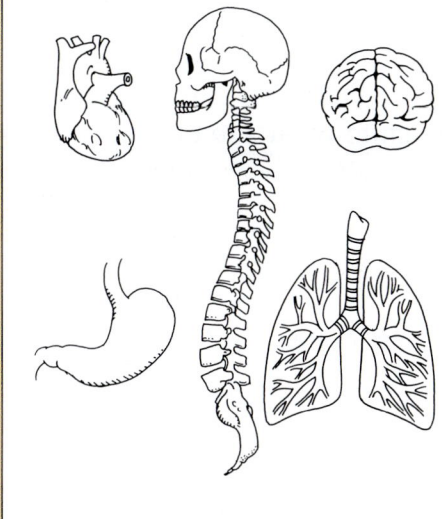

My Body on the Inside

LESSON

OBJECTIVES

- Identify the five senses and tell what they do.
- Identify ways to keep the senses safe.

VOCABULARY

- hear
- see
- smell
- touch
- taste
- senses

PROGRAM RESOURCES

- Teaching Chart 8

 Teaching Transparencies 1 and 2

- Activity Book, p. 8

MATERIALS

- blindfold
- bell, cut lemon, small crackers, crayons
- pictures from magazines that will help children identify which senses they use

Teaching Chart 8

Too much sun can be harmful to the eyes. Caution children *never* to look directly at the sun. Suggest they wear sunglasses to help protect their eyes when out in bright sunlight.

1 Motivate

Explain that the class is going to play a game, and that everyone must be very quiet while you blindfold a volunteer. Hand the blindfolded child a common classroom object that can easily be identified by touch. Ask the child what she or he is holding and how he or she knew what it was. Introduce the word *senses*.

2 Teach

Learn from Pictures

Show children Teaching Chart 8. Have children identify the different senses as you point to them.

Activity

Senses Game Have children sit in a circle. For each of the items listed, have students describe what they are sensing, and how the sense makes life more enjoyable. End the discussion of each sense by discussing ways to keep the sense organ safe.

- **Sight:** Have children cover and then uncover their eyes, describing what they see in each situation. **What would happen if we couldn't see?** Possible answers: might bump into things, could get into dangerous situations, would not be able to see beautiful things like rainbows. **How can we care for our eyes?** Possible answers: keep sharp objects away from them, wear sunglasses, make sure to get enough sleep so that they are rested.

- **Smell:** While children close their eyes, walk from child to child with a cut lemon for them to smell. Repeat the activity while children hold their noses Have them describe their experiences in each situation. **What can we do to take care of our noses?** Possible answers: never stick anything in them, blow nose gently, wear sunscreen.

- **Hearing:** While children close their eyes, ring a bell. Repeat while children hold their hands over their ears. Have children describe their experiences in each situation. **What can we do to take care of our ears?** Possible answers: avoid loud noises, don't put anything inside ears.

- **Taste:** While children close their eyes, have them eat a small cracker. *Note:* Be sure to check for any food allergies your students may have. Ask children to describe what they did, and identify the tongue as the body part that helps us taste. **What can we do to take care of our tongues?** Possible answers: avoid very hot and very cold foods, don't put anything but food in the mouth.
- **Touch:** While children close their eyes, have them pass around a crayon. Ask them to describe what they were feeling and how they knew. **What do you use to touch and feel?** fingers; Help children understand that all of the skin adds to the sense of touch. **What can we do to take care of our sense of touch?** Possible answers: avoid very hot and very cold objects, avoid sharp objects, wear sunscreen.

Use Teaching Transparencies

Use Teaching Transparency 1, The Eye, and Teaching Transparency 2, The Ear, to show the parts of these organs. The copy masters that accompany these transparencies can be used to reinforce the parts of these organs, if desired.

3 Wrap Up

Show children a variety of magazine pictures. Have children point to the senses they would use in each situation or which sense could keep them safe.

ASSESSMENT TIP Repeat the Wrap Up activity with individual children. Have them name the sense as well as point to it.

MEET INDIVIDUAL NEEDS

Vision and Hearing Impairments As you discuss the senses, be sensitive to any children in your class who have vision or hearing impairments. You may want to talk with the class about the special ways people adapt to these challenges.

Other things to do!

Language Arts Activity

My Touch Book Provide children with small pieces of sandpaper, cotton, aluminum foil (smooth and crinkled), and various fabrics (such as corduroy, silk, polyester, satin, fuzzy material) for them to glue on construction paper. One at a time, have children touch each texture and tell how it feels. Record their descriptive words under each item. Combine the pages to make a touch book. Have children decorate the covers and share the books with their families.

Math Activity

Food Graph Allow children to taste small samples of the following foods: sour (pickle or lemon), salty (pretzel), sweet (raisin), and bitter (green olives). *Note:* Be sure to check for food allergies among your students. Make a chart with a picture of each item tasted at the bottom of a column. Give children each a square piece of paper. Have them write their names on them, and glue them in the appropriate column to show which taste was their favorite.

Using the Activity Book, page 8

Children draw lines to match each sense with a picture. More than one sense may be correct.

Using My Senses

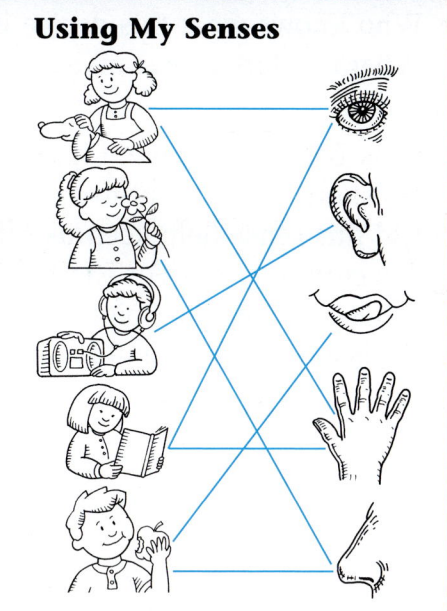

LESSON 4

OBJECTIVE
- Identify how the senses help keep people safe.

VOCABULARY
- safe
- dangerous
- smoke detector
- siren

PROGRAM RESOURCES
- Teaching Chart 9
- Activity Book, p. 9

MATERIALS
- smoke detector

Teaching Chart 9

Daily Safety Tip

Review classroom procedures for a fire drill. Remind children that the most important thing to do when there is an emergency is to follow the teacher's directions.

1 Motivate

Take down the classroom smoke detector or bring one to class. Press the button to test the detector. Most children will cover their ears when they hear the sound. (As an alternative, draw a smoke detector on the board and make the sound yourself.)

- Who knows what this device is? a smoke detector What is it for? to give an early warning of smoke or fire
- Look back at Teaching Chart 8. Ask the following question as you point to each of the sense organs. **Did this sense help keep us safe when the smoke detector went off?** For each wrong sense children should answer *No*. Point to the ears and name hearing last. Children should answer *Yes*.
- **Do you think our senses can help keep us safe?** yes

2 Teach

Learn from Pictures

Show children Teaching Chart 9. **What is happening?** A fire truck is rushing down the street. **How do you know when a fire truck is coming?** see flashing lights; hear the siren

- Point to the people in the picture. **What senses are the people using?** sight (eyes) to see the truck and the flashing lights; hearing (ears) to hear the siren
- **Which of the senses can tell you that there is dangerous smoke?** sight (eyes) and smell (nose)

Discuss

Again refer to the people in the picture. Have children identify what could happen if the following senses were not available.

- **Sight** The people could step off the curb in front of the fire engine.
- **Hearing** The people might not hear the fire engine coming and try to cross the street.

Life Skills

 **Communicate** Talk about how children can communicate what their senses are telling them. Possible situations you might suggest

38

include seeing, something scary or dangerous, hearing a warning of some kind, smelling smoke, smelling food that doesn't smell right.

- Have several children act out ways of using their eyes, ears, or noses to identify an unsafe situation and then tell the problem. Work with children to have them communicate concise, clear messages about the situation.

3 Wrap Up

Draw a large outline of a face on the board. Then describe the situations below.

- You are on a hike. There are big rocks on the ground. Better be careful! **What sense will keep you safe?** sight
- You start to cross the street. Someone yells out: "Be careful! A car is coming." **What senses will keep you safe?** hearing and sight
- Something is wrong. The cookies have been baking too long. Smoke curls out of the oven. Better tell somebody! **What senses will keep you safe?** smell and sight

Invite volunteers to come to the blank face on the board and draw the part of the face that features the senses needed. The rest of the children should touch the part of the body that expresses the correct sense.

ASSESSMENT TIP Individually, ask students to name a way one of their senses can keep them safe.

MEET INDIVIDUAL NEEDS

Kinesthetic/Visual Learners Have children practice using their eyes to keep them safe. Challenge children to walk around the classroom and tell what they need to look for to stay safe, such as things that you could trip on if you don't look where you're walking.

TEACHER TIP

Firehouse Field Trip Plan a field trip to the fire station, or invite a firefighter to come in and talk with the class. Talk about the role firefighters play as community helpers. Ask the firefighter to talk about how to use senses to identify dangers and keep safe.

Other things to do!

Language Arts Activity

Hearing Rhyme To focus on and help develop children's sense of hearing, play "Little Tommy Tittlemouse." Have one child sit on a chair with her or his back to the class. A second child comes up, knocks on the chair and says:

"Little Tommy Tittlemouse,
living in a little house,
someone's knocking, me oh my,
someone's knocking, it is I."

Tell the child in the chair to listen carefully, so she or he can recognize the voice and identify the person knocking.

Language Arts Activity

Our Senses Keep Us Safe Book Create a class big book about the ways the senses help keep children safe. Give children magazines to cut up. The book could include pictures of smoke detectors, fire trucks, police cars, ambulances, and street crossing signs. Have children paste the pictures onto white paper. Staple the pages together.

Using the Activity Book, page 9

This activity helps children identify senses used to keep them safe. Some children may indicate more than one sense.

Eyes and Ears Keep You Safe

LESSON 5

OBJECTIVES
- Describe what it means to be responsible.
- Identify ways to be responsible.

VOCABULARY
- responsible

PROGRAM RESOURCES
- Teaching Chart 10
- Story: "The Bundle of Sticks," p. RA-5
- Activity Book, p. 10

MATERIALS
- chart paper
- blocks
- magazines
- glue
- scissors

Teaching Chart 10

Daily Safety Tip

Part of being responsible is doing what you can to help keep yourself and other people safe. Show children how they can be responsible every day in class and at home. Remind them to do things such as pushing in chairs so the aisles are clear for people to walk through, and picking up toys so no one trips over them.

1 Motivate

Before children enter the classroom, scatter blocks on the floor. Ask children to come and sit on the floor for group time. (Watch as they step on or around or sit on the blocks; some might even pick up the blocks.) **Why are you having problems sitting?** Blocks are all over the group area. **What should we do about this?** Work together to clean up the area. Explain that cleaning up together is one way to be *responsible*.

2 Teach

Learn from Pictures

Show children Teaching Chart 10 and have them describe what they see. The girl is cleaning up her toys; her mother looks happy. Read the title and ask what it means. Possible answers: taking care of things, helping around the house, following rules.

Activity

Clean Up Game Tap out a beat on a drum or on your desk as you read the rhyme on the chart. Let the children practice cleaning up and putting away everything they got out today, as you tap the beat. Invite children to join in saying the words as soon as they learn them. After everything is put away, discuss how putting things away is one way to be responsible.

Life Skills

 **Resolve Conflicts and Communicate** Talk about the kinds of conflicts children get into about doing chores at home. Possible answers: It's not fair; I do more than my brother or sister; Why do I have to do chores?

- Read the story "The Bundle of Sticks," page RA-5. Discuss how the characters in the story learned that it is good to do things together and not fight about chores. **What happened when each child tried to break the bundles of sticks?** No one could do it. **What did the mother say about the sticks?** Sticks are weak when they are apart and strong when they are together. Tell children people who work together are strong, just like the bundle of sticks, and that working together is one way you can support positive family interactions.

Emphasize to children that families get along best when each family member is responsible. This responsibility includes health choices that are made by the family, such as nutritional choices, cleanliness, medical care, and so on. Ask children what health choices are influenced by their family.

3 Wrap Up

Use chart paper to make a picture chart about responsibilities and rules. Put pictures cut from magazines or drawings of classroom chores and rules on the chart. Chores may be things such as putting away what you take out, throwing away your trash in the trash basket, and hanging up your jacket. Add your classroom rules too.

- Talk about what it means to be responsible. Pass the chart around.
- Have children write their names next to chores they have done and rules they have followed.
- Hang the chart in the classroom.

ASSESSMENT TIP Look for answers that indicate children understand the meaning of responsibility and that they are beginning to be willing to accept being responsible.

TEACHER TIP

Privacy Issues As you talk about responsibility, be sensitive to any children in your class who may have too many responsibilities, or those who are not allowed to do anything responsible at home.

ART Activity

Responsibility Collage Show children some pictures of nature. Talk about the wonderful places that are on Earth. Then invite children to talk about litter and the problems litter creates. Have children work in groups to cut pictures from magazines that show people being responsible about trash and litter. Have them paste their pictures on cardboard or poster board labeled *I'm Responsible*.

Other things to do!

Language Arts Activity

Action Poem Have children learn the following poem. Teach children to point to the different parts of their bodies as they say the lines of the poem. Invite the class to perform the poem and actions together.

*Two little eyes see nice things to do,
Two little lips smile the whole day through,
Two little ears hear what others say,
Two little hands put our toys away,
A tongue to speak sweet words each day,
A loving heart for work and play,
Two feet that errands gladly run,
Make happy days for every one.*

Language Arts Activity

The Berenstain Bears and the Messy Room Read *The Berenstain Bears and the Messy Room* by Stan and Jan Berenstain (Random House, 1983). Discuss what happens when we don't take care of our things. Brainstorm ways to help Brother and Sister Bear be more responsible.

Using the Activity Book, page 10

Children color pictures that show children helping. They leave one picture uncolored.

Cleaning Up

CHAPTER  Caring *for* My Teeth

Chapter Organizer

Lesson	Objectives	Vocabulary	Program Resources
Introduce the Chapter pp. 46–47	• Preview the chapter. • Introduce chapter activity center.		• School-Home Connection, TR p. 59 • Take-Home Booklet, TR pp. 77–78
Lesson 1 **My Teeth** pp. 48–49 Pacing: 1 class period	1•5 • Describe two different types of teeth and explain their functions.	teeth bite chew gum	• Teaching Chart 11 • Teaching Transparency 8 • Poems: "Ruth Luce and Bruce Booth" and "This Tooth," p. RA-2 • Performance Assessment Summary Sheet, TR p. 48 • Activity Book, p. 11
Lesson 2 **Cleaning My Teeth** pp. 50–51 Pacing: 1 class period	1•3•7 • Demonstrate the proper way to brush teeth. • Explain how to floss teeth.	brush floss	• Teaching Chart 12 • Pattern 7, TR p. 97 • Song: "Clap Your Hands," p. RA-9 • Activity Book, p. 12
Lesson 3 **Keeping My Teeth Safe** pp. 52–53 Pacing: 1 class period	1•3•6 • Describe situations that are safe or harmful for teeth. • Identify foods that are healthful or unhealthful for teeth.	mouth guard calcium	• Teaching Chart 13 • Pattern 6, TR p. 96 • Activity Book, p. 13

National Health Education Standards
A complete list of the Standards is provided on the next page.

Key: TR = Teaching Resources

National Health Education Standards

1. Comprehend concepts related to health promotion and disease prevention.
2. Access valid health information and health-promoting products and services.
3. Practice health-enhancing behaviors and reduce health risks.
4. Analyze the influence of culture, media, technology, and other factors on health.
5. Use interpersonal communication skills to enhance health.
6. Use goal-setting and decision-making skills to enhance health.
7. Advocate personal, family, and community health.

Curriculum Integration

Use these topics to integrate health into your daily planning.

Art
- Paper Plate Teeth Puppets, p. 44
- Decorated Teeth, p. 49
- Tooth Care Mobiles, p. 51

Math
- Toothbrush Addition, p. 51
- Sorting Teeth, p. 53

Music
- Brushing Chant, p. 44
- Puppets Sing Back, p. 44

Science
- Calcium and Teeth, p. 44
- Animal Teeth, p. 49
- Toothpaste Experiment, p. 51
- Inside and Outside a Tooth, p. 53

ASSESSMENT OPTIONS

Portfolio Assessment
Have students select their best work from the following suggestions.
- **Paper Plate Teeth Puppets**, p. 44
- **Tooth Care Mobile**, p. 51
- **My Best Work Portfolio Summary Sheet**, TR p. 42
- **Portfolio Summary Sheet**, TR p. 43

Student Self-Assessment
- **Student Self-Assessment Checklist**, TR p. 38
- **Healthy Habits Checklist**, TR p. 39

Classroom Observation
- **Observation Checklist**, TR p. 36

Performance Assessment
- **Wrap Up**, pp. 49, 51, 53
- **Performance Assessment Summary Sheet**, TR p. 48

Daily Assessment
- **Assessment Tips**, pp. 49, 51, 53
- **Activity Book**, pp. 11, 12, 13

Cross-Curricular Activities

Art

Paper Plate Teeth Puppets

Give each child a paper plate to fold in half. With the long, flat side at the top, have children draw eyes and noses on the plates. Distribute small white beads, and have children glue them to the inside top and bottom curves of the plates to represent teeth.

Music

Puppets Sing Back

Have children use the puppets they made in Paper Plate Teeth Puppets or other hand puppets to sing the chorus for the song below (sung to the tune of *Frère Jacques,* also called *Are You Sleeping, Brother John?*).

(teacher) Do you brush them, do you brush them?
(puppets) Yes we do, yes we do.
(teacher) Round and round in circles.
(puppets) Round and round in circles.
(teacher) Every tooth.
(puppets) Every tooth.

Science

Calcium and Teeth

Show the children an eggshell, and tell them that eggshells are made of calcium, just like teeth. Set out two cups of equal size. Put sugared cola in one cup, and the same amount of water in the second cup. Put a piece of eggshell in each cup. Set the cups aside in a place where they will not be disturbed for two days.

- At the end of two days, have children tell what they think has happened to the eggshells. Write their predictions on chart paper. Use a slotted spoon to remove the eggshell from each cup. Have children examine the eggshells. They will find that the one sitting in the soda became brittle, while the one that was in water did not change.

- Explain that teeth, too, can become brittle if sweets are left on their surface.

Music

Brushing Chant

Have children clap out the rhythm as they chant this rhyme. You may also want to pass out copies of Pattern 7: Toothbrush, for children to use to act out toothbrushing.

When you wake up in the morning and it's quarter to one,
You want to have a little fun,
You brush your teeth, ch, ch, ch, ch, ch, ch, ch, ch, ch.

When you wake up in the morning and it's quarter to two,
And you don't know what to do,
You brush your teeth, ch, ch, ch, ch, ch, ch, ch, ch, ch.

When you wake up in the morning and it's quarter to three,
You've got a great big smile for me,
You brush your teeth, ch, ch, ch, ch, ch, ch, ch, ch, ch.

When you wake up in the morning and it's quarter to four,
You hear a knock on your bedroom door,
You brush your teeth, ch, ch, ch, ch, ch, ch, ch, ch, ch.

When you wake up in the morning and it's quarter to five,
You're so happy to be alive,
You brush your teeth, ch, ch, ch, ch, ch, ch, ch, ch, ch.

Bulletin Board

Use a strip of colored paper to divide the bulletin board into two equal sections.

- Put a picture of a large biting tooth in the center of one half, with the heading *I Bite Meat*.
- Put a picture of a chewing tooth in the center of the other half, with the heading *I Chew Plants*.
- Have children find animal pictures in magazines and books to post on the appropriate half. Use colored yarn to connect each picture to its corresponding tooth shape.

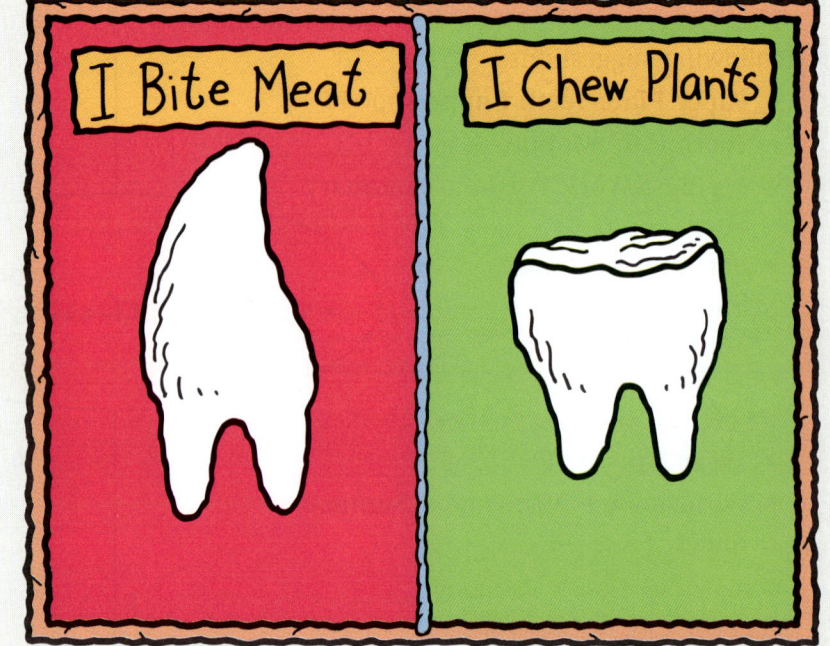

Resources

Books for Students

Read Alouds

Dowdy, Linda Cress. ***Barney Goes to the Dentist.*** Scholastic, 1997. A visit with Barney helps children feel more comfortable about dental visits. **EASY**

Langreuter, Jutta and Vera Sobat. ***Little Bear Brushes His Teeth.*** The Millbrook Press, 1995. Parents teach their cub to brush his teeth. **AVERAGE**

Bunting, Eve. ***Trouble on the T-Ball Team.*** Houghton Mifflin, 1999. Story about losing teeth. **ADVANCED**

Books for Teachers and Families

Moss, Stephen J. ***Growing Up Cavity-Free: A Parents' Guide to Prevention.*** Quintessesnce Publishing, 1994. Parents will benefit from the dental advice found here.

Swartz, Linda, ***Meet Your Teeth: A Fun Creative Dental Unit for Kids in Grades 1-4.*** Creative Teaching Press, 1996. This activity book explains in clear but entertaining terms why caring for teeth is so important.

Video

Head To Toe—A Healthy Smile. AIT Productions, 1994. (15 minutes) Shows young students good dental hygiene techniques and explains why baby teeth come out and are replaced by permanent teeth.

Arthur's Tooth. Sony Music Entertainment, 1998. (30 minutes) The aardvark has a loose tooth and tries many ingenious ways to pull it out.

A Trip to the Dentist Can Be Lots of Fun! Schlessinger Media, 2000. (25 minutes) Makes going to the dentist a positive experience as it explains dental equipment and procedures.

Your Health Webliography

The **Webliography** provides links to the Health Background and teaching resources that will support you as you teach the topics in *Your Health*. Simply choose a keyword and you will be taken to a page of links with descriptions of the content you can obtain at each site. The **Webliography** is located on the Teacher Resources page at **www.harcourtschool.com/health** Please review websites before referring your students to them.

Organizations and Agencies

American Academy of Pediatric Dentistry
211 East Chicago Avenue
Suite 700
Chicago, IL 60611–2616
312-337-2169
Provides educational materials designed for young patients.

The American Academy of Periodontology
737 North Michigan Avenue
Suite 800
Chicago, IL 60611-2690
Provides literature with detailed pictures to show students the proper way to brush and floss.

For more information about health organizations and agencies, please see the *Teaching Resources* book.

Community Health

Dentist or Dental Hygienist
Invite a dentist or a dental hygienist to visit your class to reinforce proper brushing and flossing techniques. Ask them to bring disclosing tablets if they are available, along with sample toothbrushes and toothpaste. After children hear about proper brushing techniques, have them brush their teeth, and then use the disclosing tablets. Allow them to brush their teeth again to remove any coloration. The visiting dental care professional should reinforce that some areas would be much easier to clean using floss.

Free and Inexpensive Material

The Sugar Association, Inc.
1101 15th Street, N.W. Suite #600
Washington, D.C. 20005
202-785-1122
Provides booklets and brochures that answer common questions about children's dental health.

Note that information, while correct at time of publication, is subject to change.

Visit **The Harcourt Learning Site** for related links, activities, resources, and the health **Webliography**.
www.harcourtschool.com

CHAPTER 3

Pages 42–53

"All people smile in the same language."

—Anonymous

CHAPTER SUMMARY

In this chapter children
- describe the function of different kinds of teeth.
- demonstrate how to care for their teeth and how to protect them.
- identify foods that promote dental health.

LIFE SKILLS Children *make decisions* about foods that are good for their teeth.

HUMAN BODY Children identify the different types of teeth and describe their functions.

Caring for My Teeth

Health Activity Center

The activities suggested for this chapter's Health Activity Center help reinforce the functions of teeth and how to care for them.

Learning to Floss

This activity helps children hold and use dental floss.

Materials Needed
- plastic model of teeth
- dental floss or string

What to Do Demonstrate how to pull out and break off the proper length of dental floss. Show children how to wrap the floss around each middle finger. Have children practice this wrapping technique. (Be sure children don't wrap the floss too tightly.) Using the model, show children how to slide the floss between teeth and down to the gums. Let small groups of children practice flossing, using the model. Caution them not to floss their own teeth without adult supervision.

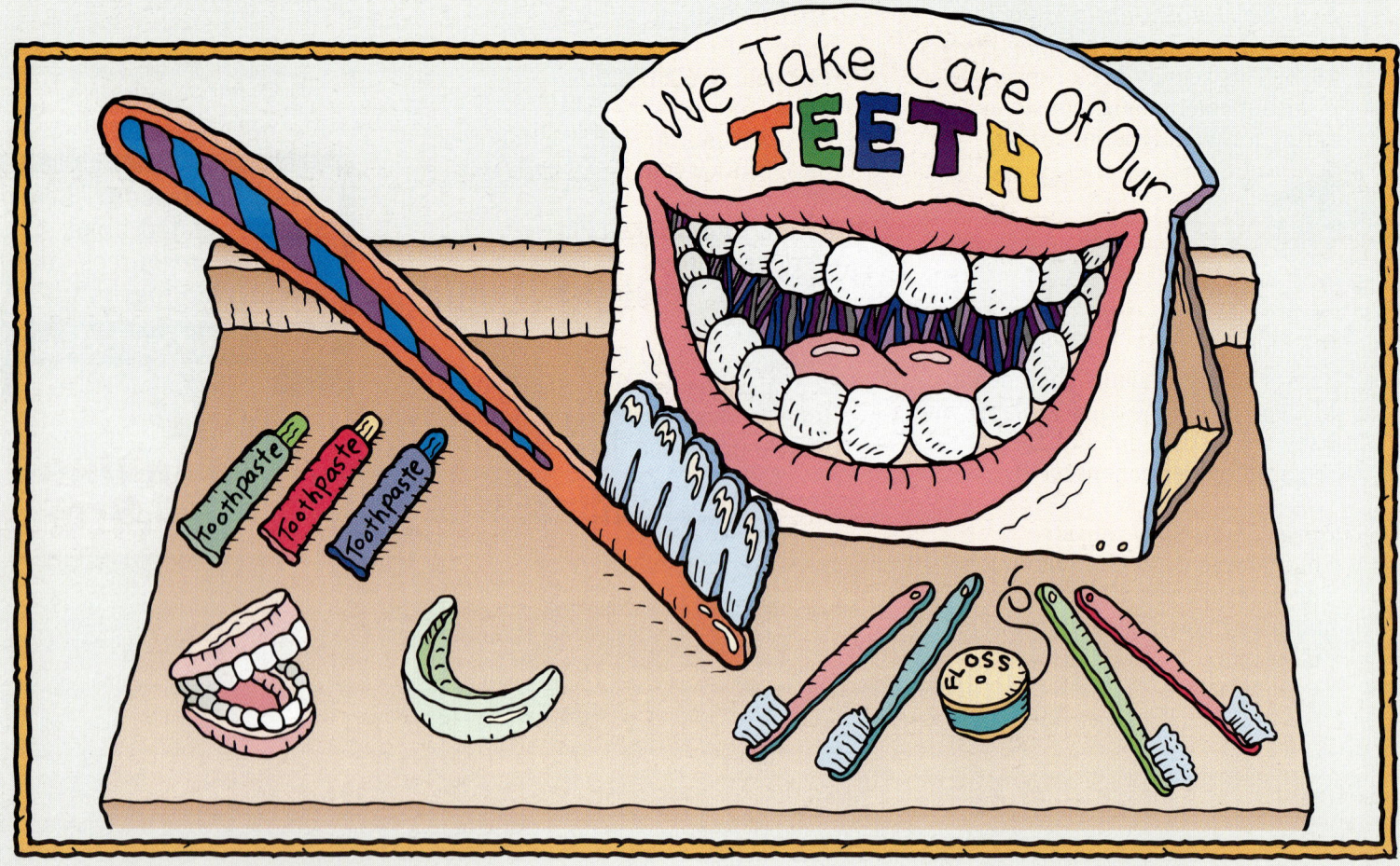

Animal Teeth

In this activity children reinforce the differences between biting and chewing teeth.

Materials Needed
- books with pictures of animals eating

What to Do Individually, have children look through the books and identify herbivores (plant eaters with grinding teeth) and carnivores (meat eaters with biting and tearing teeth). Or have children look at what the animals are eating and describe whether their teeth would be pointy (biting teeth) or flat (grinding teeth). Explain that some animals, like people, eat a variety of foods and need both biting and grinding teeth.

Class Smile

This activity helps children remember to care for their teeth every day.

Materials Needed
- large lips drawn on poster board, painted red
- white paint
- black marker

What to Do Have children collect small rocks that look like teeth. Have each child paint his or her rock white, and use the marker to label the rock with his or her initials or name. Finally, have children glue their "teeth" to the smiling mouth. Work together to label the poster *We Take Care of Our Teeth!*

Smiley Tooth

This activity helps reinforce that some foods help teeth grow strong and healthy.

Materials Needed (per child)
- Pattern 6: Tooth, TR p. 96
- magazines to cut up
- construction paper
- scissors and glue
- label that says *Smile Foods*

What to Do Review foods that are good for teeth, such as calcium-enriched orange juice, milk, fruits, and vegetables. Encourage children to name foods that are low in sugar. Have children cut out the tooth patterns and glue them on construction paper. Have children glue the labels *Smile Foods* on their papers. Finally, have them draw smiley faces on the teeth and paste pictures of foods that are good for their teeth around the smiley teeth.

Take-Home Booklet

Distribute copies of the Take-Home Booklet, TR pages 77–78. Have children fold the pages to make booklets to share with their families.

School-Home Connection

Distribute copies of the School-Home Connection (in English or Spanish), TR page 59. Have children take the page home to share with their families.

Alternative Use the page for enrichment.

LESSON 1

OBJECTIVE
- Describe two different types of teeth and explain their functions.

VOCABULARY
- teeth
- bite
- chew
- gum

PROGRAM RESOURCES
- Teaching Chart 11

Teaching Transparency 8

- Poems: "Ruth Luce and Bruce Booth" and "This Tooth," p. RA-2
- Performance Assessment Summary Sheet, TR p. 48
- Activity Book, p. 11

MATERIALS
- bite-size pieces of apple, one for each child

Daily Safety Tip

Remind children that chewing food slowly and completely, chewing with their mouths closed, and not talking with food in their mouths are not just good manners. Eating this way prevents choking on food.

---

1 Motivate

Have children wash their hands. Give each child a piece of apple to eat. Note: Check for food allergies before allowing children to eat any foods. What did you just do with the apple? ate it How did you do that? chewed; used teeth Could a baby eat that apple? Why or why not? No; babies don't have teeth.

2 Teach

Have each child turn to a partner and open their mouths. What do you see? teeth, tongue Are the teeth all the same? no

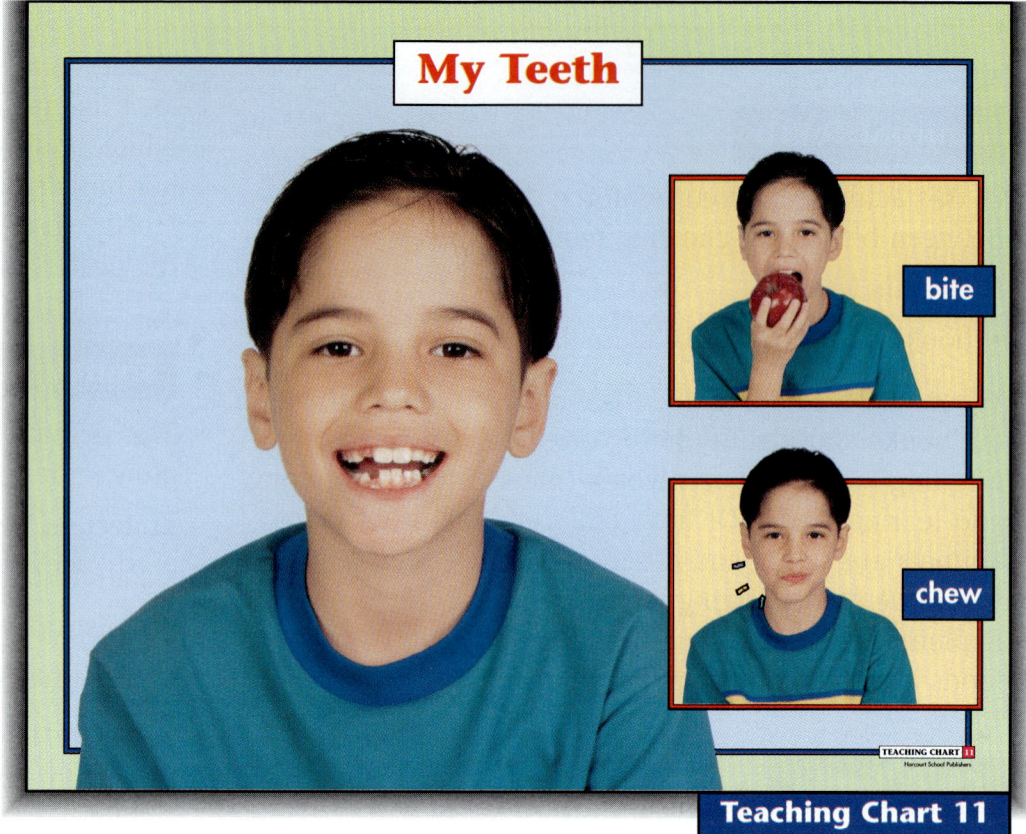

Teaching Chart 11

- Why do you think there are different kinds of teeth? Help children understand that teeth do different jobs. The teeth toward the front of the mouth are for biting. The back teeth are for chewing. These teeth grind up the food and make it small enough to swallow.

Learn from Pictures

Show children Teaching Chart 11. Point to the two small pictures. Say the words *bite* and *chew*. Have children repeat the words as you point to them in the pictures.

- Which picture shows a child using biting teeth? the top picture Which picture shows a child using chewing teeth? the bottom picture

Use Teaching Transparencies

Use Teaching Transparency 8 to show children the inside and outside of a tooth. Point out that part of a tooth can be seen and felt in the mouth and part of the tooth, the root, is under the gum. Show your own gums. Explain that teeth have roots just like flowers and plants do.

Discuss

Have children look at the large picture of the smiling child. Ask what they notice. Teeth are missing. What happened? The boy lost some of his "baby" teeth.

48

- Read the poem "Ruth Luce and Bruce Booth" page RA-2. Ask if anyone in class has a loose tooth. Does it affect the way they talk? How does it feel to wiggle the tooth back and forth in the mouth?
- What does it feel like to lose a tooth? **Possible answers: hole in mouth, tongue keeps going to the hole, empty space.** Is it difficult to eat some foods? Why? **Yes; teeth are missing.**
- Explain that after a baby tooth is lost, a permanent tooth replaces it. **How do you know when the new tooth is coming in? You can see and feel it pushing through the gum.**
- Read the poem "This Tooth" page RA-2. Ask children who have lost teeth to tell if they did all the things the child in the poem did to try and get the tooth out.

3 Wrap Up

Have children wash their hands. Tell children to feel inside their mouths and count their chewing teeth. Then have them count their biting teeth. Have children wash their hands again. Help children make a Tooth Graph that shows how many biting teeth and how many chewing teeth they have.

ASSESSMENT TIP The above activity can be used to evaluate children's performance. See the Performance Assessment Summary Sheet, TR page 48.

TEACHER TIP

More on the Tooth Graph You can make the Wrap Up activity a year-long, ongoing project. Include a column on the graph for how many teeth children lose in the course of the school year. Use this column to reinforce counting. Add a column for how many dental visits children make. Do periodic collage activities in which children cut up magazines and paste pictures of children following good dental health practices.

MEET INDIVIDUAL NEEDS

Visual and Tactile Learners Bring in a model of teeth to use throughout this chapter. Possible sources are the school science coordinator or a pediatric dentist. Children can count the teeth and look at the chewing teeth and the biting teeth. It is also useful to have mirrors the children can use to look at their own teeth.

Other things to do!

Science Activity

Animal Teeth Show children large pictures of a cow, a sheep, and a giraffe. Explain that these animals chew and eat grass and plants. Then show large pictures of a wolf, a tiger, and a lion. Explain that these animals bite and eat meat. Hold up a picture of a chewing tooth. Let children name which animals would use the chewing teeth. Do the same with a picture of a biting tooth.

Art Activity

Decorated Teeth Give each child a copy of Pattern 6: Tooth, TR page 96. Have each child cut out the tooth and write his or her name on it. Children may draw smiles on their teeth. Display the teeth in the classroom. Have children put a star on their tooth every time they lose a tooth during the school year. These teeth can also be displayed on cubbies or other places where children's possessions are labeled.

Using the Activity Book, page 11

This activity helps children reinforce the difference between the positions of biting and chewing teeth.

Teeth That Bite and Teeth That Chew

LESSON 2

OBJECTIVES
- Demonstrate the proper way to brush teeth.
- Explain how to floss teeth.

VOCABULARY
- brush
- floss

PROGRAM RESOURCES
- Teaching Chart 12
- Pattern 7, TR p. 97
- Song: "Clap Your Hands," p. RA-9
- Activity Book, p. 12

MATERIALS
- uncooked pea or a bead the size of a pea
- piece of floss or string
- toothbrush

Teaching Chart 12

Daily Safety Tip

Germs are easily spread through hand-to-mouth and mouth-to-mouth contact. Remind children not to put anything that has been in someone else's mouth or that has been handled by other people in their mouths. This includes toothbrushes.

1 Motivate

Give each child a toothbrush from Pattern 7. Have children stand in a circle with you in the middle. Lead the children in pretending to brush their teeth as you sing these words to the tune of "Clap Your Hands," page RA-9: "Brush, brush, brush our teeth, brush our teeth together."

- What were we doing? brushing our teeth, cleaning our teeth
- Why do we need to brush our teeth? Possible answers: teeth get dirty, to keep our teeth clean, so we won't get toothaches.

2 Teach

Learn from Pictures

Show children Teaching Chart 12, and draw their attention to the top row of pictures.

- What do you see in the first picture? toothbrush with toothpaste Is there a lot of toothpaste? no, just a little Explain that the picture shows the right amount of toothpaste to use, an amount about the size of a pea. Show children a toothbrush and uncooked pea or a bead that is about that size.

- What do you see in the next picture? child brushing teeth Have children wash their hands and then use their fingers on their teeth to show how the child in the picture is moving the toothbrush. Explain that they should gently brush in circles across one tooth at a time.

- What do you see in the last picture in the row? child rinsing Explain that it's not healthy to swallow toothpaste, just as it's not healthy to swallow soap after washing hands and face.

Discuss

Draw attention to the second row of pictures.

- What is the parent holding in the first picture? a container of floss What is floss used for? to help loosen the food that gets stuck between teeth

- Tell children that in the second picture the parent is stretching out the floss, getting ready to use it. Demonstrate with a piece of floss or string.
- In the third picture the parent is flossing the child's teeth. Tell children that when they get older, they will be able to floss by themselves. Right now, their parents or guardians can help. Their parents or guardians will know when it is time for the children to floss by themselves.

Discuss

Review all the pictures. Have children find the numbers in the corners of each of the photos. Review sequencing with children, and ask them to tell you the steps, in order, for brushing and flossing.

3 Wrap Up

Have children use the toothbrush pattern to practice the correct way to brush their teeth. Be sure they brush in a circular pattern.

ASSESSMENT TIP Children should be able to demonstrate the correct manner for brushing.

TEACHER TIP

A Dental Care Speaker Ask a dentist or dental hygienist to visit the class. He or she will usually bring sample toothbrushes and demonstrate proper tooth brushing. As an alternative, show children a picture of a dentist or dental hygienist and tell children what this health professional does. Note that there may be children in class who brush their teeth rarely, if at all. If you can, get some toothbrushes and sample-size toothpaste donated, and make them available to children who need them.

MATH *Activity*

Toothbrush Addition Choose up to nine children to come to the front of the room with their toothbrush patterns. Group the children into two groups. Have the rest of the class count how many toothbrushes they see in the first group. Draw that number of stick figures on the board above that group. Do the same for the other group. Put a "+" sign between the two sets on the board and an "=" sign in the appropriate place. Have the children move together under the place where the sum will be written, and guide the class in counting how many toothbrushes there are all together. Draw that number of stick figures on the board. Then have children read the math sentence together. If they have trouble understanding, re-enact the math sentence as they read it. Continue this activity using different children and different groupings and totals.

Other things to do!

Science Activity

Toothpaste Experiment Spread mustard, ketchup, and prepared oatmeal on ceramic tiles and set them aside. When food has hardened and caked on the tiles, let children try removing it with a wet toothbrush and then with a wet toothbrush with toothpaste. Point out how the toothpaste helps. Emphasize that it is important to use toothpaste when brushing teeth.

Art Activity

Tooth Care Mobiles Have children cut out from magazines pictures of toothbrushes, toothpaste, floss, dentists, children brushing their teeth, and big smiles. Then direct children to glue their pictures to copies of Pattern 6. When each child has three or four pictures ready, punch a hole near the top of each picture and attach it to a hanger using different lengths of yarn. As an alternative, children can make drawings on Pattern 6 instead of cutting out pictures.

Using the Activity Book, page 12

This activity provides an opportunity for children to show the correct order for cleaning their teeth.

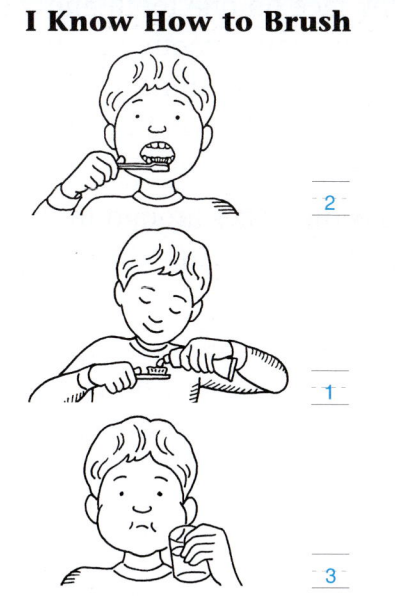

LESSON

OBJECTIVES
- Describe situations that are safe or harmful for teeth.
- Identify foods that are healthful or unhealthful for teeth.

VOCABULARY
- mouth guard
- calcium

PROGRAM RESOURCES
- Teaching Chart 13
- Pattern 6, TR p. 96
- Activity Book, p. 13

MATERIALS
- mouth guard
- two boxes, one containing a small, empty milk carton, the other containing an empty candy bar wrapper

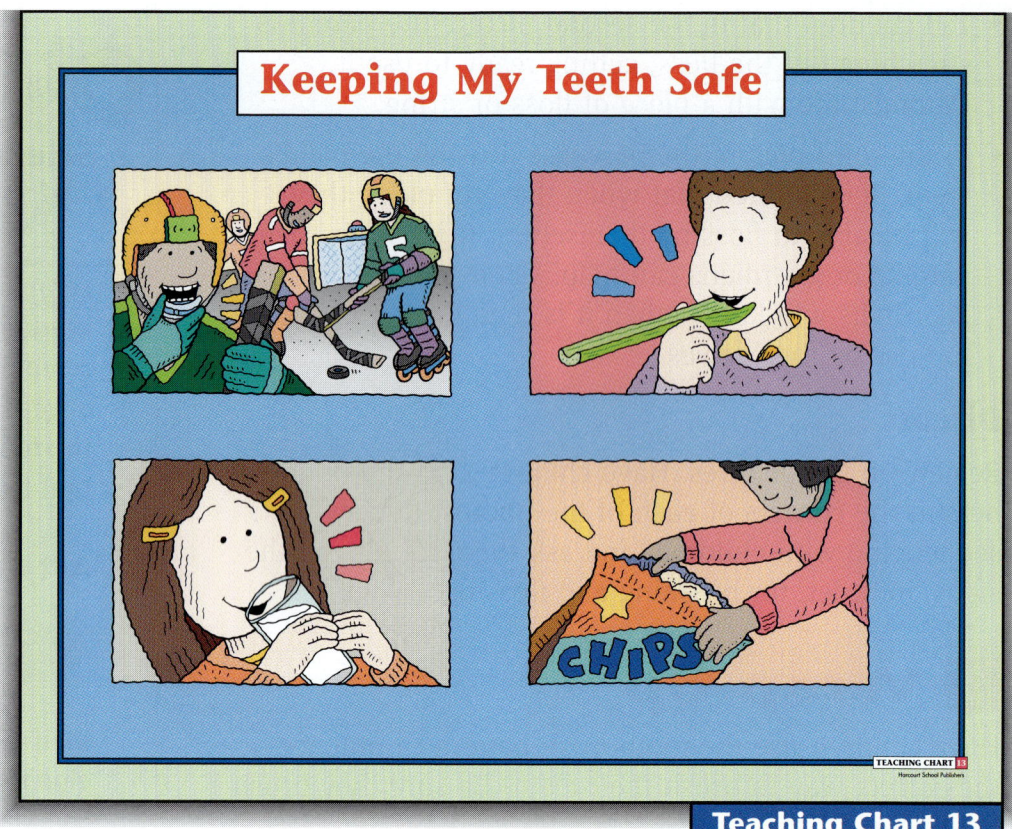

Teaching Chart 13

Daily Safety Tip

Facial injuries in almost any sport can cause damage to teeth, lips, cheeks, and tongue. Mouth guards protect the face from these injuries. Remind children to wear mouth guards when they participate in sports.

1 Motivate

Before class, make two copies of Pattern 6. Draw a happy face on one tooth and a sad face on the other. Paste the happy tooth on a box, and put a small, empty milk carton inside. Paste the sad tooth on a second box and put an empty candy wrapper inside. Tape the boxes shut.

- Pass the boxes around to the children. **What is on the boxes?** a happy tooth, a sad tooth, pictures of teeth
- Open the boxes. Let children look inside each one. **Why is a milk carton in the happy tooth box and a candy wrapper in the sad tooth box?** Possible answers: some foods are good for teeth and some are less good.

2 Teach

Remind children of what they have learned about why teeth are important. **Who remembers why teeth are important?** to bite, chew, speak

Learn from Pictures

Show children Teaching Chart 13.

- Point to the pictures, one at a time. **What are the children in each picture doing to keep their teeth safe?** wearing a mouth guard to play sports, eating celery, drinking milk, using hands to open chip bag

Discuss

Return to the picture of the mouth guard. **Has anyone ever used one (or seen one used)? If so, when?** Possible answers: all football players wear mouth guards; many children engaged in team sports wear mouth guards.

- Show children a mouth guard. Explain that dentists recommend people playing any sport wear mouth guards. Demonstrate how the mouth guard is worn. Explain that a mouth guard softens blows to the face and neck.
- **What could happen if you played sports without a mouth guard?** Possible answers: ball or stick can hit your teeth; you can fall and break your teeth.

52

Discuss

Return to the picture of the child opening the bag.

- Help children make a list of ways to open a package. Possible ways include use scissors, pull package apart, have an adult help, use teeth to tear the bag. Have each child who contributes to the list act out his or her suggestion. Guide children in sorting the list into healthful and unhealthful ways of opening packages.

- **What's wrong with opening a chip bag with your teeth?** You could break or injure teeth or gums. Remind children not to use their teeth as a tool.

Life Skills

Make Decisions Use the photos of children eating foods that are good for their teeth to reinforce decision-making skills. Explain that sugary, sticky foods and drinks are fun to eat once in a while, but they can harm the teeth over time.

- Have children list some choices they might have for a drink at snack time. Write the choices on the board. Discuss the advantages and disadvantages of each drink. Let children raise hands to vote for each drink. Repeat this process using snack foods. Encourage children to brush after all snacks.

3 Wrap Up

Give each child two copies of Pattern 6. Have children use crayons to make a happy tooth and a sad tooth. Ask children to take turns suggesting a food, a drink, or an action that is either good for or harmful to teeth. Alternatively, you suggest the foods and situations. As each action is described, have the class hold up either a happy or a sad tooth in response.

ASSESSMENT TIP Look for the proper tooth being held up in each situation. For foods, have children with different ideas about what is healthful and what is not explain their choices.

HEALTH BACKGROUND

Types of Mouth Guards *Ready-made mouth guards* can be purchased at most sporting goods stores. They are the least expensive, and the least effective. *Mouth-formed guards*, called boil and bite guards, should be fitted by a dentist. This is done by shaping a soft pre-formed guide to the contours of the teeth and allowing it to harden. *Custom-made mouth guards* are professionally designed by a dentist from a casting of your teeth. These guards cover the back teeth and cushion the entire jaw, thus preventing concussions as well as tooth injury.

Other things to do!

Math Activity

Sorting Teeth Put the happy and sad tooth boxes in the Health Activity Center. Organize the class into work groups to draw or to cut out of magazines pictures of food choices and actions that are good for teeth and harmful to teeth. Put all the pictures in a single container. As time permits, allow individual children to choose a picture and decide which box to put it into.

Science Activity

Inside and Outside a Tooth Extend the lesson by examining with the children the structure of a tooth. Use Teaching Transparency 9 to show the outside and the inside of a tooth. Remind children that a tooth has a root just like a plant. Ask a child who has lost a tooth to describe it, using the words shown on the transparency. Have children wash their hands and then feel the different parts of their teeth. Can they feel the crown? Gum? Why can't they feel the root? Have children wash their hands again after completing this activity.

Using the Activity Book, page 13

Children navigate a maze and find their way to the healthy smile by choosing the apple, milk, pretzel, and oatmeal rather than the less healthful choices.

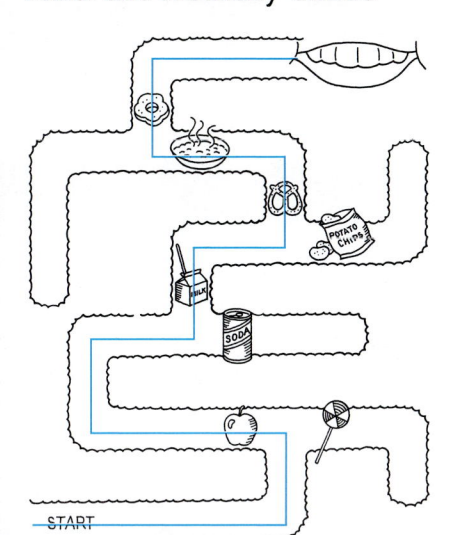

Find the Healthy Smile

CHAPTER  **Staying Fit *and* Healthy**

Chapter Organizer

Lesson	Objectives	Vocabulary	Program Resources
Introduce the Chapter pp. 58–59	• Preview the chapter. • Introduce chapter activity center.		• School-Home Connection, TR p. 61 • Take-Home Booklet, TR pp. 79–80
Lesson 1 **I Take Care of My Skin** pp. 60–61 *Pacing: 2 class periods* 1•3	• Identify ways to protect and care for skin. • Explain why cleanliness is important.	sunscreen shampoo nail clippers nail file washcloth	• Teaching Chart 14 • Pattern 8, TR p. 98 • Activity Book, p. 14
Lesson 2 **Sit Tall** pp. 62–63 *Pacing: 1 class period* 1•3•7	• Describe good posture. • Explain why good posture is important.	posture spine straight	• Teaching Charts 7 and 15 • Teaching Transparency 3 • Activity Book, p. 15
Lesson 3 **I Exercise Safely** pp. 64–65 *Pacing: 2 class periods* 3•5•6	• Describe what it means to exercise safely. • Identify a warm-up, workout, and cool-down.	warm-up workout cool-down stretching muscles	• Teaching Chart 16 • Poem: "Exercises," p. RA-3 • Teaching Transparency 7 • Activity Book, p. 16
Lesson 4 **Deal with Stress** pp. 66–67 *Pacing: 1 class period* 3•5•6	• Describe how stress feels. • Identify ways to manage stress.	stress manage stress	• Teaching Chart 17 • Pattern 3, TR p. 93 • Activity Book, p. 17
Lesson 5 **Time for Bed** pp. 68–69 *Pacing: 1 class period* 1•3•7	• Identify signs of sleepiness • Recognize that sleep and rest are necessary for good health.	sleep rest relax energy	• Teaching Chart 18 • Performance Assessment Summary Sheet, TR p. 49 • Activity Book, p. 18

National Health Education Standards
A complete list of the Standards is provided on the next page.

Key: TR = Teaching Resources

National Health Education Standards

1. Comprehend concepts related to health promotion and disease prevention.
2. Access valid health information and health-promoting products and services.
3. Practice health-enhancing behaviors and reduce health risks.
4. Analyze the influence of culture, media, technology, and other factors on health.
5. Use interpersonal communication skills to enhance health.
6. Use goal-setting and decision-making skills to enhance health.
7. Advocate for personal, family, and community health.

Curriculum Integration
Use these topics to integrate health into your daily planning.

Math
- Self-Care Graph, p. 61
- Stress Bar Graphs, p. 67
- Ten in a Bed, p. 69

Music
- Keep Our Skin Healthy Song, p. 61
- Good Posture Song, p. 63
- Sing Away Stress, p. 67

Physical Education
- Posture Movements, p. 63

Social Studies
- Exerciser's Field Trip, p. 65

Language Arts
- I Exercise Book, p. 65

Science
- Toasty Warm Verses Burnt Toast, p. 56

Drama
- Happy/Sad Puppets, p. 56
- Little Lambs Rest, p. 56

ASSESSMENT OPTIONS

Portfolio Assessment
Have students select their best work from the following suggestions:
- **Portfolio Summary Sheet,** TR p. 43
- **Our Stress Busters Collage,** p. 67
- **I Exercise Book,** p. 65
- **My Best Work Portfolio Summary Sheet,** TR p. 42

Student Self-Assessment
- **Student Self-Assessment Checklist,** TR p. 38
- **Healthy Habits Checklist,** TR p. 39

Classroom Observation
- **Observation Checklist,** TR p. 36

Performance Assessment
- **Performance Assessment Summary Sheet,** TR p. 49
- **Wrap Up,** p. 69

Daily Assessment
- **Activity Book,** pp. 14–18
- **Assessment Tips,** pp. 61, 63, 65, 67, 69

Cross-Curricular Activities

Science

Toasty Warm Verses Burnt Toast

Turn a toaster on, and let children see the element get hot. Tell children to imagine that the toaster is the sun and the bread is skin without sunscreen. What will happen to the bread when we put it into the toaster? Put one slice of white bread in at a high setting, so the bread gets very dark and children can smell it burning.

- Hold up the dark toast. **What happened?** The bread burned because the toaster was hot.

- Put one slice of white bread in at a very low setting, so the change in color is not obvious. **Did the toaster change the bread?** No, because the toaster was not hot enough. Pass the bread around. Point out that even though the children don't see a difference, the bread changed. Explain that the bread is like our skin. We need to protect it even when it will not be near heat for very long or when it is not very hot outside. We should wear sunscreen every day.

- **What do you think will happen if we put this slice of dark bread in the toaster?** Children will discover that the dark bread will feel the same as the white bread did, even though neither of them burned. Explain that everyone needs sunscreen.

Drama

Happy/Sad Puppets

Provide each child with two copies of Pattern 2, Blank Face, TR page 91. Have children make a happy face on one pattern, and a sad face on the other. Have children glue their face patterns back-to-back, with a craft stick in the middle to form a handle. When the happy/sad puppets are complete, give children a variety of stressful scenarios and ways they can manage stress. Have children hold up the face representing the way they would feel in each instance.

Drama

Little Lambs Rest

To emphasize the importance of sleep and rest, have children role-play the little lambs in this poem. One child can play the mother lamb.

Little Lambs

Little baby lambs come out to play

In a grassy field on a summer day.

They nibble the grass and jump and run,

And sleep by their mother when day is done.

Little baby lambs are fast asleep,

Beside their dear old mother sheep.

Bulletin Board

Let's Work Out

Place a banner with the above title across the top of the bulletin board. Divide the area below the title into three sections as shown.

- Have children draw or cut pictures out of magazines that represent activities they like to do for warm-ups, workouts, and cool-downs.

- Post the pictures in the appropriate sections of the bulletin board.

Books for Students

Read Alouds

Sharmat, Marjorie Weinman. *Tiffany Dino Works Out*. Simon and Schuster Books for Young Readers, 1995. Charming picture book supporting healthy habits and self-respect as links to a healthy body.
EASY

Fox, Mem. *Time for Bed*. Harcourt, 1997. The simple, rhyming text tells the story of little lamb's bedtime.
AVERAGE

Showers, Paul. *Your Skin and Mine*. HarperCollins, 1991. A lovely introduction to skin color and function.
ADVANCED

Books for Teachers and Families

Laderer, Mandy. *Fit-Kids . . . Getting Kids "Hooked" on Fitness Fun!* Allure Publishing, 1994. Wonderful for the classroom; a supportive book for good physical health.

Virgilio, Stephen J. *Fitness Education for Children: A Team Approach*. Human Kinetics Publications, 1997. A comprehensive resource that includes 100 practical activities and instructional materials for adults who work with children on good health and fitness.

Video

The Germ Busters. Kid Safety of America, 1996. (30 minutes) Shows young students how to avoid picking up germs and how to prevent spreading their own germs.

Growing Up Fit at Elliott's Gym. Schlessinger Media, 1995. (30 minutes) Children learn about exercise and how it can be fun in this live-action program.

Your Health Webliography

The **Webliography** provides links to the Health Background and teaching resources that will support you as you teach the topics in *Your Health*. Simply choose a keyword and you will be taken to a page of links with descriptions of the content you can obtain at each site. The **Webliography** is located on the Teacher Resources page at **www.harcourtschool.com/health** Please review websites before referring your students to them.

Organizations and Agencies

American Optometric Association
Communications Center
243 North Lindbergh Boulevard
St. Louis, MO 63141
Offers information on the importance of protecting your eyes.

American Skin Association
150 East 58th Street, 33rd Floor
New York, NY 10155-0002
800-499-SKIN
Promotes public education on preventing skin disorders.

National Association for the Education of Young Children
1509 16th Street, NW
Washington, D.C. 20036-1426
800-424-2460
Provides general information on keeping healthy.

For more information about health organizations and agencies, please see the *Teaching Resources* book.

Community Health

Physical Education Teacher Invite a physical education teacher or fitness trainer to visit your class. Ask the visitor to discuss the importance of exercise and demonstrate some safe, simple warm-up and cool-down stretches appropriate for children. (As an alternative invite a dermatologist to speak about ways to protect the skin.) Encourage children to ask about the value of wearing hats and other protective clothing as well as applying sunscreen frequently.

Free and Inexpensive Material

The National Grange
1616 H Street, NW
Washington, D.C. 20006-4999
Provides a program for students about sound, the ear, and how hearing works.

U.S. National Library of Medicine
8600 Rockville Pike
Bethesda, MD 20894
Provides information on the importance of proper sleep for children through its *Star Sleeper* initiative.

Note that information, while correct at time of publication, is subject to change.

Visit **The Harcourt Learning Site** for related links, activities, resources, and the health **Webliography**.
www.harcourtschool.com

CHAPTER 4

Pages 54–69

"My father had always said that there are four things a child needs—plenty of love, nourishing food, regular sleep, and lots of soap and water—and after those, what he needs most is some intelligent neglect."

—Ivy Baker Priest

CHAPTER SUMMARY

In this chapter children
- describe good posture and why it is important.
- describe how to exercise safely.
- explain what it means to be responsible and describe how they are responsible.

LIFE SKILLS Children learn how stress feels and identify ways to *manage stress.*

HUMAN BODY Children identify ways to care for the skin and explain why cleanliness is important.

Staying Fit and Healthy

Health Activity Center

The activities suggested for this chapter's Health Activity Center help reinforce the importance of skin care and taking care of oneself for good health.

Quiet as a Mouse

This activity helps children focus on a variety of quiet activities.

Materials Needed (per child)
- magazines
- glue
- construction paper

What to Do Talk about the meaning of the saying "quiet as a mouse." Ask children to think about their favorite "quiet-as-a-mouse" activities. Have children cut pictures from magazines to make collages of quiet activities they enjoy doing to relax. Title the collages "My Quiet-as-a-Mouse Activities."

Paper People

This activity reinforces the importance of protecting the skin from exposure to sun.

Materials Needed
- butcher paper
- scissors
- stapler
- crayons or markers
- newspaper
- yarn
- dress-up clothes

What to Do Invite one of the children to lie down on butcher paper. Make two tracings of the child, and cut them out. Have children draw features and glue hair on the tracings to make the front and back of a person. Staple the two outlines together, leaving an opening through which children can stuff newspapers. Then finish stapling the outlines together. Children can use clothes from the dress-up center to dress the person appropriately for a day in the sun. As an alternative, make a variety of paper people and let children draw clothes on them.

Pasta Posture

This activity reinforces how the spine should be aligned for good posture.

Materials Needed (per child)
- 33 rigatoni pasta or beads in plastic bag
- yarn or string (knotted at one end)

What to Do Have children feel a partner's upper back along the spine. Remind children that their spines help hold up their bodies. (You may wish to show Teaching Chart 7.)

- Tell children there are 33 bones in the spine. Have children string the 33 rigatoni or beads on the yarn to represent the spine and spinal cord. Tie off the loose ends of the "spines."
- Lead children in using their pasta spines to demonstrate good posture. Remind children that they should sit and stand as if an invisible string were pulling their spines into a straight line.

Animal Exercises

This activity can help incorporate body movement and stretching into your daily routine.

Materials Needed
- pictures of different, familiar animals, such as elephants, horses, cows, dogs, cats, frogs

What to Do Put the animal pictures in the activity center. Each day, ask a child to choose a picture. Talk about the animal chosen, including where it lives and what it eats. Have children stand up and move around the classroom, mimicking the way the animal moves.

Take-Home Booklet

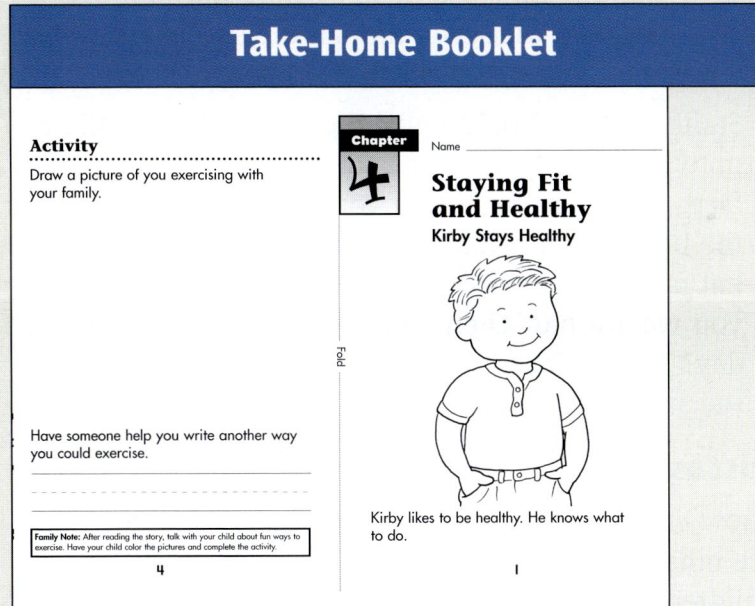

Distribute copies of the Take-Home Booklet, TR pages 79–80. Have children fold the page to make booklets to share with their families.

School-Home Connection

Distribute copies of the School-Home Connection (in English or Spanish), TR page 61. Have children take the page home to share with their families.

Alternative Use the page for enrichment.

LESSON 1

OBJECTIVES
- Identify ways to protect and care for skin.
- Explain why cleanliness is important.

VOCABULARY
- sunscreen
- shampoo
- nail clippers
- nail file
- washcloth

PROGRAM RESOURCES
- Teaching Chart 14
- Pattern 8, TR p. 98
- Activity Book, p. 14

MATERIALS
- sunscreen
- wide-brimmed hat
- nail clipper, nail file, and nail brush
- shampoo
- washcloth
- soap

Teaching Chart 14

Daily Safety Tip
The sun's rays can cause sunburn, even on cloudy days. Remind children that they should wear sunscreen whenever they are outside, not just on sunny days.

1 Motivate

Have children stand in a circle and do the "Hokey-Pokey." After the class finishes the song, ask them what they think the song and the motions are about. Explain that the song is about taking a bath.

- **Why do we take baths?** to get clean, to clean the skin
- Have children repeat the song and motions, this time altering the chorus to say, ". . . and that's how we clean our skin."

2 Teach

Learn from Pictures

Show children Teaching Chart 14. **What is the girl in the picture doing?** putting on sunscreen Show the class a bottle of sunscreen. **Why is she using sunscreen?** to protect her skin from the sun Let children imitate the girl's behavior by rubbing their arms. Tell children to notice how soft their skin is. Explain that sunscreen can help protect their skin from the sun, thus helping to keep it soft.

Discuss

Point to the sun on Teaching Chart 14. **What do we know about the sun?** hot, big, gives light **What happens if you get too close to something hot?** You get burned. Explain that even though the sun is far away, it is very hot, and its rays can burn people's skin.

- Stand under a bright light, if possible. Have children note how the "sun" shines down on your head and face. Then put the hat on your head and stand under the bright light again. Have children note how the hat provides protection from the sun. **Why should you wear a hat when you go outside on a sunny day?** The hat protects the skin on your head from the sun.

Discuss

Show children soap, shampoo, and a washcloth. **What are other ways that we take care of our skin?** Have children match each item to Teaching Chart 14 and tell how each is used.

- Discuss the importance of keeping the skin and hair clean. **Why are shampoo, soap, and washcloths important for taking care of your skin?** Washing removes germs and dirt and helps keep illness from spreading.

Activity

Washing Hands Show children the nail brush and soap. **When is it important to wash your hands?** Possible answers: before fixing food or eating, after going to the bathroom, after covering a sneeze or cough, after playing, whenever they are dirty.

- Work with small groups of children to practice hand-washing techniques. Warm water, soap, and vigorous rubbing are all needed to clean hands adequately. Suggest that children wash their hands for as long as it takes to say the ABCs.
- As children wash hands, have them pay attention to their nails. Encourage them to use a nail brush to gently remove dirt from under the nails.
- Follow up with a demonstration on how to file nails. Emphasize that an adult family member should work with children to care for their nails.
- After all children have worked on hand-washing techniques, give each child a copy of Pattern 8. Work with the class to make a list of good hand-washing tips, and copy these onto the cut-out bubble patterns. 1. Water, 2. Soap, 3. Bubbles, 4. Rinse, 5. Dry. Suggest children post these signs by their bathroom sinks at home.

3 Wrap Up

Play a *Simon Says* Skin Care game. Have children pantomime all the skin care tips they've learned as you call them out in the Simon Says format. Include washing hair and hands, filing and cleaning nails, and putting on sunscreen and hats to protect their skin.

ASSESSMENT TIP Look for answers that show children understand how to perform skin care.

TEACHER TIP

Personal Care Items Some children may not have access to the things they need to care for their skin. Keep samples of sunscreen, shampoo, soap, nail files, and even hats, on hand. Periodically, ask if anyone needs any of these things.

Other things to do!

Music Activity

Keep Our Skin Healthy Song To the tune of "Mulberry Bush," page RA-10, have children sing lyrics that remind them of the ways they can keep their skin healthy. An example is shown below. Children should do the actions as they sing the words.

> This is the way we wash our hands, . . .
> to keep our skin healthy,
>
> This is the way we clean our nails, . . .
> to keep our skin healthy,
>
> This is the way we wash our hair, . . .
> to keep our skin healthy,
>
> This is the way we put sunscreen on, . . .
> to keep our skin healthy.

Math Activity

Self-Care Graph Make the bottom of the bar graph using pictures of each personal care item pictured on Teaching Chart 14. Give each child several copies of the happy feelings faces from Pattern 2, TR page 92. Have each child glue a happy feeling face above each personal care item they have used this week.

Using the Activity Book, page 14

This activity reinforces children's understanding of when sunscreen use is appropriate.

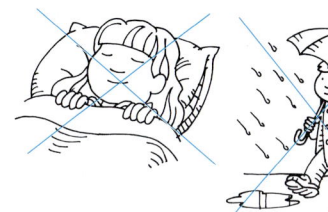

Sunny Days

LESSON 2

OBJECTIVES
- Describe good posture.
- Explain why good posture is important.

VOCABULARY
- posture
- spine
- straight

PROGRAM RESOURCES
- Teaching Charts 7 and 15

 Teaching Transparency 3

- Activity Book, p. 15

MATERIALS
- rag doll
- ruler
- footstool

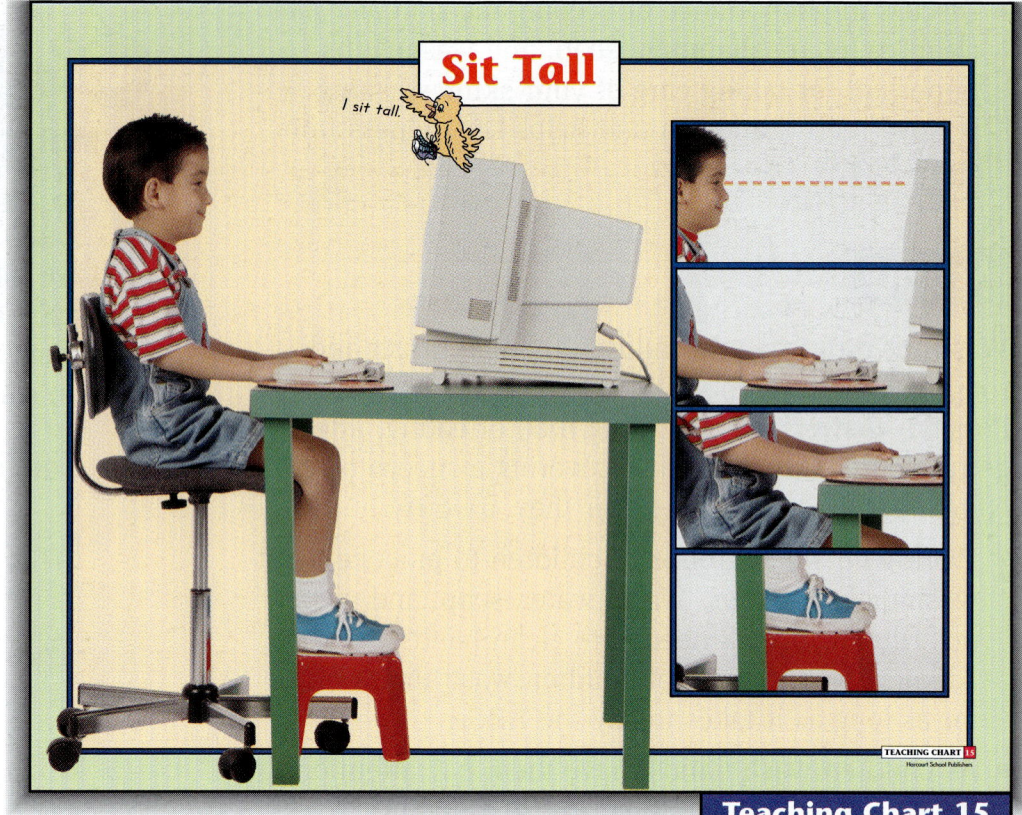

Teaching Chart 15

Daily Safety Tip

Most computer systems are designed for an adult body. Remind children of the importance of sitting square in the chair. Backs should be touching the seat the whole time. Don't slouch or lean over the keyboard while typing.

1 Motivate

Show children a rag doll. Move the doll around. **Can a rag doll sit up straight?** no **Can a rag doll stand?** No; all a rag doll can do is flop and bend.

- Put on music and have children move like a rag doll to the tempo of the music. Move the rag doll as the children move. Show the children that the rag doll can be contorted into positions that the human body cannot assume.

- **Can you flop and bend as the doll can?** no **Why not?** We have bones. **Who remembers the name of the long bone that we have in our backs?** spine Show the picture of the spine on Teaching Chart 7.

- Turn your back to the children and remind them of the spine's position. Have children touch their own spines.

2 Teach

Learn from Pictures

Direct attention to Teaching Chart 15. **What do you see?** A boy sitting up straight at the computer. Point out that the boy's feet are resting on a footstool, his eyes are level with the monitor, and his arms and hands are at a proper angle.

Teaching Transparencies

 Use Teaching Transparency 3 to remind children what their spine looks like inside their bodies.

- Point to Teaching Chart 15 again. Read what the bird sitting on the computer is saying ("I sit tall"). Explain that this boy knows how to sit tall.

Discuss

Tell children they need to help their spines stay strong and healthy. Show children a ruler. Talk about how to keep their spines straight like this ruler. Tell children that *posture* is the word that describes keeping the spine straight.

- Have children model the proper way to stand. Use the phrase "You have good posture" as children straighten their spines and stand tall.

Activity

Practice Sitting Tall Reinforce the correct way to sit at a computer (and in other chairs). Set up a "good posture" chair in front of a table. Place a footstool in front of the chair, made out of blocks, if necessary. Put another chair, the "bad posture chair," near the first one. Have the children take turns sitting in each chair, demonstrating good posture by sitting up straight, feet on the footstool, and bad posture by slumping in the chair. Let the other children call out the words "good posture" and "bad posture" to describe the child in each chair.

3 Wrap Up

Have the children sit in their own chairs. Show them Teaching Chart 15 again. Ask the children to come up to the page and match up the sections in the little pictures with the same parts of the big picture.

ASSESSMENT TIP Look for signs that children see the full picture of good posture, not just the parts.

TEACHER TIP

Transparency Alternative If an overhead projector is not available, enlarge, cut out, and laminate the spine on Pattern 5: Internal Body Parts, TR page 95. Draw a body outline on chart or butcher paper and use hook-and-loop tape to attach the spine to the outline as you discuss what the spine looks like inside the body.

MEET INDIVIDUAL NEEDS

Kinesthetic Learners Have children role-play different ways to move their bodies and spines such as arch their backs and move like a cat, slither like a snake, crawl like a baby, walk like an elephant, stretch like a giraffe, and hop like a bunny. Children can then play Follow the Leader, with the leader modeling different ways to move the body while the other children follow.

Other things to do!

Physical Education

Posture Movements Show Teaching Chart 15 again. Call out phrases that describe each of the pictures on the right side: head straight and eyes level; hands are on the keyboard, eyes straight ahead, spine straight, feet on footstool. Ask children to pantomime what you call out.

Music Activity

Good Posture Song Sing a verse of "Did You Ever See a Lassie." Have children sing it again using lyrics and actions that reinforce good posture. Use the rag doll to show children the actions. An example is shown below.

Did you ever see a slumper, a slumper, a slumper? Did you ever see a slumper go this way and that?

Children flop and slump as they sing.

Did you ever see good posture, good posture, good posture? Did you ever see good posture, stand so straight and tall?

Children stretch and reach for the sky.

Using the Activity Book, page 15

This activity provides opportunities for children to choose the best posture in sets of pictures.

Good Posture

LESSON 3

OBJECTIVES
- Describe what it means to exercise safely.
- Identify a warm-up, workout, and cool-down.

VOCABULARY
- warm-up
- workout
- cool-down
- stretching
- muscles

PROGRAM RESOURCES
- Teaching Chart 16
- Poem: "Exercises," p. RA-3
- Teaching Transparency 7
- Activity Book, p. 16

MATERIALS
- large rubber band
- recording of slow, relaxing music and player

Teaching Chart 16

Daily Safety Tip

Daily physical activity is important. For children this age, encourage daily physical activity for enjoyment. Help children see how they exercise as they play.

1 Motivate

Play some slow, relaxing music. Give children a series of directions: *Slowly stretch up tall. Slowly bend to the side. Slowly bend to the other side. Slowly turn your head from side to side.* **What parts of your bodies did you use to make those movements?** muscles Tell children that every time they move, their muscles work.

- Show children a rubber band. Slowly stretch it out and return it to its regular size. **How are muscles like this rubber band?** Muscles stretch (extend) and return (relax) just as the rubber band does. Explain that stretching muscles slowly gets the muscles ready to work out safely.

2 Teach

Use Teaching Transparencies

Use Teaching Transparency 7 to show children what muscles look like inside their bodies. Explain that exercise helps strengthen muscles, which help support the body and allow you to move.

Learn from Pictures

Direct children to Teaching Chart 16. Explain that there are three parts to exercise. The first part is called the *warm-up*. It is light exercise and stretching. Explain that the slow exercises they did are part of a warm-up.

- Look at the picture. **What comes next?** workout Explain that, to be effective, a workout needs to get your heart beating fast and your breathing rate up. **What workouts do you do?** Possible answers: running, jogging, running in place, doing jumping jacks. *Note:* Children of this age may not do any formal exercises. Active play is their most likely form of workout.

- **What comes next?** cool-down Tell children the cool-down helps their muscles relax again. A cool-down helps their heart rate and breathing rate return to normal. It helps their muscles stretch out again after exercising, so that they don't get stiff and sore.

64

Activity

A Complete Workout Have children stand up and spread out around the room. Do a warm-up activity like the picture on Teaching Chart 16. Have children extend arms over head and bend at the waist slowly from side to side, feeling muscles stretch as you count to ten. Then have children run or walk in place or do jumping jacks for five to ten minutes. If possible, have children go out on the playground to run around for this period. Now do the cool-down. Have children walk slowly for about two minutes, and then stop and stretch.

- Bring the class back together and review what you did. As you describe each part of the exercise routine, have children call out, *warm-up, workout,* or *cool-down.*

3 Wrap Up

Read the poem "Exercises," page RA-3. Have children identify the parts of a good workout described in the poem. What part of a good workout is missing?

ASSESSMENT TIP Note whether children understand that the cool-down portion of a workout is more than just sitting down and resting. The cool-down should include slow exercise followed by stretching.

TEACHER TIP

Children Who Should Not Exercise Children who have exercise-induced asthma should not be a part of classroom exercise. Children with physical disabilities, such as those who use wheelchairs, should be encouraged to exercise as they are able. When children are ill, it would be better for them to sit out of any planned exercise.

MEET INDIVIDUAL NEEDS

Kinesthetic Learners Work with the class to make a list of warm-up and cool-down activities that could be done in the classroom. When the list is complete, have children use the list as a basis for a warm-up/cool-down "Hokey Pokey." Have the class stand in a circle and practice each exercise as they sing the song.

Other things to do!

Language Arts Activity

I Exercise Book Provide each child with writing-drawing paper. Each day for a week, have children tell you a new activity for each sentence listed below.

It is fun to [name activity] to warm-up.

It is fun to [name activity] to workout.

It is fun to [name activity] to cool-down.

Have children copy the daily sentences onto the bottom of the paper and illustrate the activity at the top of the paper. At the end of the week, collect each child's papers into a booklet for them to take home.

Social Studies Activity

Exerciser's Field Trip Take a field trip to a gym or exercise facility. Arrange to have an exercise specialist teach the class some warm-up, workout, and cool-down exercises. Caution children that workout machines are not designed for children to use. These machines are built for adult bodies, and can cause serious harm if used improperly.

Using the Activity Book, page 16

Children order the steps of a safe workout. Children color pictures and number them.

I Know How to Exercise

2 Workout

1 Warm-Up

3 Cool-Down

LESSON 4

OBJECTIVES
- Describe how stress feels.
- Identify ways to manage stress.

VOCABULARY
- stress
- manage stress

PROGRAM RESOURCES
- Teaching Chart 17
- Pattern 3, TR p. 93
- Activity Book, p. 17

MATERIALS
- old magazines
- drawing paper
- crayons

Teaching Chart 17

Daily Safety Tip

Stress occurs in everyone. Even young children have worries and feel stress. Remind children that talking to someone is a good way to deal with stress. Two other stress busters include exercise and taking time to laugh and have fun.

1 Motivate

Make a hand puppet using Pattern 3. Have children listen as you use the puppet to act out this story.

- Puppet: "Oh, no, I can't find my new sweater! I can't go home without it! My parents will be so angry with me!" Have Puppet clutch its stomach and show other signs of distress.

- Ask children to pantomime what Puppet is feeling in its body. stomachache, pounding heart Then have Puppet begin to cry and say, "I know I'll never find my brand new sweater. Boo hoo, boo hoo!" Have children pantomime the crying.

- How might Puppet be feeling? Possible answers: worried, scared, panicked, very upset, sick. When are times you might feel this way? Possible answers: when parent is ill, when there's too much to do, when it's time to get a shot, when I get in trouble.

- Explain that there is a word for these feelings. The word is *stress*. Stress is something that everyone feels sometimes.

2 Teach

Learn from Pictures

Show children Teaching Chart 17. Explain that the pictures show some ways to manage stress. *Managing stress* means to find ways to feel better, to get your mind off the problem that is bothering you, and to relax.

- How are the children in this picture dealing with stress? quiet time, exercise, painting, music, talking to someone who can help

- Talk about ways that the children in your class deal with stress. Encourage them to list a variety of activities that help them relax. Emphasize that talking to adult family members, teachers, or other trusted adults may be one of the best ways to handle stress.

- Children may wish to draw pictures of the person they would most like to talk to when feeling stress about something.

Life Skills

Manage Stress Emphasize that physical activity is one of the ways to deal with stress. Brainstorm with the class a list of physical activities that children can do when they are feeling stressed.

- Work together to find pictures in magazines or draw pictures of these physical activities. Compile the pictures into a collage entitled, "Our Stress Busters." Encourage children to choose one of these activities whenever they feel overwhelmed or stressed-out.

3 Wrap Up

Remind children of the story with Puppet. Explain that Puppet's teacher has found Puppet upset and stressed-out. Puppet has explained the problem to the teacher. The story continues.

Teacher: "I don't see your sweater anywhere. I'm sure we'll find it, but school is over for today. Everyone has to leave now."

Puppet continues to cry. **How can Puppet deal with stress?** Talk with an adult family member about the problem.

Have another dialogue with Puppet talking with parents about the problem. Ask children for ways the family could deal with the problem of the lost sweater that would make Puppet feel better.

ASSESSMENT TIP Look for ideas that show understanding that talking a problem over with someone, and then doing things to get your mind off your problem, are good ways to deal with stress.

MEET INDIVIDUAL NEEDS

Visual and Auditory Learners Have pairs of children act out ways to deal with stress. Tell the children this scenario: You are ready for school. Your mom's car won't start. You have to wait for someone to come and fix the car. You feel stress because you are going to be late for school. Have children review the ideas on Teaching Chart 17 and those brainstormed for the Stress-Busters Collage. Assign one of the ways to deal with stress to each pair. Depending on class size, you may need to assign some stress-busters to several groups. Have each group make up a simple skit showing how they would deal with the stress. Have pairs perform their skits for the rest of the class.

Other things to do!

Math Activity

Stress Bar Graphs Use the pictures shown on Teaching Chart 17, on the Stress-Busters Collages, or from other lists made during this lesson to make the base of a pictograph. Give each child a sticker with his or her name on it. Have children place their stickers on the graph to show their favorite ways to relieve stress.

Music Activity

Sing Away Stress Use the song "If You're Happy and You Know It, Clap Your Hands" to reinforce ways to deal with stress. Substitute different words and appropriate actions. Have children use body language to show the actions. For example,

If you're feeling too much stress, read a book. . . .

If you're feeling too much stress, have a talk. . . .

If you're feeling too much stress, take a walk. . . .

Using the Activity Book, page 17

This activity helps children make choices about ways of dealing with stress.

I Can Deal with Stress

LESSON 5

OBJECTIVES
- Identify signs of sleepiness.
- Recognize that sleep and rest are necessary for good health.

VOCABULARY
- sleep
- relax
- rest
- energy

PROGRAM RESOURCES
- Teaching Chart 18
- Performance Assessment Summary Sheet, TR p. 49
- Activity Book, p. 18

MATERIALS
- *Goodnight Moon* by Margaret Wise Brown (Harperfestival, 1991) or any other story suitable for bedtime

Teaching Chart 18

Daily Safety Tip

Most experts agree that young children need twelve or more hours of sleep a night. Adequate sleep helps children stay alert and improves learning. Encourage children to get a good night's rest.

1 Motivate

Tell children you have a story to read to them. Have them sit quietly as you read *Goodnight Moon* (or any other suitable bedtime story). **How are you feeling?** Possible answers: quiet, relaxed, peaceful.

2 Teach

Learn from Pictures

Show children Teaching Chart 18. **What do you see?** a father reading a story to a child **What time do you think it is?** nighttime, bedtime **Why do you think the father is reading the book?** to help the child relax and fall asleep easily Explain that the body and mind need a transition time from the active day to sleep. This time works much like a cool-down after a workout. It lets your mind and body slow down and begin to relax.

- Make a class list of quiet activities children like to do before going to bed. Have children pantomime these activities as you add them to the list. Encourage children NOT to watch TV or do very physical activities right at bedtime. These activities excite the mind and body, making it more difficult to relax and fall asleep.

Discuss

Just as it is important for the body to get exercise and work hard, the body also needs time to sleep and rest. When the body is sleeping, it grows and repairs itself. The mind is able to clear itself and the body relaxes.

- **What do you feel like when you're tired and need to go sleep?** Possible answers: cranky, sleepy, no energy, bad mood. Explain that these feelings are the body's signals for telling a person he or she needs rest.

Quiet Time Explain that sleeping is a quiet activity. Quiet activities done throughout the day can help a person rest and recover from periods of physical activity. Many of the activities children listed for dealing with stress are good quiet-time activities.

- Work as a class to list children's favorite quiet-time activities. (These may be very similar to the before-bed activities listed on page 68.)
- **Problem Solving** A child stayed up very, very late one night. The next day the child was cranky, and sleepy by lunchtime. **What could the child do?** Possible answers: take a nap, have some quiet time alone, lie on the bed and rest. Explain that taking a nap or resting when tired during the day can help give the body time to "catch up," giving more energy for the rest of the day.

Discuss

Talk about how the body feels after a period of quiet activity or a good night's sleep. Have children stand up, yawn, and stretch. Explain that these motions help wake up the body after resting, and help get the muscles stretched out and the blood moving.

3 Wrap Up

Give each child a sheet of drawing paper. Explain that you will be comparing the steps in sleeping to those of a good workout. Have each child fold his or her paper into three parts to form a triptych.

- Help children label the first section "wind-down." Have them draw or paste pictures cut from magazines of their favorite relaxation activity.
- Help children label the second section "sleep." Have them show themselves sleeping.
- Help children label the last section "wake-up." Have them draw themselves stretching, getting ready to start a new day.

ASSESSMENT TIP This activity can be used for performance assessment. See the Performance Assessment Summary Sheet, TR page 49.

TEACHER TIP

Sharing Good Night Tips Read the poem "Good Night," page RA-2. Print the words *Good Night* at random on two sheets of chart paper or poster board. Divide the class into two groups to make collages of things they like to say "good night" to. Have each group cut and paste magazine pictures onto the chart paper or poster board to create a collage. Display the collages in the classroom.

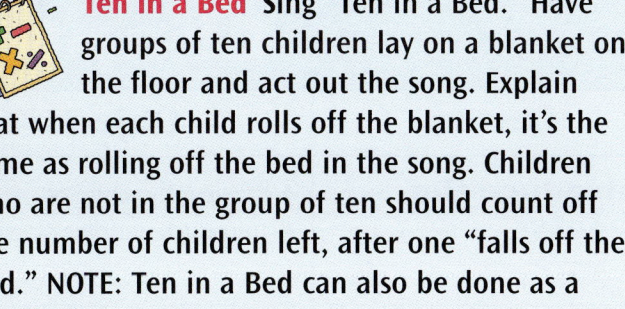

Math Activity

Ten in a Bed Sing "Ten in a Bed." Have groups of ten children lay on a blanket on the floor and act out the song. Explain that when each child rolls off the blanket, it's the same as rolling off the bed in the song. Children who are not in the group of ten should count off the number of children left, after one "falls off the bed." NOTE: Ten in a Bed can also be done as a finger play.

"There were ten in the bed, and the little one said, 'roll over, roll over'; So they all rolled over, and one fell out.

There were [children call out the number] in the bed, and the little one said, 'roll over, roll over' . . .

(repeat until there is one in the bed)

There was one in the bed, and the little one said, 'Good Night!'"

Using the Activity Book, page 18

This activity helps children count up the hours they sleep. On a clock, children mark the time they go to bed and the time they get up and count up the hours.

Bed Time!

I sleep _____ hours every night.

CHAPTER 5

Food for Health

Chapter Organizer

Lesson	Objectives	Vocabulary	Program Resources
Introduce the Chapter pp. 74–75	• Preview the chapter. • Introduce chapter activity center.		• School-Home Connection, TR p. 63 • Take-Home Booklet, TR pp. 81–82
Lesson 1 **Food Gives Me Energy** pp. 76–77 *Pacing: 1 class period* — 1•7	• Recognize that the body needs food for energy.	energy	• Teaching Chart 19 • Activity Book, p. 19 • Teaching Transparency 4
Lesson 2 **The Food Guide Pyramid** pp. 78–79 *Pacing: 1 class period* — 1•2•6	• Identify food groups. • Explain why the food groups are arranged in a pyramid.	Food Guide Pyramid food groups	• Teaching Chart 20 • Teaching Transparency 9 • Poem: "Oh, my goodness, oh my dear," p. RA-3 • Activity Book, p. 20
Lesson 3 **Choose Healthful Snacks** pp. 80–81 *Pacing: 1 class period* — 3•5•6	• Identify healthful snacks.	healthful snack	• Teaching Charts 20 and 21 • Teaching Transparency 9 • Pattern 9, TR p. 99 • Performance Assessment Summary Sheet, TR p. 50 • Activity Book, p. 21
Lesson 4 **Food Safety Hints** pp. 82–83 *Pacing: 1 class period* — 1•2•7	• Demonstrate ways to be safe when eating. • Identify ways to handle food safely.	germs storage spoil	• Teaching Charts 14 and 22 • Activity Book, p. 22

National Health Education Standards
A complete list of the Standards is provided on the next page.

Key: TR = Teaching Resources

National Health Education Standards

1. Comprehend concepts related to health promotion and disease prevention.
2. Access valid health information and health-promoting products and services.
3. Practice health-enhancing behaviors and reduce health risks.
4. Analyze the influence of culture, media, technology, and other factors on health.
5. Use interpersonal communication skills to enhance health.
6. Use goal-setting and decision-making skills to enhance health.
7. Advocate for personal, family, and community health.

Curriculum Integration

Use these topics to integrate health into your daily planning.

Math
- Memory Matching Game, p. 72
- Fruits and Vegetables Patterns, p. 81

Music
- Hokey-Pokey Energy Dance, p. 77
- Food Safety Song, p. 83

Science
- Moldy Bread, p. 72

Social Studies
- Classroom Kitchen, p. 81

Art
- Picnic Fun, p. 72
- Good Food for Breakfast, p. 77

Language Arts
- Poetry Fun, p. 79
- Food Safety Booklet, p. 83

ASSESSMENT OPTIONS

Portfolio Assessment
Have students select their best work from the following suggestions:
- **Good Food for Breakfast,** p. 77
- **Food Safety Booklets,** p. 83
- **My Best Work Portfolio Summary Sheet,** TR p. 42
- **Portfolio Summary Sheet,** TR p. 43

Student Self-Assessment
- **Student Self-Assessment Checklist,** TR p. 38
- **Healthy Habits Checklist,** TR p. 39

Classroom Observation
- **Observation Checklist,** TR p. 36

Performance Assessment
- **Wrap Up,** p. 81
- **Performance Assessment Summary Sheet,** TR p. 50

Daily Assessment
- **Assessment Tips,** pp. 77, 79, 81, 83
- **Activity Book,** pp. 19–22

Cross-Curricular Activities

Science

Moldy Bread
Explain that one of the things that can cause food to spoil is mold.

- Have children help you prepare several self-sealing bags with pieces of slightly damp bread. Homemade or bakery bread works best for this experiment. Make sure all bags are tightly closed.

- Place the bags in different places around the classroom. Put one in a dark, warm spot, one in a cool spot (a refrigerator, if possible), and one in a sunny spot.

- Each day, check the bread for mold. IMPORTANT: Instruct children NOT to open the bags at any time. By comparing mold growth in the different bags, have the class determine which conditions are most conducive to mold growth. Tell children that they should never eat bread that shows mold growth.

Math

Memory Matching Game
Children can use laminated fruits and vegetables cards to play a memory game.

- Make several copies of Pattern 10: Fruits and Vegetables. Have children color the pictures, then cut them apart and laminate them to make cards.

- Place the cards face-down in rows. One child turns over two cards to see if they match. If the cards don't match, the child replaces the cards face-down in the same locations.

- The next child then turns over two cards, trying to find a match. If the cards match, the child keeps them. If not, the cards are returned face-down to the same locations, and the next child takes a turn.

Art

Picnic Fun
Invite children to a pretend picnic. Explain that there will be lots of games to play at the picnic and they will need lots of energy.

- Have children help set up utensils for the picnic. Give each child a paper plate and crayons. Have children suggest healthful picnic foods, and then have them draw these food on their plates.

- Ask for suggestions for a healthful drink for the picnic. Use pretend cups for the drink.

- Have children pretend to eat the picnic foods, then play some energetic picnic games, such as Simon Says, Follow-the-Leader, and Hide-and-Seek.

Bulletin Board

Use colorful paper to make a representation of the Food Guide Pyramid on the bulletin board. Label each section with its group name.

- Divide the class into six groups, and assign each a different food group.

- Have children cut pictures out of magazines or draw pictures representing the foods in their group, and glue them to the proper section of the Food Guide Pyramid.

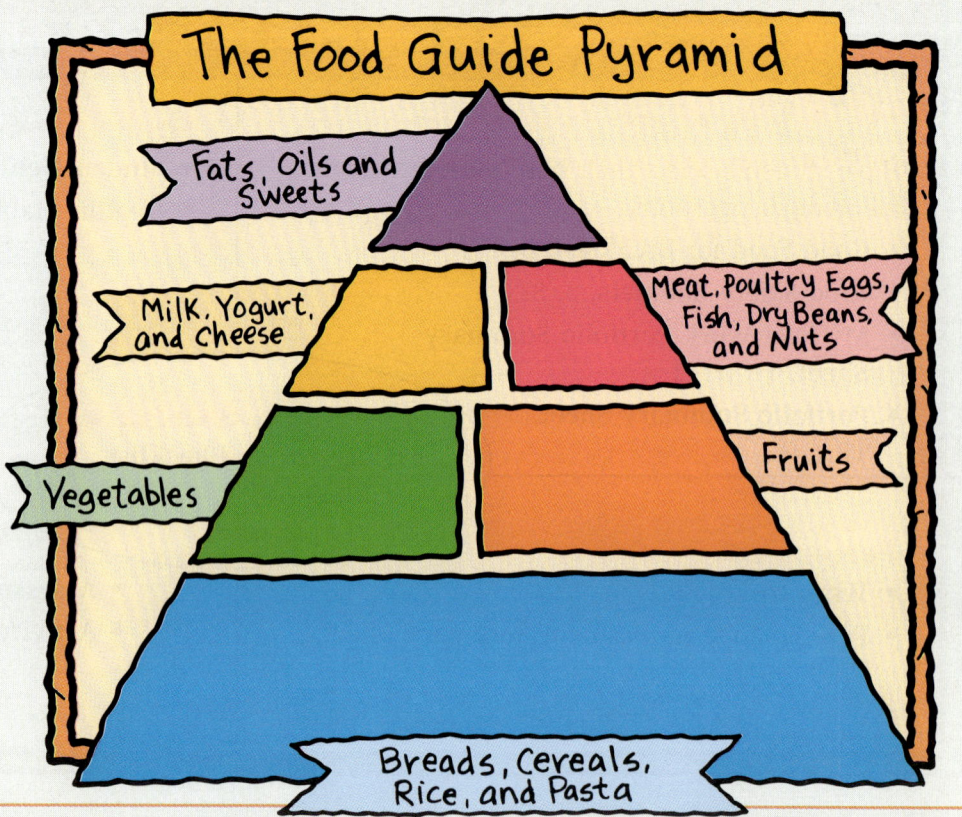

 ## Books for Students

Read Alouds

Blos, Joan W. **The Hungry Little Boy.** Simon & Schuster Books for Young Readers, 1995. Enjoy the idea of comfort food, as good nutrition and love go hand in hand. **EASY**

Hoberman, Mary Ann. **The Seven Silly Eaters.** Harcourt Children's Books, 2000. Whimsical story of seven fussy eaters told through the rhythm of a clever, rhyming text. **AVERAGE**

Leedy, Loreen. **The Edible Pyramid.** Holiday House, 1994. At The Edible Pyramid Restaurant, the animal guests receive only the best foods. **ADVANCED**

Marotz, Lynn R., Marie Z. Cross, and Jeanettia M. Rush. **Health, Safety, and Nutrition for the Young Child.** Delmar Publishing, 2000. Discusses the power of good nutrition.

Tamborlane, William V., M.D., Ed. **The Yale Guide to Children's Nutrition.** Yale University Press, 1997. A comprehensive guide to the best nutrition for children and young adults.

Go, Grow, Glow.—Well, Well, Well With Slim Goodbody AIT Productions, 1985. (15 minutes) Explains that food is the body's source of energy and introduces the concept of digestion.

Food Power—Well, Well, Well With Slim Goodbody. AIT Productions, 1985. (15 minutes) Identifies food groups and explains why eating a variety of foods is so important.

Your Health Webliography

The **Webliography** provides links to the Health Background and teaching resources that will support you as you teach the topics in *Your Health*. Simply choose a keyword and you will be taken to a page of links with descriptions of the content you can obtain at each site. The **Webliography** is located on the Teacher Resources page at **www.harcourtschool.com/health** Please review websites before referring your students to them.

United States Department of Agriculture
Food and Nutrition Information Center, National Agricultural Library, Room 304
10301 Baltimore Blvd.
Beltsville, MD 20705
703-305-2286
Provides print and audiovisual materials on topics in human nutrition, food service management, and food technology.

For more information about health organizations and agencies, please see the *Teaching Resources* book.

Community Health

Finding Out About Food Field Trip
Show children where pasta is on the Food Guide Pyramid on the Teaching Chart 20. Have children make macaroni necklaces, using yarn and different kinds of pasta. Invite children to put on their necklaces for a field trip to the school cafeteria. Arrange for staff to talk to the class about how they plan healthful lunches and snacks. If your school doesn't have a cafeteria, arrange for a nutritionist to visit your class. Nutritionists can be located by contacting local health departments.

American Crop Protection Association Publications
1156 Fifteenth Street, NW
Suite 400
Washington, D.C. 20005
Supplies teachers with games, projects, and whole language story ideas emphasizing foods grown in the United States

International Reading Association
800 Barksdale Road
P.O. Box 8139
Newark, DE 19714-8139
302-731-1600
Provides brochures explaining the connection between what children eat and how they learn.

California Strawberry Commission
P.O. Box 269
Watsonville, CA 95077-0269
Offers a classroom lesson on nutrition and the food pyramid.

Note that information, while correct at time of publication, is subject to change.

Visit **The Harcourt Learning Site** for related links, activities, resources, and the health **Webliography**.
www.harcourtschool.com

CHAPTER 5
Pages 70–83

"There is no sincerer love than the love of food."

—George Bernard Shaw

CHAPTER SUMMARY

In this chapter children
- explain that the body needs food for energy.
- identify food groups and explain why they are arranged in a pyramid.
- identify healthful snacks.
- identify ways to handle food safely.

LIFE SKILLS Children *make decisions* about food choices.

 HUMAN BODY Children learn about the digestive system and its role in providing energy for the body.

Food for Health

Health Activity Center

The activities suggested for this chapter's Health Activity Center help reinforce the importance of choosing healthful foods.

The Healthful Snack Store

This activity lets children practice choosing healthful snacks. They also practice counting money and making change.

Materials Needed
- empty healthful snack containers
- play money

What to Do Children can use the empty healthful snack containers to play store. Have them choose healthful snacks they like and use the play money to pay for them.

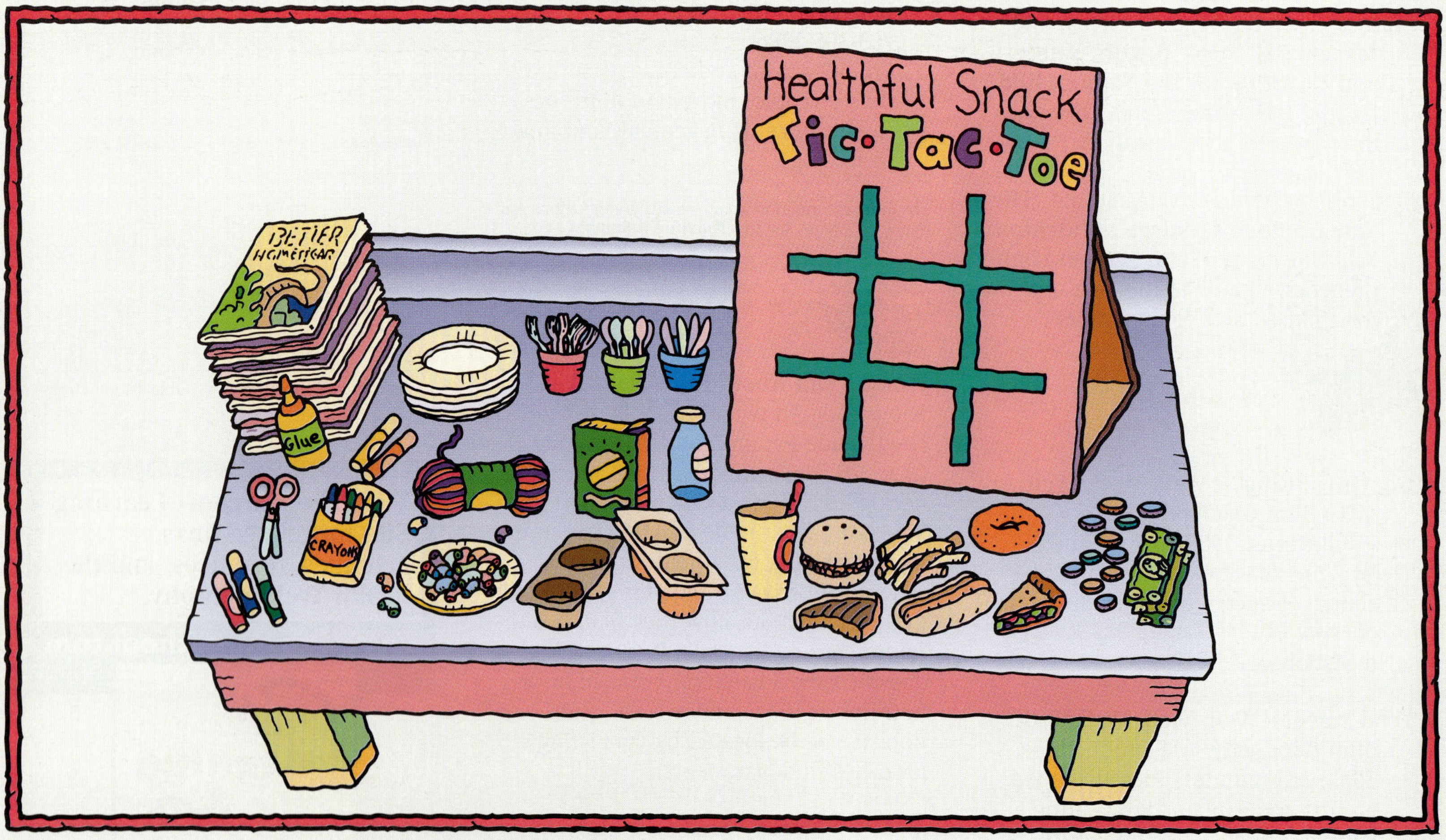

Snack Tree

This activity is used to reinforce and suggest foods that make healthful snacks.

Materials Needed
- large tree branch "planted" in a coffee can of rocks or a tree trunk and branches cut from construction paper and attached to the wall
- magazines with pictures of snacks
- paper and crayons
- tape

What to Do Construct the Snack Tree in a corner of the classroom. Divide the tree approximately in half. Hang a sign on one half that reads "Anytime Snacks." Label the other half "Sometimes Snacks."

- Work with children to brainstorm a list of snacks they enjoy. When the list is complete, have children draw pictures of the snacks or find pictures of them in magazines. Have children cut out the pictures they find or draw.
- Work with children to help them decide which part of the tree they should hang their snack on. After they decide, let them tape their snack to the tree.
- As an option, have children bring in empty packages from their favorite snacks to hang on the tree.

Healthful Snack Tic-Tac-Toe

This activity reinforces the different food groups.

Materials Needed
- tic-tac-toe board
- container with several play foods from each food group or pictures of these foods

What to Do When partners go to play, they should each pick a food group. For example, one could be fruits and the other vegetables. Each child must use foods from his or her chosen group to mark squares. The first child to get three foods from his or her group in a row is the winner. Challenge children to pick a different food group each time they play.

How Many Servings?

Materials Needed
- large Food Guide Pyramid with the sections and the number of servings indicated
- pictures of foods from each pyramid section

What to Do Post the Food Guide Pyramid on the wall. Hide the food pictures around the room. Hide the same number of pictures as servings indicated on the Food Guide Pyramid. Have children search for the foods and post them in the correct section of the pyramid. As a class, count the number of foods posted to see if all the pictures have been found.

Take-Home Booklet

Distribute copies of the Take-Home Booklet, TR pages 81–82. Have children fold the pages to make booklets to share with their families.

School-Home Connection

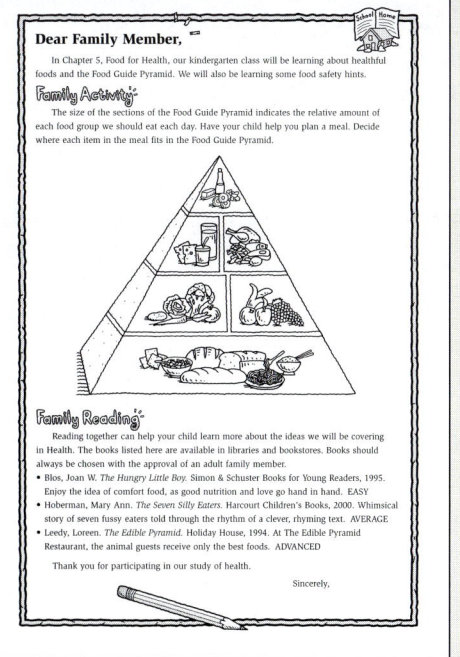

Distribute copies of the School-Home Connection (in English or Spanish), TR page 63. Have children take the page home to share with their families.

Alternative Use for in-class enrichment.

LESSON 1

OBJECTIVE
- Recognize that the body needs food for energy.

VOCABULARY
- energy

PROGRAM RESOURCES
- Teaching Chart 19

Teaching Transparency 4

- Activity Book, p. 19

MATERIALS
- wind-up toy
- chart paper

Teaching Chart 19

Daily Safety Tip

The importance of food as a source of energy cannot be overemphasized. Empty stomachs can result in a loss of energy. Encourage children to start every day with breakfast.

1 Motivate

Gather children in a circle. Place a wind-up toy (not yet wound) in the center of the circle. (As an alternative, have children imagine that they are wind-up toys. You can "wind" them up with pretend keys on their backs.)

- Ask for suggestions on how to make the toy go. push it, attach a string and pull it, wind it Ask children what to try first. Follow children's suggestions until they suggest winding the toy. Let the toy run until it runs down. Have children imitate the actions of the toy, including running down at the end.

- Ask children what they saw and felt. toy slowed down, they slowed down; toy stopped, they stopped Ask what would make the toy go again. Winding the toy will make it run again.

- Explain that winding the toy gives it energy to run. *Energy* makes the toy move. **What do you think gives you energy?** Children will most likely suggest the food they eat.

2 Teach

Learn from Pictures

Show children Teaching Chart 19. **What are the children in the picture doing?** playing, having fun, eating snacks at a picnic table

- Draw children's attention to the title above the bird. Explain that even during sleep or while doing a quiet activity, the body needs energy from food. **Where are the children in the picture getting their energy?** from the food they eat

- Point to the foods in the picture. Emphasize that eating a variety of foods is important in order for the body to get everything it needs for energy and growth.

Discuss

Problem Solving Have children imagine a group of children who started their day by eating breakfast so they have lots of energy. The children played and played. Then, around lunchtime, they started feeling a little tired. **What should the children do? Can they be wound up like a toy?** No; they should eat lunch. Reinforce that food is like a wind-up knob on the toy—food gives people energy. We need to eat on a regular basis (three meals and snacks) in order to keep the body fully fueled with readily available energy.

Activity

Draw a large clock face on a sheet of chart paper. Then have children list the three meals they eat each day (breakfast, lunch, dinner). Indicate on the clock face the approximate time for these meals (8:00 A.M., 12:00 noon, 5:00 P.M.).

- Why do you think meals are spaced like this? **to provide energy for the body throughout the day**
- What might you want to do if one of your meals, such as dinner, were going to be late? **eat a snack**

Use Teaching Transparencies

Show Teaching Transparency 4, The Digestive System. Explain that the digestive system is the part of the body that processes the food we eat into the energy our body uses.

- On the transparency, trace the path of food from the mouth, down the food tube, and into the stomach. Have children trace the path, on their bodies, touching their mouths, their throats, and ending up at their stomachs.

3 Wrap Up

Tell children to copy your motions. Pantomime eating a banana. Then walk in place briskly for a few moments. Begin to slow down, and then finally slump over like a rag doll. Have children tell you what each of your actions were, and why they happened.

ASSESSMENT TIP Children should indicate they understand that food gives their bodies energy. When it's been a while since you ate, your body starts to run low on ready energy, and needs to be replenished.

MEET INDIVIDUAL NEEDS

Kinesthetic Learners Read the story *Body on Strike*, page RA-6. Then divide the class into three groups. Assign the role of *Mouth* to one group, *Hands* to another, and *Teeth* to the third. You take the part of *Tummy*. Re-read the story and, as you read, have each group act out the role of their body part.

Other things to do!

Art Activity

Good Food for Breakfast Review the clock drawn in the Activity in the lesson. Point out how long it is from dinner until breakfast, and how important it is to give the body energy after its long fast. Work with the class to make a list of favorite breakfast foods. Then give each child a copy of Pattern 1: Blank Face, TR page 91. Have children make a happy face on their patterns. Then have children cut out pictures from magazines or draw pictures of favorite breakfast foods. Children should draw or paste their pictures around the happy face.

Music Activity

Hokey-Pokey Energy Dance Use the *Hokey-Pokey* to demonstrate both a lack of energy and lots of energy. Sing a verse of the song in slow motion and have children dance in slow motion, with little energy. Then, sing a verse at normal speed as children dance with lots of energy. You might want to write a verse of the song on chart paper and have the children follow along and sing as you point to each word.

Using the Activity Book, page 19

Children color pictures that show activities where food is needed for energy. Note that *all* pictures should be colored, as everything we do requires energy.

Food Gives Me Energy

LESSON 2

OBJECTIVES
- Identify food groups.
- Explain why the food groups are arranged in a pyramid.

VOCABULARY
- Food Guide Pyramid
- food groups

PROGRAM RESOURCES
- Teaching Chart 20

  Teaching Transparency 9

- Poem, "Oh, my goodness, oh my dear," p. RA-3
- Activity Book, p. 20

MATERIALS
- Large number of blocks, math counters, or other objects such as macaroni that are all the same size.
- chart paper
- pointer or yardstick

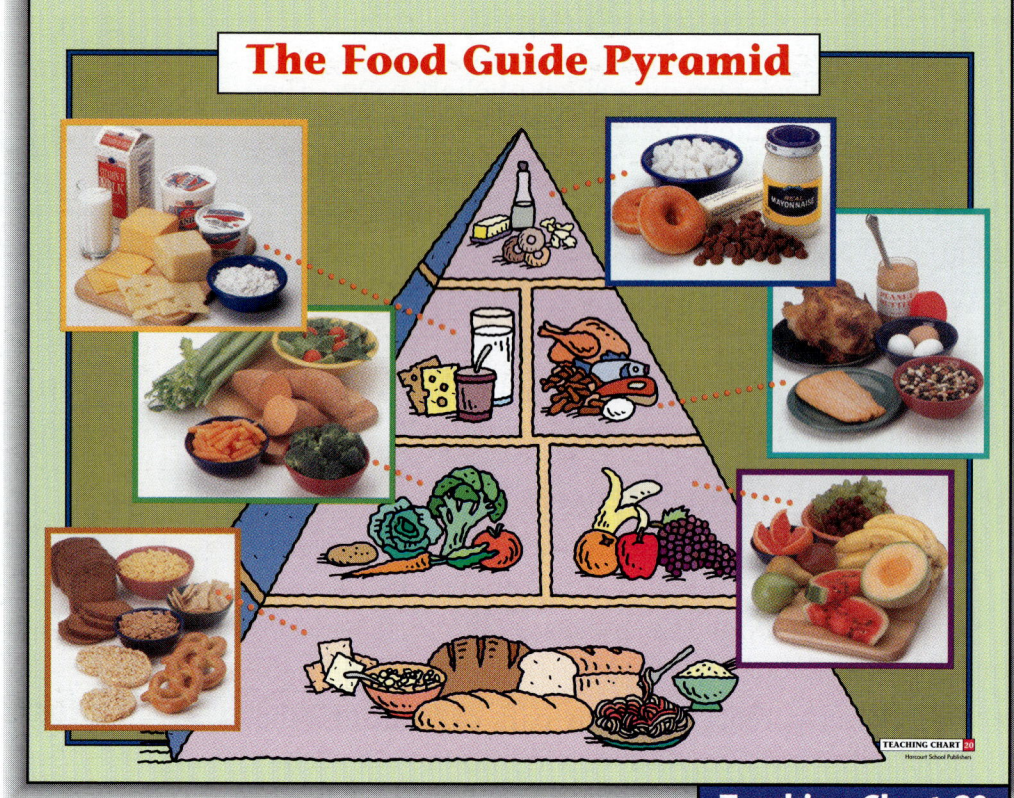

Teaching Chart 20

Eating fruits and vegetables that are in season is a good thing to do, because the food is usually fresh. Frozen fruits and vegetables are good too, because they have been frozen soon after harvesting. Encourage children to eat at least five servings of fruits and vegetables every day.

1 Motivate

Gather the children in the group area. Read the poem, "Oh, my goodness, oh my dear," page RA-3.

- Ask children to act out how they would feel if they ate all the food described in the poem before lunch. Children should clutch their stomachs and moan and groan.
- Why is it a problem if you eat chocolate cake and apple punch instead of your lunch? Accept reasonable answers at this point in the lesson. Some children may say that sweets aren't "good" for you.

2 Teach

Learn from Pictures

Show Teaching Chart 20. Who remembers what the body needs for energy? food What do you notice about these foods? They are arranged in groups. Read the name of each *food group* with children. Have volunteers identify the different foods shown. After children understand the types of foods in the different groups, point to each group and have children tell you another food that belongs in the group but is not shown on Teaching Chart 20.

Discuss

Read the title and point to the Food Guide Pyramid on Teaching Chart 20. What shape is this? pyramid or a triangle What part of the pyramid is biggest? the bottom Smallest? the top

- Have children make a triangle shape with their fingers and compare their finger pyramids to the Food Guide Pyramid. Again, have them determine what is the largest and smallest portion of the pyramid.
- Explain that some foods give the body more of the things it needs to grow and provide more energy than others. The Food Guide Pyramid can help them choose foods to help their bodies stay healthy and grow strong.

Activity

Block Pyramids Draw a large triangle on chart paper. Include the divisions shown on the Food Guide Pyramid. Working on the floor, have children help you fill each section with blocks or other objects that are all the same size.

- Work with children to count the number of blocks in each section of the pyramid, starting with the bottom. As you complete each section, record the number of blocks each held.

- When finished, direct attention to the Food Guide Pyramid. **Is each section that makes up the pyramid the same size?** no Explain that you can use the size of each part of the pyramid to determine how much of each type of food you should eat. Compare the larger number of blocks in the bottom section of the block pyramid to the larger number of servings of foods you should eat from the bottom section of the Food Guide Pyramid. Do the same for each section as you go up the pyramid. Emphasize that you should eat the fewest foods from the top section.

- Reuse the Food Guide Pyramid outline as the basis for the bulletin board described on page 72.

3 Wrap Up

Use Teaching Transparencies

 Project Teaching Transparency 9: The Food Guide Pyramid. Call out the names of specific foods. Let children go to the projection and use the pointer or yardstick to point to the group to which the food belongs.

ASSESSMENT TIP Children should be able to locate the different food groups in the pyramid. When finished, read "Oh, my goodness, oh my dear" again, and ask the Motivate question again. Children should now understand that eating sweets instead of a healthful lunch will not provide their bodies with the materials it needs to grow and stay healthy.

HEALTH BACKGROUND

Food Guide Pyramid for Young Children In 1999 the USDA developed a Food Guide Pyramid for Young Children ages two to six. The adaptations are geared for more understanding at this age. To view the Food Guide Pyramid for Young Children, see Webliography, keyword *Food Guide Pyramid*.

Other things to do!

Language Arts Activity

 **Poetry Fun** Read "Nell and Jack Horner," page RA-3, to the class. Show Teaching Chart 20 again. Ask children to point to the place on the food pyramid where Jack Horner would find his Christmas pie, and Nell Horner would find her tarts and jam. Invite groups of children to come up to the picture and choose some good foods for Jack and Nell to eat. Write the children's choices on the board. Add children's favorites to the list as well. When the list is complete, let children work in groups to make three healthful meals for Jack and Nell to share. An example is shown below.

Nell and Jack's Healthful Meals

Breakfast	Lunch	Dinner
peanut butter toast	chicken sandwich	spaghetti with meat sauce
milk	carrots and celery	green beans
banana	milk	salad
	apple	cookie

Using the Activity Book, page 20

Children match foods to the proper section of the Food Guide Pyramid.

Pyramid Match

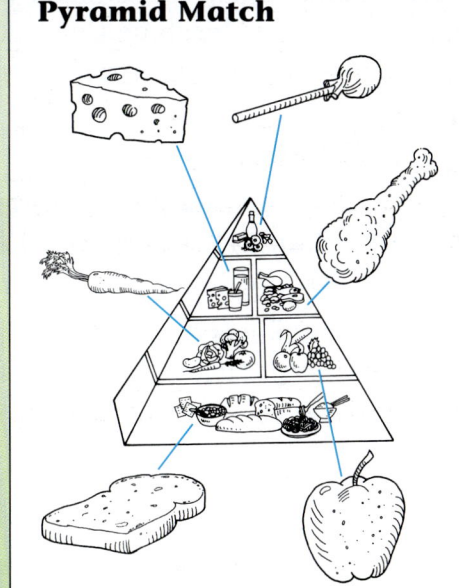

OBJECTIVE
- Identify healthful snacks.

VOCABULARY
- healthful
- snack

PROGRAM RESOURCES
- Teaching Charts 20 and 21

 Teaching Transparency 9

- Pattern 9, TR p. 99
- Performance Assessment Summary Sheet, TR p. 50
- Activity Book, p. 21

MATERIALS
- pointer or yardstick
- glue
- magazines to cut up
- crayons

Teaching Chart 21

Daily Safety Tip

There are lots of yummy snacks that are good for you too. Fresh fruits and vegetables are always tasty. Remind children to wash all fruits and vegetables before peeling or eating.

1 Motivate

Have children again make finger triangles with their fingers. Re-show Teaching Chart 20, and direct attention to the Food Guide Pyramid. Have volunteers point to the area showing foods they should eat most of and least of.

- Remind children that foods toward the bottom are more *healthful,* meaning they have more of the things that give the body energy and help it grow.
- Invite volunteers to take turns telling what they had for breakfast. Help them locate the part of the pyramid where each food would be located.

2 Teach

Learn from Pictures

Show Teaching Chart 21 and have children describe what they see. A boy who is thinking about a lot of different foods.

- Explain that the boy is trying to decide what to have for a snack. **When do you eat snacks?** after school, after dinner, between meals Explain that *snacks* can help give our bodies energy between meals.

Use Teaching Transparencies

 Project Teaching Transparency 9: The Food Guide Pyramid on the wall. As you point to each snack choice shown on Teaching Chart 21, have children take turns using a pointer or yardstick to point to the food group on the transparency where that snack would fit in.

Life Skills

 **Make Decisions** Ask for volunteers to help the boy choose a healthful snack from the Teaching Chart. Encourage children to consider the choices they see, and think about the consequences of each choice. Examples: Fruits or vegetables help your body stay healthy. Foods high in sugar and fat have less of what your body needs to grow and stay healthy.

80

- If less healthful choices are suggested, response can be, "That tastes good and is OK to eat once in awhile, but try to find some foods that have more of what the body needs to grow and stay healthy."

3 Wrap Up

Give each child a copy of Pattern 9: Apple. Have them cut and glue pictures from magazines of three healthful snacks they like to eat onto the apple. Children can also draw their snacks, if desired.

ASSESSMENT TIP This activity can be used for performance assessment. See the Performance Assessment Summary Sheet, TR page 50.

TEACHER TIP

Healthful Snack Party Using the Food Guide Pyramid, let the class plan a snack party. Guide the children to choose simple, healthful snacks, such as celery with peanut butter or tossed fruit salad, so they themselves can prepare the food under supervision. So children will try a variety of foods, use some of the ethnic selections the children suggest. *Note:* Be sure to check for any food allergies among children.

MEET INDIVIDUAL NEEDS

Auditory and Visual Learners Display Teaching Chart 21. Have children work in pairs to role-play situations in which one child wants to choose a less healthful snack, and the second child convinces the first to choose a more healthful snack. Encourage children to think of many reasons for choosing the more healthful snack, including tasting good, being good for the body, and not ruining other meals.

MULTICULTURAL LINK

Breads of Many Lands Different cultures eat many different foods, but most rely on bread to make up a substantial portion of the diet. If you have a multiculturally diverse student population, invite children to bring a sample of the bread they usually eat at home. Or bring pictures (or samples) of breads such as tortillas, matzos, and bagels. Have a tasting party. *Note:* Check for food allergies before allowing children to taste any foods.

Other things to do!

Social Studies Activity

Classroom Kitchen Make the classroom kitchen area into a healthful meals and snacks center. Post a laminated Food Guide Pyramid, available on many cereal boxes. Have children bring in washed, empty containers from foods they have eaten at home. *Safety note:* If children bring in cans, watch for sharp edges. Check all containers for cleanliness. Encourage children to use the packages, as well as any play food in the kitchen, to assemble meals and snacks. Have them compare their choices to the Food Guide Pyramid to determine how healthful their choices are.

Math Activity

Fruits and Vegetables Patterns Make several copies of Pattern 10: Fruits and Vegetables, TR page 100. Cut apart the fruits and vegetables and laminate. Place all the laminated pieces in a bag or other container. Working in pairs, have one child make a pattern of fruits and vegetables for the other child to replicate. You can control the level of difficulty by varying the number of different fruits and vegetables in the container.

Using the Activity Book, page 21

Children circle and color the healthful snacks, and cross out the less healthful snacks.

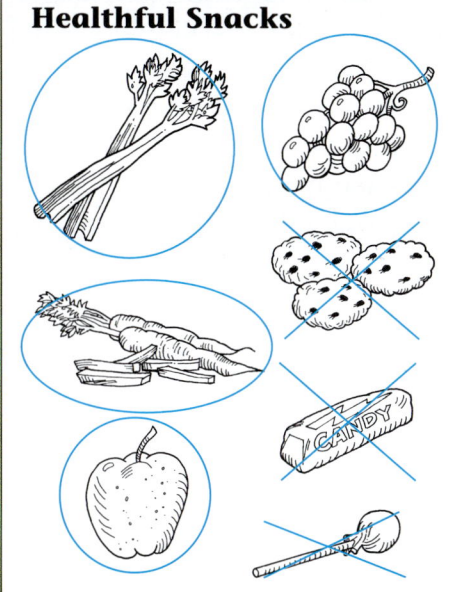

Healthful Snacks

LESSON 4

OBJECTIVES
- Demonstrate ways to be safe when eating.
- Identify ways to handle food safely.

VOCABULARY
- germs
- storage
- spoil

PROGRAM RESOURCES
- Teaching Charts 14 and 22
- Activity Book, p. 22

MATERIALS
- crackers
- several sets of food storage materials, including plastic containers, self-sealing plastic bags, and pre-cut aluminum foil.

Teaching Chart 22

Daily Safety Tip

Because lunch containers sit unwashed for much of the day, they can be a breeding ground for germs. Remind children to make sure their lunch boxes, food containers, and drink containers are washed every day with very hot, soapy water.

1 Motivate

Tell children to imagine that dinner is ready. **What should you do?** Accept all answers. Children may suggest coming to the table, turning off the TV, cleaning up playthings, and so on. Remind children, if not suggested, that there is one thing they should always do before eating—wash their hands. **Why?** to remove dirt and germs that could get into the body when eating

- Review hand-washing procedures with children using Teaching Chart 14. Have children make corresponding motions to demonstrate the procedure. Remind children that they should wash their hands with warm water and soap for as long as it takes them to say the ABCs. Drying hands thoroughly when finished is also important.

2 Teach

Learn from Pictures

Show Teaching Chart 22. Explain that there are other things everyone should do to stay safe when eating.

- Point to the first picture. **What is happening?** Someone is washing his or her hands. Remind children they should also wash raw fruits and vegetables they may eat as snacks before peeling or eating.

- Move on to the next picture. **What do you see?** Girl sitting at a table to eat. Have children stand up and jump around for a few minutes. When finished, have them sit again and think about how their bodies feel. breathing harder, out of breath, and so on Ask if anyone has accidentally swallowed food wrong and choked. Explain that it is easier to swallow incorrectly and choke on food when moving around while trying to eat.

- Talk about the picture of a girl chewing. Give each child a cracker. *Note:* Check for food allergies before distributing food in the classroom. **What's the safe way to eat the cracker?** Take little bites; chew the cracker completely before swallowing; don't talk while eating it. Have children eat their crackers in the safe way. (You may wish to review biting and chewing teeth at this time.)

- Look at the last picture. Ask children why the child is putting food in the refrigerator. Explain that food can spoil and that eating spoiled food can make people ill. Refrigerating food helps slow the growth of germs that cause food to spoil.

Activity

Storing Food Demonstrate safe food *storage*. Provide plastic containers, aluminum foil (pre-cut), and self-sealing plastic bags. Brainstorm a list of different types of foods. For each food mentioned, help children determine if it needs to be refrigerated or not, and if it needs to be wrapped or not. Help children determine appropriate wrappings for those foods that need it.

3 Wrap Up

Again, tell children that dinner is ready. Have children take turns acting out the steps to follow to be safe when eating. Encourage children to use play food and food storage containers as props.

ASSESSMENT TIP Make sure that children include all four steps covered in this lesson—washing hands before eating, sitting down to eat, chewing slowly, and storing food appropriately when the meal is completed.

TEACHER TIP

Food Storage After completing this lesson, you may wish to place the food storage items in the classroom kitchen. Encourage children to practice storing the play foods using the proper containers.

HEALTH BACKGROUND

Keeping Food Safe Experts recommend following these safety tips when preparing food. In all cases, the most important tip is: "When in doubt, throw it out!"

- Wash hands in warm, soapy water before preparing food and after preparing each dish.
- Defrost meat in the microwave or the refrigerator.
- Keep raw meat, poultry, fish, and their juices away from other food.
- Wash cutting boards, knives, and countertops immediately after cutting up meat, poultry, or fish. Never use the same cutting board for meats and vegetables without washing the board first.

Other things to do!

Music Activity

Food Safety Song Have children sit in a circle to sing and act out the steps of food safety. Use these words to the song "If You're Happy and You Know It."

*If you're hungry and you know it,
wash your hands, . . .
If you're hungry and you know it,
sit and eat, . . .
If you're hungry and you know it,
chew real slow, . . .
If you've eaten and you know it,
store the food, . . .*

Language Arts Activity

Food Safety Booklet Extend the lesson by helping children make food safety booklets. Make copies of Pattern 9: Apple, TR page 99, or provide children with writing or drawing paper. Have children write a different safety tip, listed below, at the bottom of each page, and illustrate the tip in the apple.

*I wash my hands before I eat.
I sit down to eat.
I chew my food slowly.
I put leftover food away.*

Using the Activity Book, page 22

Children color happy faces yellow under pictures of good food-handling practices. They color unhappy faces blue under pictures of poor food-handling practices.

I'm Safe with Food

CHAPTER 6 **Staying Well**

Chapter Organizer

Lesson	Objectives	Vocabulary	Program Resources
Introduce the Chapter pp. 88–89	• Preview the chapter. • Introduce chapter activity center.		• School-Home Connection, TR p. 65 • Take-Home Booklet, TR pp. 83–84
Lesson 1 **I'm Ill** pp. 90–91 **Pacing: 1 class period** — 1•2•5	• Describe what it feels like to be ill. • Identify symptoms of illness.	ill symptoms	• Pattern 3, TR p. 93 • Teaching Chart 23 • Activity Book, p. 23
Lesson 2 **Wash Away Germs** pp. 92–93 **Pacing: 1 class period** — 1•3•7	• Describe ways to keep disease from spreading.	germs immunization	• Teaching Chart 24 • Poem: "Sneeze," p. RA-3 • Song: "Clap, Clap, Clap Your Hands," p. RA-9 • Activity Book, p. 24
Lesson 3 **Staying Well** pp. 94–95 **Pacing: 1 class period** — 1•3•6	• Describe ways to stay well.	staying well	• Poem: "Rainy Day," p. RA-4 • Teaching Chart 25 • Performance Assessment Summary Sheet, TR p. 51 • Activity Book, p. 25

National Health Education Standards
A complete list of the Standards is provided on the next page.

Key: TR = Teaching Resources

National Health Education Standards

1. Comprehend concepts related to health promotion and disease prevention.
2. Access valid health information and health-promoting products and services.
3. Practice health-enhancing behaviors and reduce health risks.
4. Analyze the influence of culture, media, technology, and other factors on health.
5. Use interpersonal communication skills to enhance health.
6. Use goal-setting and decision-making skills to enhance health.
7. Advocate for personal, family, and community health.

Curriculum Integration

Use these topics to integrate health into your daily planning.

Art
- Collages: Feeling Well or Feeling Ill?, p. 86

Social Studies
- A Cold in Our Classroom, p. 86

Science
- Check the Temperature, p. 86
- Exercise Strengthens the Body, p. 95

Math
- Illness Graph, p. 91
- Staying Well Graph, p. 95

Drama
- Role-Play Disease Prevention, p. 93

Music
- Symptoms Song, p. 91
- Tissue Dance, p. 93

ASSESSMENT OPTIONS

Portfolio Assessment
Have students select their best work from the following suggestions.
- **Collages: Feeling Well or Feeling Ill,** p. 86
- **Staying Well Graph,** p. 95
- **My Best Work Portfolio Summary Sheet,** TR p. 42
- **Portfolio Summary Sheet,** TR p. 43

Student Self-Assessment
- **Student Self-Assessment Checklist,** TR p. 38
- **Healthy Habits Checklist,** TR p. 39

Classroom Observation
- **Observation Checklist,** TR p. 36

Performance Assessment
- **Wrap Up,** p. 95
- **Performance Assessment Summary Sheet,** TR p. 51

Daily Assessment
- **Assessment Tips,** pp. 91, 93, 95
- **Activity Book,** pp. 23–25

Cross-Curricular Activities

Science

Check the Temperature
Have two glasses of water, one very cold, the other warm.

- Hold up the thermometer and lead children to discuss what it is used for. Explain that you are going to use it to check the temperature of the water.
- Ask children to predict which glass of water will have a bigger number for its temperature. List predictions on the board.
- Test the two glasses of water, and record the results.
- Have children feel the temperature of each glass of water, and compare it to the numerical temperature readouts.

Art

Collages: Feeling Well or Feeling Ill?
Organize the class into four work groups.

- Have two work groups make collages, using pictures they have cut out of magazines, of people who look ill.
- Have the other two groups make collages of people who look well.
- Encourage the groups to look for pictures of both children and adults to include in their collages.
- When finished, have each group present their collage, explaining why the people look ill or well.

Social Studies

A Cold in Our Classroom
Work with children to help them write a story about a cold in the classroom.

- Help them draw a simple map of the classroom, showing the different areas, where people sit, the rest rooms, and so on.
- Have them indicate on the map how a cold could spread from one person to another in the classroom.
- Reinforce ways children can help keep a cold from spreading from person to person.

Bulletin Board

Use a Tissue
Have each child cut out a copy of Pattern 1: Blank Face, TR page 91, and draw a face on it. Then direct children to trace one of their hands on colored construction paper and cut out the tracing. Help children place the tissue over the nose and mouth of the face pattern and staple the hand on top. Attach each finished piece to the bulletin board entitled "Keep Germs from Spreading."

- Extend this activity by giving each child a copy of Pattern 8: Bubbles, TR page 98. Again, have them trace a hand, cut out the tracing, and attach to the pattern. Add these to the bulletin board.

Resources

Books for Children

Read Alouds

Royston, Angela. *Healthy Me (A Lift-the-Flap Book).* Barrons Juvenile, 1995. Offers important information about common health concerns. **EASY**

Slate Joseph. *Miss Bindergarten Stays Home From Kindergarten.* Dutton Children's Books, 2000. Tells about the teacher's illness and her absence from school. **AVERAGE**

Kohlenberg, Sherry. *Sammy's Mommy Has Cancer.* American Psychological Association, 1993. Nurtures honest discussion and the gift of love as healing. **ADVANCED**

Books for Teachers and Families

Cheung, Lilian W.Y. and Julius B. Richmond, M.D. *Child Health, Nutrition, and Physical Activity.* Human Kinetics Publications, 1995. An excellent resource, in essay form, that helps adults support healthy children.

Komaroff, Anthony. *Harvard Medical School Family Health Guide.* Simon & Schuster, 1999. A complete reference book on the health and medical needs of families.

Rona, Zoltan P. *Childhood Illness and the Allergy Connection: A Nutritional Approach to Overcoming and Preventing Childhood Illness.* Prima Publications, 1996. This book offers helpful suggestions for treating chronic illness with sound nutrition and specific diets.

Videos

All About Health and Hygiene. Schlessinger Media, 2001. (23 minutes) A good all-encompassing video that explains how good hygiene promotes good health.

Head to Toe—Fighting Germs and Diseases. AIT Productions, 1994. (15 minutes) Tells students how germs can get in the body and make one ill.

Your Health Webliography

The **Webliography** provides links to the Health Background and teaching resources that will support you as you teach the topics in *Your Health*. Simply choose a keyword and you will be taken to a page of links with descriptions of the content you can obtain at each site. The **Webliography** is located on the Teacher Resources page at www.harcourtschool.com/health Please review websites before referring your students to them.

Organizations and Agencies

Asthma and Allergy Foundation of America
1233 20th St. NW Suite 402
Washington, D.C. 20036
A voluntary health agency that works to solve the health problems associated with allergies.

Candlelighters Childhood Cancer Foundation
3910 Warner St.
Kensington, MD 20895
800-366-2223
Educates, supports, serves, and advocates for families with individuals touched by cancer. Several publications including *Educating the Child with Cancer*.

For more information about health organizations and agencies, please see the *Teaching Resources* book.

Community Health

Nurse Invite your school nurse or a pediatric nurse to talk to children about how disease spreads. Ask the nurse to emphasize the importance of hand washing and to talk about how often doctors and nurses wash their hands to help prevent the spread of disease.

Free and Inexpensive Material

American School Health Association
7263 State Route 43
P.O. Box 708
Kent, OH 44240
330-678-1601
Offers posters on hand washing.

Pharmacia Corporation
100 Route 206 North
Peapack, NJ 07977
Distributes brochures to educate young children and parents on health matters.

Note that information, while correct at time of publication, is subject to change.

Visit **The Harcourt Learning Site** for related links, activities, resources, and the health **Webliography**.
www.harcourtschool.com

Pages 84–95

"Look to your health: . . . for health is . . . a blessing that money cannot buy."

—Izaak Walton

CHAPTER SUMMARY

In this chapter children
- explain what to do when they feel ill.
- learn ways to prevent the spread of disease.
- discuss ways to stay well.

LIFE SKILLS Children *communicate* when they are ill.

 **HUMAN BODY** Children learn about the symptoms of illness.

Staying Well

Health Activity Center

The activities suggested for this chapter's Health Activity Center help reinforce how germs are spread and how people can stay well.

 What's My Temperature?

In this activity children learn what normal body temperature is.

Materials Needed
- fever strips

What to Do Allow children to use the fever strips to take their temperatures by pressing the strips on their foreheads. Assist them in reading the temperatures shown. You may wish to record the temperature of everyone in the class and discuss how "normal" body temperature can vary from person to person. Reinforce that when children are ill, their body temperatures often rise. This rise in temperature indicates that the body is fighting germs.

What's in Water?

This activity helps children understand that, even though they can't see them, germs are all around them.

Materials Needed
- microscope
- slides and cover slips
- pond water or water from a fish tank
- dropper

What to Do Place a drop of the pond or fish tank water on the slide and cover with the cover slip. Place the assembled slide on the microscope, and focus so that the organisms in the water are visible through the lens. Have a small jar of pond water or fish-tank water available for comparison. (Be sure that any sediments have settled from the water so that it looks clear.)

Explain that the water, which looks clear, contains hundreds of tiny living things. Allow children to look through the microscope to see the tiny living things in the water. Compare the living things in the water to germs all around us. You can't see the germs, but they are still there.

Stepping Stones to Wellness

This activity helps reinforce actions that can help keep a person well.

Materials Needed
- large ovals cut from cardboard
- paints and crayons
- magazines, scissors, and glue

What to Do Have children decorate the oval stepping stones with pictures of things that help them stay well. You may want to provide Teaching Chart 25 for reference. When all the stones are complete, help children make a path. Let children take turns leading the class along the path. The followers must imitate how the leader moves—hopping, jumping, skipping, "swimming," and so on.

Take-Home Booklet

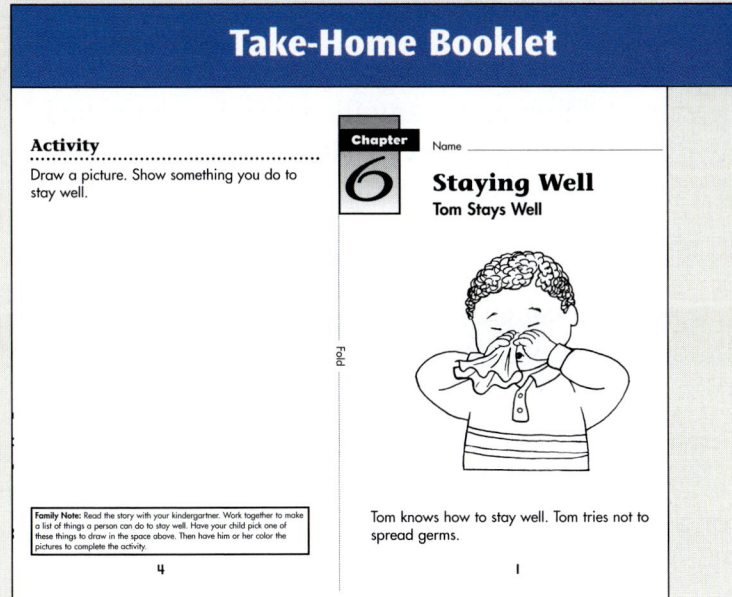

Distribute copies of the Take-Home Booklet, TR pages 83–84. Have children fold the pages to make booklets to share with their families.

School-Home Connection

Distribute copies of the School-Home Connection (in English or Spanish), TR page 65. Have children take the page home to share with their families.

Alternative Use the page for enrichment.

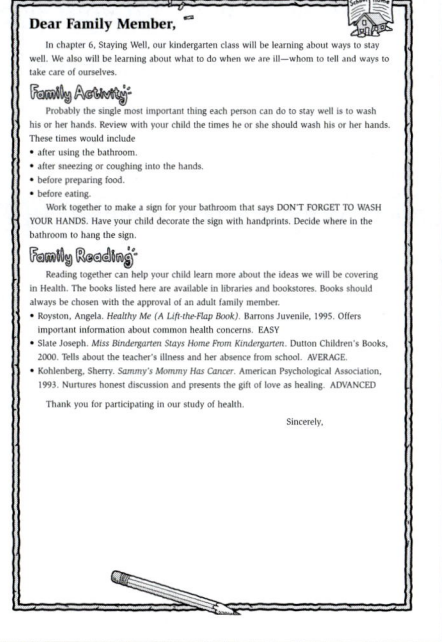

LESSON

OBJECTIVES
- Describe what it feels like to be ill.
- Identify symptoms of illness.

VOCABULARY
- ill
- symptoms

PROGRAM RESOURCES
- Pattern 3, TR p. 93
- Teaching Chart 23
- Activity Book, p. 23

MATERIALS
- small scrap of fabric for puppet blanket
- facial tissue
- cushion for puppet's bed

Teaching Chart 23

Daily Safety Tip

A child who has a fever may have a contagious illness. He or she should be separated from other children and sent home, if possible.

1 Motivate

Make a puppet out of Pattern 3. Lay the puppet on a cushion, and cover it with a blanket. Put a tissue in its hand. Show the puppet to the children. Say that the puppet is not feeling well today.

Teacher: "Puppet, why are your eyes closed?"

Puppet: "The light hurts my eyes."

Teacher: "Why are you holding a tissue?"

Puppet: "My nose is running."

Teacher: "Why are you covered up?"

Puppet: "I am so cold."

What do you think is wrong with the puppet? It has a cold; it has the flu; it is sick. Explain that the puppet is *ill*. Tell children that ill is another word for sick.

2 Teach

Learn from Pictures

Show children Teaching Chart 23. **What is happening in the picture?** The boy is ill; his mother is taking care of him.

- **What things do you see in the picture that tell you the boy is ill?** box of tissues, glass of water, thermometer in boy's mouth Explain that using a thermometer is a way to check if someone has a fever. A fever is a sign of illness.

Discuss

Talk with children about any illnesses they have had. **How did you know you were ill?** Possible answers: I had a fever; I was cold; my throat hurt; I coughed; I had a runny nose; I was sneezing; I had a stomachache and a headache. Tell children the things they mentioned are called *symptoms*. Symptoms are signs that help an adult know what is wrong with you.

- **What do you do to feel better when you are ill?** Provide these suggestions if children don't mention them: Tell an adult; lie quietly in bed; eat cool things for a sore throat; lower lights if your eyes hurt; drink plenty of liquids, such as water and juice.

Life Skills

Communicate Tell children it's important to tell an adult when they feel ill. Invite pairs of children to come up and practice telling you their symptoms, as if they were ill. Have one child in the pair pantomime symptoms, such as putting hand on head, clutching stomach, and rubbing ear. The other child puts into words what the child is pantomiming. Finish up by saying that using words to tell symptoms is a better way of communicating than just using actions.

3 Wrap Up

Extend the communication activity, and give children more practice in describing symptoms. Demonstrate a number of actions which indicate you're feeling ill: hand on forehead, hand on throat, groaning, pretend sneezing, coughing. After each action, ask children to put your symptoms into words.

ASSESSMENT TIP Children should be able to recognize and describe symptoms of illness.

HEALTH BACKGROUND

The Common Cold Colds are a frequent childhood illness. Many children of kindergarten age average five to eight colds per year. By age six, most children's immune systems have developed sufficiently to reduce the number of colds experienced each year.

Causes and Symptoms of Colds More than 200 different viruses cause the common cold. Most of these viruses affect the nose and throat, although some of them can cause bronchitis and laryngitis. Symptoms of a cold usually include congested head, sneezing, sore throat, cough, and sometimes fever. Most cold symptoms will disappear on their own in one to three days. Coughs, however, may linger for several weeks.

Treat a Cold In general, there is little that can be done to cure a cold. Because colds are caused by viruses, antibiotics are of no use. Some doctors recommend saline nosedrops, available without a prescription, to help relieve congestion. If aches and fever accompany a cold, children can be given acetaminophen. Children should NOT be given aspirin, which has been linked with Reye's syndrome, a life-threatening condition.

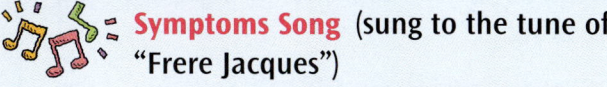

Other things to do!

Music Activity

Symptoms Song (sung to the tune of "Frere Jacques")

"Jack" (choose a child) is ill,
"Jack" is ill,
Yes, he is,
yes, he is.
What are all his symptoms?
What are all his symptoms?
"Jack" has _____. ("Jack" suggests symptom.)
"Jack" has _____. (Use same symptom.)

Continue the song, selecting different children.

Math Activity

Illness Graph Invite children to tell which parts of their body have been affected by illness. Some children may have had earaches, some stomachaches, and so on. Make a chart showing body parts that are affected by illness. Put a picture of each body part at the bottom of each column. Give children small paper rectangles. Have them write their names on the rectangles and paste them to the columns showing the parts of their bodies affected when they were ill.

Using the Activity Book, page 23

This activity gives children practice in identifying who is ill and who can help when they are ill.

Who Is Ill?

Who Can Help?

LESSON 2

OBJECTIVE
- Describe ways to keep disease from spreading.

VOCABULARY
- germs
- immunization

PROGRAM RESOURCES
- Teaching Chart 24
- Poem: "Sneeze," p. RA-3
- Song: "Clap, Clap, Clap Your Hands," p. RA-9
- Activity Book, p. 24

MATERIALS
- spray bottle filled with water

Wash Away Germs

Teaching Chart 24

Daily Safety Tip

Remind children that they should wash their hands before cooking, eating, or handling eating utensils, after using the bathroom, and after playing.

1 Motivate

Read the poem, "Sneeze," page RA-3. After reading the last words, "so pardon me, please, while I sneeze," have children pretend to sneeze.

- Set a spray bottle to fine-mist setting. Spray a gentle mist over the class. Tell children that this is how far an uncovered sneeze will reach.

2 Teach

Learn from Pictures

Show children Teaching Chart 24. **What is happening?** Hands are being washed with a bar of soap.

- **Why is hand washing an important thing to do?** Washing removes dirt and germs. **Why is it important to remove germs?** Germs spread illness.

- Spray the spray bottle again. Ask children what happens when someone sneezes without covering his or her mouth. Germs get spread. Tell them that coughing spreads germs in the same way.

Activity

Controlling the Spread of Germs Have children pretend to sneeze again and then to cough. This time, tell them to cover their noses and mouths with their hands. **Where would all the germs be that came from your sneezes and your coughs?** in our hands

- Have children look around the classroom and make a list of all the things they touch. **Why is it important to wash your hands after you cough or sneeze into them?** Lead children to understand that the germs in their hands can be spread to everything they touch.

- **Critical Thinking** Hand washing is one way to keep germs from spreading. **What are some other ways?** Possible answers: covering coughs or sneezes, throwing used tissues in the trash, staying home when ill.

Discuss

Talk about another thing that can help people stay well. Ask children what they know about getting shots. Invite children to share their experiences with immunizations. **Why did you need a shot if you weren't sick?** to keep from getting sick

- Explain that special shots protect people from certain illnesses for a very long time. They are called *immunizations*. (See Health Background.)

3 Wrap Up

Hand-Washing Song Sing a disease prevention song to the tune of "Clap, Clap, Clap Your Hands." Use these lines or any suggestions children have for keeping disease from spreading.

> Germs, germs, keep them out, . . .
> Wash, wash, wash our hands, . . .
> When we sneeze, use a tissue, . . .
> When we cough, cover our mouths, . . .
> Get, get, get, our shots, . . .

ASSESSMENT TIP Children should understand that there are ways to avoid spreading germs and illnesses.

TEACHER TIP

Classroom Germ Prevention Young children are often unaware that their noses are running or that they are coughing with wide open mouths in someone else's face. Some children don't know they're going to sneeze until after they've done it. Keep tissues in the classroom, and encourage children to use them. Prepare a lined wastebasket to be used only for tissue disposal. Remind children not to drink out of each other's glasses or juice containers. Sharing is good, but sharing germs is not!

HEALTH BACKGROUND

Immunization Schedule Healthy infants and children usually are immunized according to the schedule shown below.

Vaccine	When Needed
Hepatitis B Protects against hepatitis B virus	birth-2 months, 1-4 months 6-18 months
DTP Protects against diphtheria, tetanus, pertussis bacteria	2 months, 4 months, 6 months, 15-18 months, 4-6 years, 11-16 years (tetanus and diphtheria only)
MMR Protects against measles, mumps, and rubella viruses	12-15 months, 4-6 years
Hib Protects against *Haemophilus influenzae* bacterium	2 months, 4 months, 6 months, 12-15 months
IPV Protects against polio virus	2 months, 4 months, 6-18 months, 4-6 years
Pneumococcal Conjugate Protects against pneumococcal bacteria	2 months, 4 months, 6 months, 12-15 months
Varicella Protects against chicken pox	12-18 months

Other things to do!

Drama Activity

Role-Play Disease Prevention Describe situations similar to the ones that follow. Have children role-play how to prevent germs from spreading.

- Two children are doing jumping jacks together. One child has a runny nose. She wipes her nose with her hand. What could the other child do?
- Two children are making mud pies in the backyard. It's lunchtime. What should the children do?

Music Activity

Tissue Dance Reinforce concepts developed in this lesson with a "tissue dance." Play some lively music. Have children take tissues and dance around with them, pretend to sneeze into them, and then dance over to the lined wastebasket and throw away their tissues.

Using the Activity Book, page 24

In this activity children cross out pictures showing children spreading germs.

Don't Spread Germs

LESSON 3

OBJECTIVE
- Describe ways to stay well.

VOCABULARY
- staying well

PROGRAM RESOURCES
- Poem: "Rainy Day," p. RA-4
- Teaching Chart 25
- Performance Assessment Summary Sheet, TR p. 51
- Activity Book, p. 25

MATERIALS
- rain gear, snow gear, and summer clothing

Teaching Chart 25

Daily Safety Tip

Remind children that germs can be spread by sharing food and drink. If they are going to share food or drink with someone, they should use clean dishes or utensils to split the portions before they have tasted any of the food or drink.

1 Motivate

Read the poem "Rainy Day," page RA-4. After reading the selection, show some rain gear, snow gear, and summer clothes to the class. On the board, make three drawings: a sun, some clouds with rain falling from them, and snowflakes.

- Stand in front of the sun, and hold up the raincoat. **Is this a good thing to wear on a hot, sunny day? What *should* I wear?** Invite children to come up and choose the right clothes. Do this for each of the drawings. (As an alternative, bring some pictures of the different types of clothing, and let children choose from the pictures.)

- **What happens if you don't dress appropriately for the weather?** can get cold, wet, too hot Lead children to understand that dressing for the weather helps us stay well.

2 Teach

Learn from Pictures

Show Teaching Chart 25. **What does this picture remind you of?** a game, a path Point to the picture of the children dressed in rain gear. Read the poem "Rainy Day" again. **What are these children and the child in the poem doing to stay well?** They are wearing clothes appropriate for the weather. Explain that this "game" shows ways of staying well.

Activity

Follow the Leader Prior to class starting, select a starting point and a destination point in the classroom. Mark off points along the path to correspond to the ten spaces on Teaching Chart 25. Number small pieces of paper one through ten, and place them in a paper bag or hat.

- Lead the class in "Follow the Leader." When you get to each predetermined space, have a volunteer choose a number from the hat and count off the corresponding number of spaces on the path on Teaching Chart 25.

- Have that child talk about the way to stay well shown in that space. If a child lands on a blank, ask the class to help him or her think of things not shown on the chart that they do to stay well. Suggestions might include being immunized, seeing the doctor or dentist for checkups, telling an adult when ill.

Discuss

After completing the activity, review the things that people can do to stay well.

- washing hands before eating and after using the restroom
- dressing appropriately for the weather
- exercising regularly
- getting enough rest
- wearing sunscreen, hats, and sunglasses
- eating healthful foods

3 Wrap Up

Give each child a sheet of construction paper, scissors, glue, and crayons. Ask them to find pictures in magazines to cut out and glue to the paper or to draw pictures of three things they can do to help stay well.

ASSESSMENT TIP This activity can be used for performance assessment. See Performance Assessment Summary Sheet, TR page 51.

TEACHER TIP

Indoor Exercise In inclement weather exercise offers a way for children to release energy. On days that you are unable to go outside for recess, have children spread out and pretend to be jack-in-the-boxes, do bend and stretch exercises, or jump and count. Active games of "Simon Says" or "Follow the Leader" are also good alternatives to quiet play.

TEACHER TIP

Reinforce Ways to Stay Well Have children help you make up new verses to the song "Clap, Clap, Clap Your Hands," page RA-9, that reinforce ways of staying well. Here are some examples you might want to suggest.

Wear, wear, wear your boots, wear them when it's raining. . .

Play, play, play outside, exercise your body. . .

Eat, eat, eat good foods, good foods for your body. . .

Wash, wash, wash your hands, wash before you eat. . .

Other things to do!

Math Activity

Staying Well Graph On chart paper, make a class graph of favorite ways to stay well. Across the bottom of the graph, depict the ways shown on Teaching Chart 25. Include the additional ideas that children generated for the blank spaces. When the graph is prepared, ask: What is your favorite way to stay well? Give each child a sticker, and have them vote for their favorite way. Help children total all the numbers after everyone has voted.

Science Activity

Exercise Strengthens the Body Explain that when people are well and are able to exercise, all their body parts benefit. Have children take deep breaths. Explain that the lungs work hard during exercise. Ask children to sit quietly for a minute, and have them note that their breathing is slow and quiet. Then ask them to jump up and down for a minute or so. When they are done, have them again notice their breathing, which most likely is more rapid. Explain that during exercise, the lungs work hard to bring more oxygen (air) into the body. Have children think of other body parts that exercise affects. This might include the heart (beats faster) and the muscles.

Using the Activity Book, page 25

This activity reinforces that dressing appropriately for the weather is one way to stay well.

What Should I Wear?

CHAPTER 7 # Medicines Help—Drugs Hurt

Chapter Organizer

Lesson	Objectives	Vocabulary	Program Resources
Introduce the Chapter pp. 100–101	• Preview the chapter. • Introduce chapter activity center.		• School-Home Connection, TR p. 67 • Take-Home Booklet, TR pp. 85–86
Lesson 1 **What Are Medicines?** pp. 102–103 *Pacing: 1 class period* ✓ 1•2•7	• Describe why medicines are used. • Identify different forms of medicines.	medicines pharmacist prescription	• Poem: "Sneeze", p. RA-3 • Teaching Chart 26 • Activity Book, p. 26
Lesson 2 **Take Medicines Safely** pp. 104–105 *Pacing: 1 class period* ✓ 1•3•7	• Describe how to take medicines safely.	trusted adult	• Pattern 3, TR p. 93 • Teaching Chart 27 • Activity Book, p. 27
Lesson 3 **Say NO to Drugs** pp. 106–107 *Pacing: 1 class period* ✓ 3•5•6	• Use refusal skills to say **no** to drugs.	refuse drugs alcohol tobacco caffeine	• Teaching Chart 28 • Performance Assessment Summary Sheet, TR p. 52 • Activity Book, p. 28
Lesson 4 **Tobacco Harms the Body** pp. 108–109 *Pacing: 2 class periods* ✓ 3•5•6	• Recognize that tobacco and tobacco smoke harm the body. • Use refusal skills to say **no** to tobacco products.	tobacco throat brain lungs heart mouth gums nicotine environmental tobacco smoke	• Teaching Charts 28 and 29 ▪ Teaching Transparencies 5 and 6 • Activity Book, p. 29

✓ National Health Education Standards
A complete list of the Standards is provided on the next page.

Key: TR = Teaching Resources

National Health Education Standards

1. Comprehend concepts related to health promotion and disease prevention.
2. Access valid health information and health-promoting products and services.
3. Practice health-enhancing behaviors and reduce health risks.
4. Analyze the influence of culture, media, technology, and other factors on health.
5. Use interpersonal communication skills to enhance health.
6. Use goal-setting and decision-making skills to enhance health.
7. Advocate for personal, family, and community health.

Curriculum Integration

Use these topics to integrate health into your daily planning.

Math
- Sort: What's Safe, What's Not, p. 98
- Liquid Measures, p. 103

Social Studies
- No Smoking Walk, p. 98

Science
- Chemical Reactions, p. 98

Physical Education
- Model How Smoking Affects the Body, p. 109

Art
- We Take Medicines Safely, p. 105
- We Say NO to Drugs, p. 107

Drama and Music
- Role-Play Taking Medicines, p. 105
- No, No, No to Drugs, p. 107

Language Arts
- Refuse Tobacco Big Book, p. 109

ASSESSMENT OPTIONS

Portfolio Assessment
Have students select their best work from the following suggestions:
- **We Take Medicines Safely,** p. 105
- **Refuse Tobacco Big Book,** p. 109
- **My Best Work Portfolio Summary Sheet,** TR p. 42
- **Portfolio Summary Sheet,** TR p. 43

Student Self-Assessment
- **Student Self-Assessment Checklist,** TR p. 38
- **Healthy Habits Checklist,** TR p. 39

Classroom Observation
- **Observation Checklist,** TR p. 36

Performance Assessment
- **Wrap Up,** p. 107
- **Performance Assessment Summary Sheet,** TR p. 52

Daily Assessment
- **Assessment Tips,** pp. 103, 105, 107, 109
- **Activity Book,** pp. 26–29

Cross-Curricular Activities

 ## Science

Chemical Reactions

Some medicines work by causing chemical changes in the body. To help children understand what a chemical reaction is, show them some of the following reactions. Allow children to observe the fizzing that occurs in each case.

- Drop vinegar onto baking soda.
- Drop antacid tablets into a glass of water.

 ## Social Studies

No Smoking Walk

Take the class for a walk around the school. Continue out into the community, if possible. Have children look for *No Smoking* signs.

- After the walk, talk about why these signs are posted in different places. Explain that many businesses and public buildings are smoke free to help people avoid the dangers of environmental tobacco smoke.
- Write the words *No Smoking* on the board. Draw the international NO sign over the words. Have children make their own *No Smoking* signs to take home.

 ## Math

Sort: What's Safe, What's Not

Provide two bags. Label one bag SAFE, and put a happy face on the bag. Label the second bag UNSAFE, and put the international NO sign on the bag (see Teaching Chart 28).

- Have children look through magazines or draw pictures of items that are safe to put in the mouth (food, beverages, eating utensils) and unsafe to put in the mouth (alcohol, drugs, tobacco products, poisons).
- Have children paste each picture to a different piece of poster board, and then sort the pictures into the two bags.
- Allow children to sort the pictures of unsafe items in different ways, such as tobacco, alcohol, and drugs.

 ## Bulletin Board

Divide the bulletin board in half. Label the left half "We take medicines safely." Label the right half "We say NO to drugs."

- In Lesson 2, have children complete the Art Activity: We Take Medicines Safely. Hang the finished pictures on the left half of the bulletin board.
- In Lesson 3, have children complete the Art Activity: We Say NO to Drugs. Hang the finished pictures on the right half of the bulletin board.
- You may want to discuss with children where people get reliable information about medicines and other drugs. Brainstorm a list of information sources such as doctors and nurses, pharmacists, the Internet, magazines, and so on.

Resources

Books for Students

Read Alouds

Zoehfeld, Kathleen W. *Pooh Plays Doctor.* Disney Press, 1999. Christopher Robin takes Pooh to see Owl for his annual checkup. **EASY**

Daly, Niki. *My Dad.* Margaret K. McElderry Books, 1995. A father's drinking causes his family pain and embarrassment until he begins to attend AA meetings. **AVERAGE**

Vigna, Judith. *I Wish Daddy Didn't Drink So Much.* Albert Whitman Company, 1988. Lisa's daddy makes a sled for Christmas, but his drinking nearly spoils the holiday. **ADVANCED**

Books for Teachers and Families

Sifton, David W. *The PDR Family Guide to Over-the-Counter Drugs.* Ballantine, 1998. This Physician's Desk Reference is a consumer guide for OTC drugs.

Graedon, Joe and Teresa Graedon. *The People's Pharmacy.* Griffin, 2001. A handy reference on available medicines.

Video

Monica & The Powerful Drug. AGC Educational Media, 1993. (17 minutes) An animated musical cartoon that educates young children about alcohol.

Happy Healthy, Drug-Free Me, Part 1. Rainbow Educational Media, 1997. (10 minutes) Explains that rules help children make the right decisions and that there are rules against children using tobacco and alcohol.

Happy Healthy, Drug-Free Me, Part 2. Rainbow Educational Media, 1997. (10 minutes) Explains how children can deal with the stresses in their lives without turning to drugs.

Your Health Webliography

The **Webliography** provides links to the Health Background and teaching resources that will support you as you teach the topics in *Your Health*. Simply choose a keyword and you will be taken to a page of links with descriptions of the content you can obtain at each site. The **Webliography** is located on the Teacher Resources page at **www.harcourtschool.com/health** Please review websites before referring your students to them.

Organizations and Agencies

American Cancer Society
National Home Office
1599 Clifton Road, NE
Atlanta, GA 30329-4251
800-ACS-2345
Provides information on the effects of tobacco use on the human body.

American Lung Association
National Office
1740 Broadway
New York, NY 10019
212-315-8700
Conducts educational programs that focus on the prevention and control of lung disease.

For more information about health organizations and agencies, please see the *Teaching Resources* book.

Community Health

Pharmacist Ask a pharmacist to visit the class to talk about medicine safety rules. If possible, have the pharmacist show some medicines that are easily confused with candy to emphasize the importance of children not taking medicines on their own or eating things they find that look like candy.

Free and Inexpensive Material

Parents' Resource Institute for Drug Education
PRIDE Youth Programs
4684 S. Evergreen
Newaygo, MI 49337
800-668-9277
Provides information on drug abuse prevention.

National Family Partnership
2490 Coral Way
Miami, FL 33145-3449
800-705-8997
Network committed to nurturing children by opposing the illegal use of tobacco, alcohol and other drugs and by promoting a healthy lifestyle.

Note that information, while correct at time of publication, is subject to change.

Visit **The Harcourt Learning Site** for related links, activities, resources, and the health **Webliography**.
www.harcourtschool.com

CHAPTER 7
Pages 96–109

"You can't make someone else's choices. You shouldn't let someone else make yours."

—Secretary of State Colin Powell

CHAPTER SUMMARY

In this chapter children
- describe medicines and how to use them safely.
- demonstrate how to refuse drugs, including alcohol and tobacco.
- describe how tobacco harms the body.

LIFE SKILLS Children practice *refusal skills* as they apply to drug use. They *make decisions* about safe ways to take medicines.

HUMAN BODY CONNECTION Children examine the effects of alcohol and tobacco on body systems.

Medicines Help— Drugs Hurt

Health Activity Center

The activities for this chapter's Health Activity Center help reinforce the difference between OTC (over-the-counter) and prescription medicines. They also help children understand the dangers of drug use.

Prescription Medicines

This activity helps children understand that prescription medicines are personalized for individuals.

Materials Needed
- empty, clean prescription and OTC drug containers

What to Do Tell children that prescription drugs are given by a doctor. OTC drugs can be bought in a supermarket or pharmacy without a doctor's prescription.
- Show children the label on one of the prescription drug containers. Point out the patient's name and other information on the label. Then show children

an OTC container and point out that it is not intended for a specific individual.

- Give small groups of children several prescription and OTC drug containers.
- Have children sort the containers into two groups: ones that have prescription labels and ones that do not.

I Can Say NO!

In this activity children use advertisements for tobacco and alcohol products to practice refusal skills.

Materials Needed

- magazine advertisements for things children should refuse, such as tobacco and alcohol products
- box for the advertisements

What to Do Place the advertisements in the box. Have children work in pairs.

- The first child removes an advertisement from the box and offers it to the second child. For example, he or she might offer an advertisement for cigarettes.
- The second child says *no*, and gives a reason why he or she is refusing the offer. He or she can say, "No, I don't smoke cigarettes. The smoke hurts my lungs."

Dropper Art

This activity gives children experience with using droppers.

Materials Needed (per child)

- droppers
- art paper
- paints

What to Do Explain that pharmacists sometimes use droppers to prepare liquid medicines.

- Demonstrate the use of a dropper, showing how it can drop small drops, larger drops, or a continuous stream of water. Have children use droppers and water to practice filling and emptying the droppers.
- When children are comfortable with their use, give each child a sheet of art paper. Have children use droppers and paints to make designs on their papers.
- Encourage them to experiment with using different-sized drops and combining colors.

Take-Home Booklet

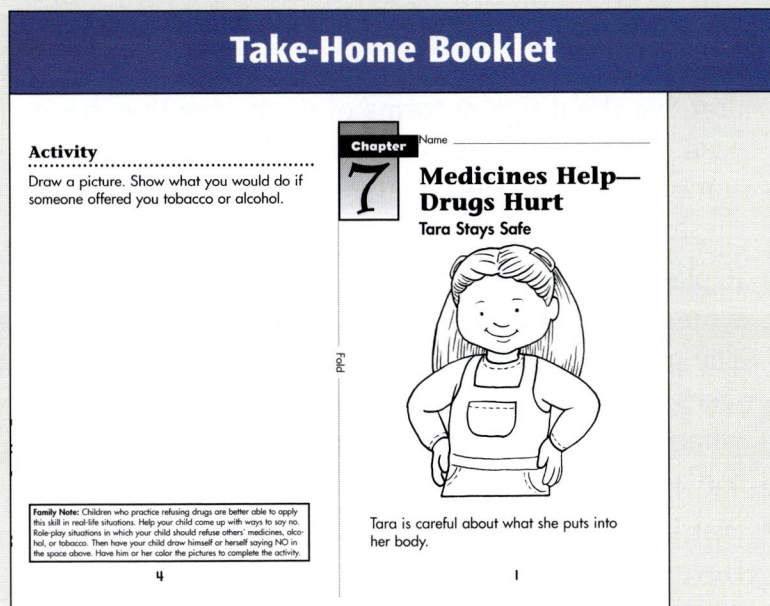

Distribute copies of the Take-Home Booklet, TR pages 85–86. Have children fold the pages to make booklets to share with their families.

School-Home Connection

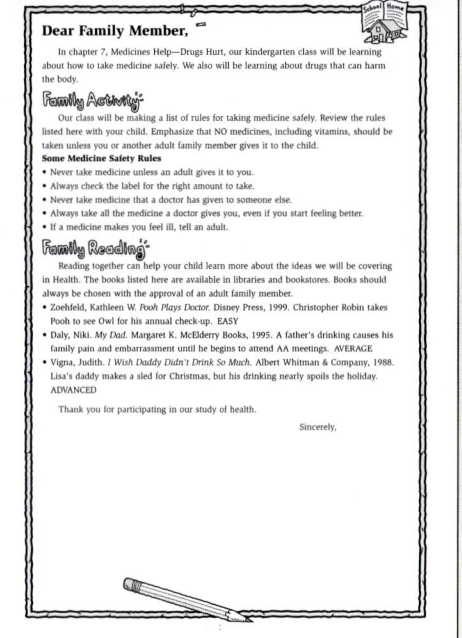

Distribute copies of the School-Home Connection (in English or Spanish), TR page 67. Have children take the page home to share. Alternative Use the page for enrichment.

LESSON 1

OBJECTIVES
- Describe why medicines are used.
- Identify different forms of medicines.

VOCABULARY
- medicines
- pharmacist
- prescription

PROGRAM RESOURCES
- Poem: "Sneeze," p. RA-3
- Teaching Chart 26
- Activity Book, p. 26

MATERIALS
- pictures of different forms of medicines (pills, liquids, creams) cut from magazines and mounted on pieces of poster board
- several empty, clean prescription bottles showing the prescription labels
- pictures of OTC medicines cut from magazines and mounted on pieces of poster board
- several empty, clean OTC medicine bottles

Daily Safety Tip
Getting a good night's sleep helps bodies grow strong. Rest and sleep also help the body fight infection. Remind children to get plenty of rest at the first sign of a cold or other illness.

1 Motivate

Read the poem "Sneeze," page RA-3. As you read the poem a second time, ask children to add actions that mirror the words. For example, children may make faces, wiggle like eels, and finally produce some make-believe sneezes.

- **What is sneezing often a sign of?** catching a cold, coming down with the flu, getting sick or ill Explain that sometimes when children are ill, they need medicine.

What Are Medicines?

Teaching Chart 26

2 Teach

Learn from Pictures

Show children Teaching Chart 26. Direct attention to the left side of the picture and ask children what they see. Possible answer: a drugstore, a pharmacy. **Who is the person in the picture?** pharmacist Explain that a *pharmacist* prepares medicines for people who are ill. *Medicines* are drugs used to treat illnesses.

Discuss

- **Do you ever take medicines?** Let volunteers share their experience with different medicines. Have children list the different forms of medicines they have seen. Some medicines come as pills, some as liquids, some as creams. Display the pictures of each of these forms of medicine for children to identify.

- Explain that sometimes when a person is ill, a doctor writes an order called a *prescription* for a medicine. The person who is ill (or an adult family member) takes the prescription to a pharmacist. The order tells what kind of medicine is needed. The pharmacist reads the prescription and prepares the medicine.

- Distribute the empty prescription medicine bottles. Have children locate the name of the person for whom the medicine was prescribed. Explain that medicines should only be used by the person for whom they were prescribed. Taking another person's medicine is not safe. It can make you ill.

Learn from Pictures

Direct attention to the picture on the right side of Teaching Chart 26. **How is this picture different from the one with the pharmacist?** *The medicines are on a shelf; there isn't anyone to give out the medicine; an adult can get the medicine by himself or herself.*

- Show the pictures of the OTC medicines and the OTC medicine bottles. Have children compare them to the prescription bottles. Work together to make a list of differences. For example, the prescription medicine is for one person's specific illness. The OTC medicines are available to anyone. They are for many illnesses. Emphasize that only adults should purchase medicines.

3 Wrap Up

Show a bottle of prescription medicine and a bottle of OTC medicine. Using Teaching Chart 26, have children tell you how an adult could obtain each of these drugs.

ASSESSMENT TIP Children should be able to identify differences between prescription and OTC medicines. They should be able to explain that a prescription from a doctor is needed for prescription medicines and that a pharmacist prepares these medicines.

TEACHER TIP

Dispensing Medicines Many schools have specific rules regarding the dispensing of any medicines to children. In some, medicines must be dispensed by the school nurse or office secretary. If you are responsible for dispensing medicines to children, obtain written instructions from the child's parent or guardian. Over-the-counter drugs, too, should not be brought to school without directions to you from a parent or guardian.

Remember that children and teenagers should NOT be given aspirin or medicines that contain aspirin. Aspirin can trigger Reye's syndrome, a life-threatening condition. Caregivers should check medicines to see whether they contain aspirin before administering them to children and teenagers. Children may be treated with acetaminophen, available under the brand name Tylenol® or as a generic ingredient. Caregivers must be careful to give only the correct dosage for the child's age and weight. They must also be aware that children can accidentally get too high a dosage of acetaminophen if they are given different medicines containing the drug simultaneously.

Other things to do!

Math Activity

Liquid Measures Explain that a pharmacist measures medicines carefully when filling a doctor's order. Discuss the meaning of the words *more* and *less*. Fill a pitcher with colored water. Have a 1-cup glass measuring cup on hand. Using plastic measuring cups, demonstrate how the $\frac{1}{4}$-, $\frac{1}{3}$-, $\frac{1}{2}$-, $\frac{3}{4}$-, and 1-cup containers fill the 1-cup glass measure to different heights. Discuss which of the measuring cups hold more or less water. Have children take turns pouring more or less liquid into the glass measuring cup than the amount you tell them. For example, hold up the $\frac{1}{2}$-cup measure, and say, "pour in an amount that is less than this."

Using the Activity Book, page 26

This activity reinforces the difference between prescription medicines and OTC medicines.

Get Prescription Medicines

Drug store   Pharmacy

103

LESSON 2

OBJECTIVE
- Describe how to take medicines safely.

VOCABULARY
- trusted adult

PROGRAM RESOURCES
- Pattern 3, TR p. 93
- Teaching Chart 27
- Activity Book, p. 27

MATERIALS
- fabric scraps for hand puppets
- 15 index cards
- chart paper
- medicine bottles (both prescription and OTC) gathered for Lesson 1

Teaching Chart 27

Daily Safety Tip

Many children's medicines, and some adult medicines, are flavored. Children sometimes enjoy the taste of these medicines (such as antacid tablets). Stress that medicine is *not* candy. Emphasize that even though some medicines taste good, they should only be taken when needed and only when given by a trusted adult.

1 Motivate

Use Pattern 3 and fabric scraps to make two hand puppets. Have puppets act out this scenario.

- The first puppet offers medicine to the second puppet. The first puppet says that the medicine tastes just like candy. The second puppet says in a big voice, "*No,* I only take medicines from my parents or other trusted adults!" Invite children to echo this remark.

2 Teach

Discuss

Talk about taking medicines. **When do you take medicines?** when ill **Who gives you your medicine?** Possible answers: adult family members, doctor, nurse. Describe for children who a *trusted adult* might be—someone whom your parent or guardian says it is OK for you to take medicine from.

Learn from Pictures

Show children Teaching Chart 27. **What is happening in the picture?** A child's father is giving him medicine. **Is the boy taking medicine safely? Explain how you know.** Yes, because he is receiving medicine from a trusted adult. Work with children to make a list of people who might be trusted adults. These might include parents, other adult family members, babysitters, after-school or before-school care providers, nurses, doctors, and teacher (if allowed by school policy). Explain that children should not take medicines from anyone unless an adult family member has said it is OK.

Activity

Name Game Ahead of time, write names such as Mom, Dad, Aunt Rita, Dr. Smith, Nurse Susan, Friend Jeremy, Friend Laura, and Ice Cream Store Worker on index cards. Have children sit in a circle. Mix up the cards.

- Hold up a card and read the name aloud. Ask the child on your right: **Should you take medicine from this person?** Have each child say *yes* or *no*, and explain his or her answer.

- Continue around the circle until each child has had a turn.
- Finish up by emphasizing again that they should take medicines only from trusted adults.

Life Skills

Make Decisions Hang the chart paper where everyone in the class can see it. Work to make a list of other medicine safety rules. Show again the medicine bottles from Lesson 1.

- Who should purchase medicines? *adults*
- Show the prescription medicine bottle. **Who should take this medicine?** *The person whose name is on the label.* Re-emphasize that a person should only take his or her own medicine.
- Show both types of medicine bottles. **When should you take these medicines?** *when you are ill and a trusted adult gives the medicine to you* **What should you do if you are ill and your parent isn't home?** *Get help from another trusted adult. Do not take medicine on your own.*

3 Wrap Up

Bring out the hand puppets again. Have the first puppet ask the second puppet to take medicines in different situations. For each situation, have children help the second puppet decide whether or not it is safe to take the medicine.

Safe Situations: a parent giving a child cough medicine; a nurse or doctor giving medicine; a parent giving a child his or her own prescription medicine.

Unsafe Situations: a child offering another child any medicine; a child feeling ill and taking any medicine.

ASSESSMENT TIP Children's responses should indicate that they understand the following: Only take medicine from a trusted adult. Never take another person's medicine. Never take medicine by yourself.

TEACHER TIP

Emphasizing Medicine Safety Rules Write this sentence on the board.

"I can take medicine from _____."

Have children take turns coming up to the board and writing the name (or title: Mommy, Daddy, Doctor) of a trusted adult to finish the sentence. Offer help with spelling. As an alternative, have children say the name of the person. Appoint one child to erase the name after each turn.

Other things to do!

Drama Activity

Role-Play Taking Medicines Have children sit in a circle. Assign the roles of parent birds and a stranger bird. Tell children: You are baby birds who are ill. You need medicine. Open your mouths when mother or father bird brings your medicine. Close your mouth tight when a stranger bird brings your medicine. Have the parent birds and the stranger bird take turns trying to give medicine to the babies.

Art Activity

We Take Medicines Safely Using two copies of Pattern 1: Blank Face, TR page 91, write two versions of the following rule: _____ *never takes medicine on his (her) own.* Then make a copy for each child in your class. Have each child draw his or her face on the pattern and write his or her name in the blank. Provide a variety of yarn and other craft materials for hair, if available. Display the finished pictures on the bulletin board. (See page 98.)

Using the Activity Book, page 27

In this activity, children circle the people who can safely give them medicines. They cross out the people from whom they should not take medicines.

Take Medicines Safely

LESSON 3

OBJECTIVE
- Use refusal skills to say *no* to drugs.

VOCABULARY
- refuse
- drugs
- alcohol
- tobacco
- caffeine

PROGRAM RESOURCES
- Teaching Chart 28
- Performance Assessment Summary Sheet, TR p. 52
- Activity Book, p. 28

MATERIALS
- magazines to cut up
- scissors
- paste

Teaching Chart 28

Daily Safety Tip

Remind children that they should never eat or drink anything unless they know a trusted adult approves. They should not accept food or drink from strangers.

1 Motivate

Pose these hypothetical questions to the children: If someone offered you a bowl of worms to eat, what would you do? If someone offered you some raw meat, what would you do? If someone offered you some spoiled milk, what would you do? Encourage children to respond, "Say *NO!*" in loud voices.

- Why would you say *no* to these things? because they aren't good for us Reinforce the idea that people should say *no* when offered things that aren't good for them. Explain that saying *no* means that you r*efuse* something.

2 Teach

Learn from Pictures

Show children Teaching Chart 28. **What does the circle with a line through it mean when it is over a picture?** It shows that something is bad for you or that it is something you shouldn't do. This sign is the international NO sign.

- Help volunteers point to drugs shown on the page as you name them. Introduce the terms *alcohol, tobacco,* and *drugs.* Explain that alcohol and tobacco contain drugs. Although alcohol and tobacco are legal for adults to use, they are illegal for children. *Drugs* are substances that can harm the body.

- Explain the difference between medicines and drugs. Medicines are given to help when you are ill. If medicines are taken in unsafe ways, they can act as drugs and harm the body.

- Now have children look at the girl's face pictured on Teaching Chart 28. **What is the girl doing?** She is saying *no!*

Discuss

Why might the girl be saying *no*? Someone might have offered her one of the harmful things. Help children understand that they should say *no* to anyone offering them the things pictured.

106

Life Skills

Refuse Have children practice saying *no* in a loud voice. Have them mime the same body language shown on Teaching Chart 28. Encourage children to use firm tones of voice, not angry tones, as they practice saying *no*.

- After children have practiced saying *no*, explain that there are other ways to refuse drugs. Work together to make a list of ways, including telling the other person that the drug isn't good for their body, walking away from the person, making a joke, suggesting something else to do, and seeking help from a parent or other trusted adult.

- When children understand some different ways of refusing, help them role-play situations where they are offered the items on Teaching Chart 28 and use refusal skills to say *no*.

Discuss

Explain that there are drugs in some foods that aren't good for their growing bodies. *Caffeine* is one of these drugs. Caffeine is a drug found in some food and drinks such as chocolate, coffee, tea, and some sodas. Explain that caffeine affects the way the body works, and that children should avoid foods with caffeine.

3 Wrap Up

Have children cut advertisements and other pictures from magazines. Have them paste pictures of things that harm the body, such as cigarettes, alcohol, and drugs, on drawing paper. Talk individually to children and ask them to explain their pictures. After everyone has explained his or her picture, have a ceremony in which the children tear up their pictures and say a loud *no* as they drop their torn-up pictures in the recycling bin or waste can.

ASSESSMENT TIP This activity can be used for performance assessment. See Performance Assessment Summary Sheet, TR page 52.

MEET INDIVIDUAL NEEDS

Kinesthetic Learners Have volunteers demonstrate different ways to say *no* with body language, such as shaking their heads, holding up their hands, turning their backs, folding their arms in front of them, stamping a foot while shaking their heads. Elicit these motions in a game of "Simon Says."

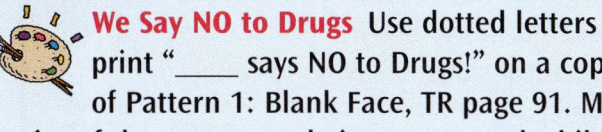

Art Activity

We Say NO to Drugs Use dotted letters to print "____ says NO to Drugs!" on a copy of Pattern 1: Blank Face, TR page 91. Make copies of the pattern and give one to each child. Have children trace the dotted letters and print their names in the blank. Allow children to make representations of their faces using crayons, yarn, and other craft supplies. Display the finished pictures on the bulletin board. (See page 98.)

Music Activity

NO, NO, NO to Drugs Have children sing about saying *no* to drugs. (Tune: "Row, Row, Row Your Boat")

> NO, NO, NO to drugs,
> That is what I say.
> They make me ill,
> They're bad for me,
> Say NO and walk away.

Work with children to come up with additional verses.

Using the Activity Book, page 28

In this activity, children draw circles with lines through them (the international NO sign) over substances that hurt their bodies.

I Say NO to Drugs

No   No

No   No

LESSON 4

OBJECTIVES

- Recognize that tobacco and tobacco smoke harm the body.
- Use refusal skills to say *no* to tobacco products.

VOCABULARY

- tobacco
- throat
- brain
- lungs
- heart
- mouth
- gums
- nicotine
- environmental tobacco smoke

PROGRAM RESOURCES

- Teaching Charts 28 and 29

 Teaching Transparencies 5 and 6

- Activity Book, p. 29

MATERIALS

- pointer or yardstick

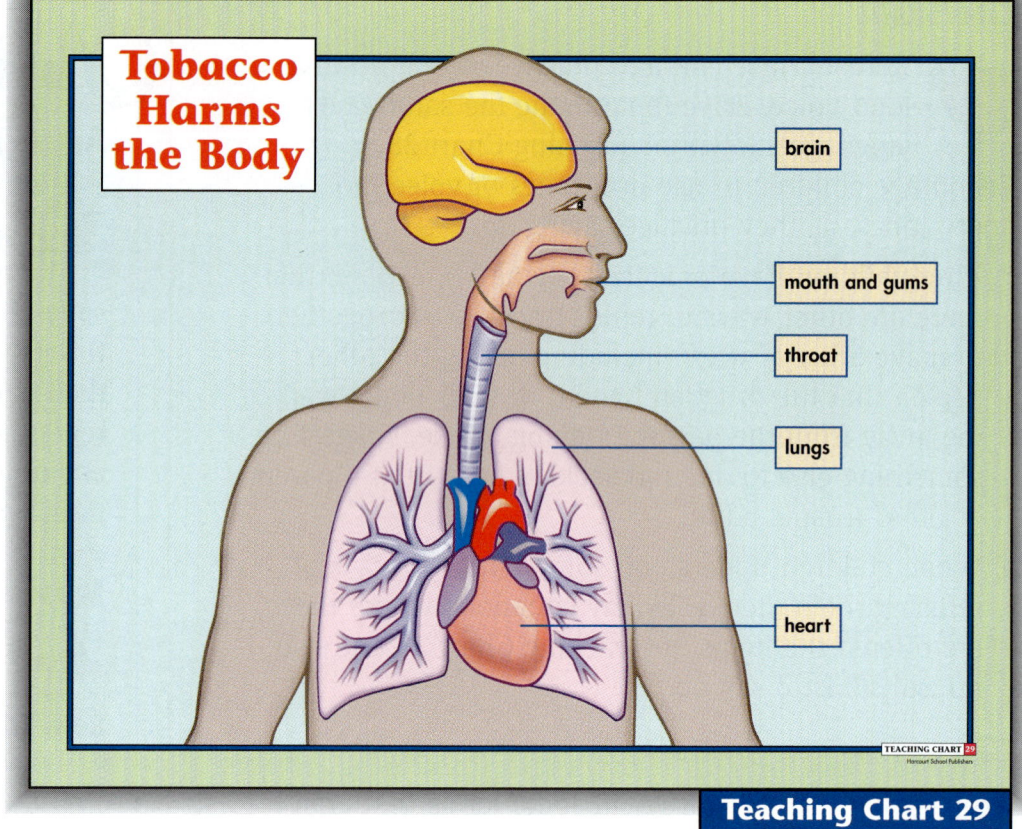

Teaching Chart 29

Tell children that adults at school want children to stay healthy. That is why they have made rules about not smoking.

1 Motivate

Show children Teaching Chart 28. Review the meaning of the international NO sign. Have a volunteer identify the tobacco products.

- What should you say if someone offers you a cigarette? **NO!**

- Point to each tobacco product shown. Help children identify each product. Explain that snuff is finely ground tobacco that users place between the lips and gums. Chewing tobacco is moist, shredded tobacco. A wad of chewing tobacco is placed in the mouth and chewed like chewing gum. This produces a dark juice that must be spit out of the mouth periodically. Pipe smokers also use moist, shredded tobacco, which they pack in pipes and smoke. Cigarettes are made of dried, shredded tobacco wrapped in paper. Cigars are tobacco leaves twisted into a roll.

2 Teach

Learn from Pictures

Turn to Teaching Chart 29. As a way of assessing children's prior knowledge, ask them what they know about how tobacco harms the body. Some children will likely know that tobacco smoke causes harm. Fewer children will be familiar with the harm that smokeless tobacco causes.

Critical Thinking Why do you think these body parts are shown? *These body parts are harmed by tobacco.* Point to each of the body parts on the chart and name them, one at a time. Ask children to touch those parts of their own bodies as you name them.

Discuss

Explain that any way of using tobacco causes the body harm.

- Tobacco smoke hurts the inside of the nose, makes allergies worse, hurts teeth and gums, causes people to have trouble breathing, and may lead to lung diseases. Some substances in tobacco smoke replace the oxygen in the blood. This affects how the brain and all other organs work. Tobacco smoke not only harms the person who is smoking, but anyone who breathes it in. Smoke in the air is called *environmental tobacco smoke*.

108

- Smokeless tobacco harms the gums, mouth, and teeth.
- All tobacco products contain the drug nicotine. Nicotine makes a person want to keep using tobacco. This drug speeds up the body, causing the heart to beat faster. This causes the body to work harder, and can lead to heart diseases.

Critical Thinking What might happen if someone fell asleep in bed while holding a lit cigarette? Explain that many fires are started by cigarettes that fall into bedding or upholstery.

Life Skills

Refuse Tobacco Have children practice refusing offers of tobacco. Provide different scenarios, starting simply and then becoming less obvious, such as "Would you ever try a cigarette?" and building to "I know how you can look really cool," and "I'll bet that you are afraid to try this cigarette." Have children respond by adding words to finish this sentence: *No, I'm smart, I'd rather . . .* Possible answers: go and play, draw a picture, dance, look at a book.

3 Wrap Up

Use Teaching Transparencies

Project Teaching Transparencies 5 and 6. Have volunteers use the pointer or yardstick to point out body parts affected by tobacco. As an alternative, have volunteers finish this sentence using different body parts. "I won't use tobacco, it hurts my (heart, lungs, mouth, brain)." Have children point to the approximate location of each body part as it is mentioned.

ASSESSMENT TIP Children should identify the nose, mouth, and lungs on the respiratory system transparency, and the heart on the circulatory transparency.

TEACHER TIP

Smoking at Home Be sensitive to the fact that some of your children may live with adults who use tobacco products. Emphasize that, even though these products harm the body, it is legal for adults to smoke. Help children understand that the nicotine in tobacco makes it very hard for a person to quit using tobacco products. The best way to stop smoking is to never start.

Other things to do!

Language Arts Activity

Refuse Tobacco Big Book Make a class big book. Provide each child a sheet of chart paper that says: I will not use tobacco because _____. Help each child finish the sentence. Then let children illustrate their pages. Encourage children to take a positive approach, such as: "I will not use tobacco because I want to be able to run and play."

Physical Education

Model How Smoking Affects the Body Take the class to the playground, and divide into two groups. Assign one group to be tobacco users, and the other non-tobacco users. Have the non-tobacco users do a series of activities, such as jumping jacks, jumping rope, and running in place. Have the pretend tobacco users go through the same routine. Tell them to cough, pretend to be having trouble breathing, and put their hands on their hearts as if they hurt. Then let groups switch and do the same routines.

Using the Activity Book, page 29

In this activity, children cross out people using tobacco products and circle people engaging in healthful activities.

I Have Better Things to Do!

109

CHAPTER 8 Keeping Safe

Chapter Organizer

Lesson	Objectives	Vocabulary	Program Resources
Introduce the Chapter pp. 114–115	• Preview the chapter. • Introduce chapter activity center.		• School-Home Connection, TR p. 69 • Take-Home Booklet, TR pp. 87–88
Lesson 1 Stop, Look, and Listen pp. 116–117 *Pacing: 1 class period* — 1•5	• Identify ways to stay safe when crossing streets or playing.	traffic crosswalk helmet safety gear	• Teaching Chart 30 • Song: "Wheels," p. RA-9 • Poem: "I Did a Nutty Somersault," p. RA-4 • Activity Book, p. 30
Lesson 2 Staying Safe pp. 118–119 *Pacing: 1 class period* — 1•5	• Identify steps to stay safe. • Explain how to use steps to stay safe.	stranger trusted adult password respect disrespectful	• Pattern 11, TR p. 101 • Teaching Chart 31 • Teaching Transparency 10 • Activity Book, p. 31 • Story: "Benjamin Rabbit and Stranger Danger," p. RA-6
Lesson 3 Stay Away from Poisons pp. 120–121 *Pacing: 1 class period* — 1•3•5	• Explain the dangers of poisons. • Recognize that anything may be a poison if used unsafely.	poisons	• Poem: "Jellybeans Up Your Nose," p. RA-4 • Teaching Charts 28 and 32 • Performance Assessment Summary Sheet, TR p. 53 • Activity Book, p. 32
Lesson 4 Know How Fires Start pp. 122–123 *Pacing: 1 class period* — 1•2•7	• Recognize how fires start. • Identify ways to prevent fires. • Describe a fire safety plan.	prevent fire 911 escape	• Teaching Chart 33 • Pattern 12, TR p. 102 • Activity Book, p. 33
Lesson 5 Stop, Drop, and Roll pp. 124–125 *Pacing: 1 class period* — 3•5•6	• Demonstrate how to stop, drop, and roll in case of fire. • Demonstrate how to stay low when escaping from a fire.	stop, drop and roll	• Teaching Chart 34 • Teaching Transparency 11 • Activity Book, p. 34
Lesson 6 Water Safety pp. 126–127 *Pacing: 1 class period* — 3•5•6	• Describe safe ways to behave near or in the water.	safe unsafe	• Teaching Chart 35 • Activity Book, p. 35
Lesson 7 Dangerous Things pp. 128–129 *Pacing: 1 class period* — 3•5•6	• Explain why it is not safe to pick up anything lying on the street or sidewalk.	dangerous	• Teaching Chart 36 • Activity Book, p. 36
Lesson 8 Car Safety and Bus Safety pp. 130–131 *Pacing: 1 class period* — 3•5•6	• Explain ways to stay safe when riding in vehicles.	safety vehicle	• Teaching Chart 37 • Activity Book, p. 37

National Health Education Standards
A complete list of the Standards is provided on the next page.

Key: TR = Teaching Resources

National Health Education Standards

1. Comprehend concepts related to health promotion and disease prevention.
2. Access valid health information and health-promoting products and services.
3. Practice health-enhancing behaviors and reduce health risks.
4. Analyze the influence of culture, media, technology, and other factors on health.
5. Use interpersonal communication skills to enhance health.
6. Use goal-setting and decision-making skills to enhance health.
7. Advocate for personal, family, and community health.

Curriculum Integration

Use these topics to integrate health into your daily planning.

Physical Education
- Arms that Travel, p. 131

Social Studies
- Signs in Our Neighborhood, p. 112
- Calling 911, p. 123
- Community Travel, p. 131

Drama
- Buckle Up, p. 112
- Benjamin Rabbit Role-Play, p. 119

Math
- No-Touch Matching, p. 112
- Poisons at Home Graph, p. 121
- Favorite Water Activities Graph, p. 127

Science
- Safe and Unsafe Leaves, p. 121

Music
- Safety Song, p. 129

Art
- Stranger Safety Pictures, p. 112
- Traffic Lights, p. 117
- Fire Prevention Posters, p. 123

Language Arts
- Class Safety Sign Book, p. 117
- Stop, Drop, and Roll Booklets, p. 125
- Journal Writing, p. 127

ASSESSMENT OPTIONS

Portfolio Assessment
Have students select their best work from the following suggestions:
- **Stranger Safety Pictures,** p. 112
- **Class Safety Sign Book,** p. 117
- **Fire Prevention Posters,** p. 123
- **Stop, Drop, and Roll Booklets,** p. 125

Student Self-Assessment
- **Student Self-Assessment Checklist,** TR p. 38
- **Healthy Habits Checklist,** TR p. 39

Classroom Observation
- **Observation Checklist,** TR p. 36

Performance Assessment
- **Wrap Up,** p. 121
- **Performance Assessment Summary Sheet,** TR p. 53

Daily Assessment
- **Assessment Tips,** pp. 117, 119, 121, 123, 125, 127, 129, 131
- **Activity Book,** pp. 30–37

Cross-Curricular Activities

 ## Social Studies

Signs in Our Neighborhood

Talk to children about signs. Explain that the purpose of signs is to provide information. Take a sign-watching walk around the neighborhood. At each sign, discuss the meaning of the sign and why it is important.

- On the playground, play a version of Red Light, Green Light. The goal is for all children to cross the playground safely, following the signs. Children should stand in a line opposite the teacher. Hold up red, yellow, or green pieces of construction paper to represent lights on a traffic signal. Have children practice crossing the street safely, obeying the signal.

 ## Math

No-Touch Matching

Collect pictures of things that are dangerous for children to touch. Examples include knives, guns, needles, prescription drug bottles, and cleaning products. Make duplicates of the pictures so that you have pairs. Paste pictures on cards that are the same size and arrange the cards face-down on a table.

- Children randomly choose two cards and turn them over. They are looking to make a No-Touch Match. If the pictures do not match, they turn the pictures over again and the next child tries. When a match is made, the child should explain why children should not touch this item.

 ## Drama

Buckle Up

Have children assist in creating a set that includes a car with four seats. Then let groups of four pretend to get into the "car." One child plays the driver while the other children get into the car safely. The driver should check that safety belts are fastened and doors are closed. Rotate children into the driver role so all can get an opportunity to play the lead.

 ## Art

Stranger Safety Pictures

Return to the Stranger Danger *Do*s and *Don't*s described in *Benjamin Rabbit and Stranger Danger,* page RA-6. Have each child choose a safety rule to illustrate.

- Help each child write, "_____ stays safe around strangers," at the bottom of his or her picture.
- Post the pictures around a list of Stranger *Do*s and *Don't*s. Use colored yarn to connect the pictures to the appropriate safety tips.

 ## Bulletin Board

Label the bulletin board, "We Say NO to Poisons."

- Place a large international NO sign in the center of the bulletin board.
- Have children bring in labels and box fronts from household items that can be poisonous if ingested.
- Post them around the sign on the bulletin board.

Resources

Books for Students

Read Alouds

Marzollo, Jean. *I Am Fire.* Turtleback Books, 1996. This book explains the difference between "good" fire, which can be used safely for cooking and providing warmth, and "bad" fire, which can cause burns or destroy property. **EASY**

Marston, Hope Irvin. *Fire Trucks.* Cobblehill, 1996. Discusses firefighting vehicles and procedures, and has instructions for fire safety. **AVERAGE**

Brown, Marc and Stephen Krensky. *Dinosaurs, Beware! A Safety Guide.* Little, Brown, and Company, 1984. Dinosaurs illustrate safety tips in various situations—home, car, street, and so on. **ADVANCED**

Books for Teachers and Families

Einzig, Mitchell J., M.D., Ed. *Baby and Child Emergency First-Aid Handbook: Simple Step-by-Step Instructions for the Most Common Childhood Emergencies.* Meadowbrook Press, 1995. This practical reference offers easy instructions and treatments for common injuries.

Giggans, Patricia Occhiuzzo and Barrie Levy. *50 Ways to a Safer World: Everyday Actions You Can Take to Prevent Violence in Neighborhoods, Schools, and Communities.* Seal Press Feminist Publications, 1997. An all-purpose guide to safer homes, reduced stress, and safer communities.

Videos

Fire Trucks in Action. High Profile Video Productions, 1995. (25 minutes) Children learn about fire trucks and fire safety including important safety tips.

Safety 4 Kids: Volume 1. Boo-Boo Productions, 1998. (18 minutes) Educates children using positive messages about safety including safety songs.

Your Health Webliography

The **Webliography** provides links to the Health Background and teaching resources that will support you as you teach the topics in *Your Health*. Simply choose a keyword and you will be taken to a page of links with descriptions of the content you can obtain at each site. The **Webliography** is located on the Teacher Resources page at **www.harcourtschool.com/health** Please review websites before referring your students to them.

Organizations and Agencies

California Highway Patrol
Office of Public Affairs
P.O. Box 942898
Sacramento, CA 94298-0001
916-657-7261
Offers several brochures that stress the importance of traffic safety.

National Lead Information Center
1019 19th Street, NW
Washington, D.C. 20036
800-424-5323
A resource center that provides the general public with information about lead hazards and their prevention.

For more information about health organizations and agencies, please see the *Teaching Resources* book.

Community Health

Police Officer Visit Many communities have special programs through the local police department to educate children about personal safety. Ask a police officer to visit the class and talk about staying safe. Ask the officer to discuss when and why people call 911. Make a copy of Pattern 11, 911 for each child.

Free and Inexpensive Material

American Automobile Association Contact your local AAA office. Offers a booklet that contains activities designed to stress the importance of pedestrian, bicycle, and passenger safety.

Pharmacia Corporation
100 Route 206 North
Peapack, NJ 07977
Offers a delightfully illustrated children's first book on first aid.

Note that information, while correct at time of publication, is subject to change.

Visit **The Harcourt Learning Site** for related links, activities, resources, and the health **Webliography**.
www.harcourtschool.com

Pages 110–131

"Simple precautions and an awareness of the consequences on one's choices and decisions can help to prevent many unintentional injuries."

—Page 42, CA Health Framework

CHAPTER SUMMARY

In this chapter children
- demonstrate how to cross the street safely.
- describe poisons and how to avoid them.
- identify ways to help prevent fires.
- describe and demonstrate ways to stay safe in case of fire.
- describe safe ways to behave near or in water.
- explain that it is not safe to pick up anything off the street.
- describe how to ride safely in a car or bus.

LIFE SKILLS Children practice *communicating* in emergency situations, including calling 911.

HUMAN BODY Children review the need for helmets to protect their heads when playing on bikes or skates, and the need for life jackets when participating in water activities. They also learn about the effect smoke has on the lungs.

Keeping Safe

Health Activity Center

The activities suggested for this chapter's Health Activity Center help reinforce rules for staying safe in many situations that young children encounter.

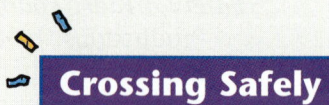

Crossing Safely

This activity helps reinforce the idea that children should cross the street only at corners.

Materials Needed
- simple map drawn for Lesson 1
- small stop signs and traffic lights made for Lesson 1
- toy cars

What to Do At the conclusion of Lesson 1, put the maps, traffic signs and signals, and toy cars in the activity center. Encourage small groups of children to set up a variety of traffic situations on the map, and then tell how to cross the street safely at each intersection.

More Trusted Adults

This activity helps reinforce the concept of a trusted adult.

Materials Needed
- labeled pictures of adults made for the Health Activity Center in Chapter 8
- additional labeled pictures of a teacher, a principal, a police officer, a firefighter, a crossing guard

What to Do Pair children for this activity. Have the first child pick a person from the cards and say, "A stranger has bothered you. Can you tell me?" The second child identifies whether or not the person shown is a trusted adult. Then children switch roles.

Safe and Unsafe Products

This activity helps reinforce the difference between things children can and can't eat.

Materials Needed
- magazines to cut up
- scissors
- index cards
- glue

Have children cut pictures from magazines showing items that are safe and unsafe to eat. Have them paste each picture on a separate index card. Mix the cards in a box. Allow children to sort the pictures into safe and unsafe categories.

Ordering Safety Steps

In this activity children practice the steps for staying safe around strangers and in uncomfortable situations.

Materials Needed
- steps for staying safe from Teaching Transparency 10

What to Do Make a copy of the steps for staying safe that accompanies Teaching Transparency 10. Color the copy, cut the pictures apart, and laminate them. Have children take turns mixing up the pictures and then placing them in the proper order.

Calling 911

This activity reinforces when and how to call 911.

Materials Needed
- play telephone
- cards showing different emergencies, such as a fire or a cut knee

What to Do Have children choose cards from the pack. They should then decide if the situations depicted are serious enough to call 911. If the answer is yes, they should call 911, and practice communicating their names, addresses, phone numbers, and what the problems are.

Take-Home Booklet

Distribute copies of the Take-Home Booklet, TR pp. 87–88. Have children fold the pages to make booklets to share with their families.

School-Home Connection

Distribute copies of the School-Home Connection (in English or Spanish), TR page 69. Have children take the page home to share with their families.

Alternative Use the page for enrichment.

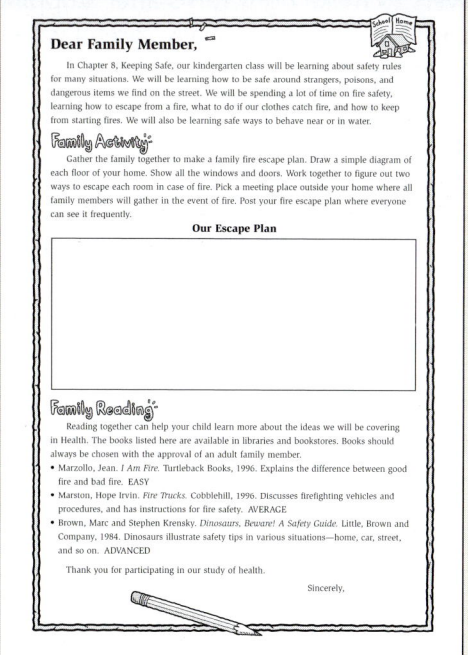

LESSON 1

OBJECTIVE
- Identify ways to stay safe when crossing streets or playing.

VOCABULARY
- traffic
- crosswalk
- helmet
- safety gear

PROGRAM RESOURCES
- Teaching Chart 30
- Song: "Wheels," p. RA-9
- Poem: "I Did a Nutty Somersault," p. RA-4
- Activity Book, p. 30

MATERIALS
- one large and several small stop signs made out of construction paper
- one large and several small traffic lights made out of construction paper
- large sheet of chart paper
- crayons
- toy cars
- bicycle helmet, knee pads, elbow pads, shin guards, wrist guards, mouth guard
- masking tape

Daily Safety Tip
Most states have right-turn-on-red laws. These laws allow drivers to make right turns after stopping. Emphasize that children must be especially careful when crossing the street due to these laws. They must watch for cars turning corners, even when traffic from that direction is stopped.

1 Motivate

Draw a simple street map on the chart paper. Include several corners. Have a volunteer take a toy car and "drive" it along the roads.

- When the driver comes to a corner, ask: **What should the driver do now?** Discuss how the driver needs to slow down and look for traffic when he or she approaches a corner. Explain that *traffic* is the cars, buses, and trucks that are driven on a street.

Teaching Chart 30

- Place a small stop sign at one of the corners. Have a different "driver" approach the corner. **What should the driver do now?** Stop. **When can the driver move ahead?** when there is no traffic coming from another direction

- Place a small traffic light at a different corner. Have a different "driver" approach the corner. **What should the driver do now?** Obey the traffic signal. Hold up the large construction paper traffic light. Remind children that when the light is red, the traffic stops. When the light is green, the traffic goes. Explain that when the light is yellow, traffic slows down and prepares to stop.

Critical Thinking Why do you think it is safer to cross the street at the corner than in the middle of the block? Explain that because drivers must look for oncoming traffic at corners, they are more apt to see people crossing the street at corners. This is why the corner is the safest place to cross.

2 Teach

Learn from Pictures

Show children Teaching Chart 30. Ask volunteers to make up a story about what is happening in the main picture on Teaching Chart 30. Possible story: The children are going to school. The crossing guard is helping

116

them. Be sure everyone knows that a crossing guard walks out in the street to stop the cars so that people can cross safely.

- What do the words *stop, look,* and *listen* mean? Stop before you cross the street, look to see that no cars are coming, and listen for any cars. Talk about how to cross a street safely if there's no crossing guard. Point to the different signs as you discuss how they control traffic and pedestrians at corners. Emphasize that even when using a *crosswalk*, people should stop, look, listen, and look again before crossing.

Activity

Cross Safely Use masking tape to make a corner on the floor of your classroom. Have children take turns standing at the side of the road at the corner, waiting to cross. Give each child a different situation, such as a corner with a crossing guard, a corner with a traffic light, a corner with *walk* and *don't walk* signs, and a corner with a STOP sign. Have each child act out crossing (or not crossing) the street safely.

Discuss

Play and sing "Wheels," page RA-9, and have the children sing along. **When do you play on wheels?** when riding a bike, skating, skateboarding

- Hold up each piece of *safety gear* (bicycle helmet, knee pads, elbow pads, shin guards, wrist guards, mouth guard). Have children point to the part of their bodies each object protects. **When would you wear each of these safety items?** Possible answers: riding bikes; playing soccer, softball, or street hockey; skating; skateboarding.

- Read "I Did a Nutty Somersault," page RA-4. Explain that the child described in the poem is wearing skates, which are causing the child to fall. **What could happen if you don't wear safety gear when you skate?** You could be injured.

3 Wrap Up

Have children come up to Teaching Chart 30 and point to the proper signs to answer these questions: Which signs mean that you can walk? Which signs mean that you should stop and wait?

ASSESSMENT TIP Children should be able to point to and interpret the signs that indicate ways to move safely in the street.

Other things to do!

Art Activity

Traffic Lights Have children use black, red, yellow, and green construction paper to make their own traffic lights. Cut sheets of black construction paper in half lengthwise to create two long panels. Use cardboard to make patterns for 2-inch circles. Have children trace around the patterns on each of the different colors of paper, and then cut out the circles. Have children use the traffic light shown on Teaching Chart 30 as a pattern for finishing their traffic lights. Have children glue labels on each colored circle with the appropriate color word.

Language Arts Activity

Class Safety Sign Book Children should use drawing paper and crayons to make pictures of street signs and signals they have seen. Help them record a word or two describing each sign or signal. Gather the pictures into a class Safety Sign book. As an alternative, have children each make several signs for individual books they can take home to share with their families.

Using the Activity Book, page 30

Children identify and color pictures of children acting safely.

I Stay Safe

LESSON 2

OBJECTIVES
- Identify steps to stay safe.
- Explain how to use steps to stay safe.

VOCABULARY
- stranger
- trusted adult
- password
- respect
- disrespectful

PROGRAM RESOURCES
- Pattern 11, TR p. 101
- Teaching Chart 31

 Teaching Transparency 10

- Activity Book, p. 31
- Story: "Benjamin Rabbit and Stranger Danger," p. RA-6

MATERIALS
- copies of page with large areas for the following information: Name, Address, City, State, Phone Number
- poster-sized list of the Stranger *Do*s and *Don't*s shown on p. RA-6

Most young children love pets. Be sure they understand not to respond to a stranger who asks them for help finding a lost pet. Explain that adults should ask other adults for help.

Teaching Chart 31

1 Motivate

Gather the children in your story area. Begin reading the story "Benjamin Rabbit and Stranger Danger," page RA-6. Stop where the reader learns that Benjamin Rabbit knows his phone number and his address.

- Ask how many know their phone numbers and addresses. Make and distribute copies of Pattern 11. Help children print their full names in the proper spots. Encourage children to share the papers with family members who can help children fill in and learn the rest of the information.

2 Teach

Discuss

Continue reading. Stop at: "Now, I'm going to give you a list of Stranger *Do*s and *Don't*s."

- Ask children if they know what a stranger is. After some discussion, explain that a *stranger* is *any* person they don't know well. Stress the importance of never going anywhere with a stranger and never taking anything from a stranger.

- Go over the list of Stranger *Do*s and *Don't*s. Re-emphasize that a stranger can be a delivery person or someone asking for help.

- Explain that sometimes strangers will tell a child that a parent has sent the stranger to pick the child up from school. Ask if children know what a *password* is. Encourage children to talk with their families and come up with a secret family password.

Learn from Pictures

Show children Teaching Chart 31. Read the title and each of the numbered sentences. Explain that the three rules on Teaching Chart 31 will help children stay safe from strangers who won't leave them alone.

- Point to the picture of the boy saying "NO!" and ask what is happening. Emphasize that children should be firm in refusing attention from a stranger.

- Have children describe the second picture. Emphasize that children should run and scream if a stranger is threatening them. They should run toward a place they know is safe.
- Ask what they think is happening in the third picture. Explain that it is important for children to tell a *trusted adult* if something happens to frighten them or if someone makes them feel uncomfortable. Explain that a trusted adult in this situation could include a police officer, a firefighter, a crossing guard, a teacher, or a neighbor.

Use Teaching Transparencies

Transparency 10 also shows the three steps shown on Teaching Chart 31, and can be used to present this information.

Life Skills

Communicate Role-play some situations involving strangers. Emphasize that children should use the three steps shown on Teaching Chart 31 to handle the situations.

Discuss

Explain that the steps shown on Teaching Chart 31 can be used in any situation that makes you uncomfortable or afraid. Review the idea of *respect*. Respect is being thoughtful in the way you touch, talk, and act toward others. Disrespectful touches, talk, or actions can cause a person to feel uncomfortable. If another person touches you in a way that makes you feel uncomfortable, you have the right to say NO, run away, and tell an adult.

3 Wrap Up

Continue reading the story. Have children call out "No" at each situation where the animals in the story call out "No." Have children act out what Benjamin Rabbit should do when he is approached by a stranger.

ASSESSMENT TIP Children should be able to apply the safety steps covered in this lesson. Finish reading the story through to the end.

TEACHER TIP

Good and Bad Secrets Include a discussion of good secrets and bad secrets. Good secrets are those for special occasions such as a surprise party. Bad secrets are those that make a person feel bad. They include not telling about dangerous situations, disrespectful touches, and other situations that make a child uncomfortable. Emphasize that anytime an adult or older child tells a child to keep a bad secret the child should immediately tell a trusted adult.

Other things to do!

Drama Activity

Benjamin Rabbit Role-Play These necktie bunny puppets can be used to act out the Benjamin Bunny story.

- For each puppet, you will need an old necktie, a cotton ball, scraps of construction paper, yarn, scissors, and glue.
- Cut across the wide end of the tie about 14 inches above the point.
- Cut a nose, ears, and eyes from construction paper. Glue two pieces of yarn across the point of the tie. Glue the nose on top of the "whiskers." Position the eyes above the nose.
- About 2 inches about each eye, cut a small slit for each ear. Glue the ears into the slits.
- Glue a cotton ball tail to the body of the bunny.
- To work the puppet, slip your hand between the fabric and the lining of the necktie all the way to the point.

Using the Activity Book, page 31

Children draw lines from the pictures of trusted adults to the places where they can be found.

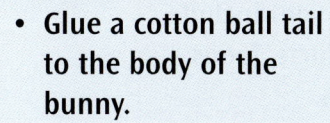

LESSON

OBJECTIVES
- Explain the dangers of poisons.
- Recognize that anything may be a poison if used unsafely.

VOCABULARY
- poisons

PROGRAM RESOURCES
- Poem: "Jellybeans Up Your Nose," p. RA-4
- Teaching Charts 28 and 32
- Performance Assessment Summary Sheet, TR p. 53
- Activity Book, p. 32

MATERIALS
- Well-washed and sealed containers from products that are safe and unsafe to touch or eat. Products might include cleaning or lawn care products, foods, and personal care products.
- play telephone
- scissors
- construction paper
- glue
- magazines to cut up
- plastic gloves
- labels *poison, safe, unsafe*

Daily Safety Tip
Help children understand that some of the things they put in their mouths may be dangerous, even poisonous. Remind children not to put leaves from any outdoor plant or houseplant in their mouths.

1 Motivate

Ask children to name some safe things to play with at home. *toys and games, crayons and paper*

- **What are some things in your home that you should NOT play with?** *stoves, other appliances, medicines, tools, cleaning supplies*
- Read "Jellybeans Up Your Nose," page RA-4. Have children describe what happened in the poem. *Johnny took something safe, a jellybean, and didn't use it the way it was supposed to be used, which made the jellybean unsafe.* Explain that there are many things that can be unsafe if not used properly.

Teaching Chart 32

2 Teach

Learn from Pictures

Show children Teaching Chart 32. Explain that *poison* is something that can make people very ill if they eat or drink the products. Review the meaning of the international NO sign (described in Chapter 7, Lesson 3). Explain that this sign indicates children should stay away from all of these products.

- Name the products in the pictures. As you name each one, ask children to raise their hands if they have seen the product in their homes. (Keep track of the data for the Math Activity described on page 121.) Explain that all of the products shown on this page are poisons that are dangerous if not used the way they are supposed to be used.

- Make a list of additional products that can be poisonous. Remind children that medicines, if taken incorrectly, can be harmful. Show Teaching Chart 28. **What would happen if the girl used any of the things in the circles?** *They are poisons; she would get sick.*

Activity

Safe or Not? Display the washed and sealed containers. As you name each one, invite volunteers that have

120

plastic gloves on to group them according to whether they are safe or unsafe. Point out that poisons are sometimes stored unsafely in familiar containers such as milk cartons. Emphasize that children should never touch anything if they are not sure it is safe.

- Help children cut construction paper into label-sized pieces. Glue copies of the word *poison* on each label. Have children draw the universal NO sign over each word. Ask children to ask an adult family member to help them place the labels on poisons in their homes.

Discuss

Talk about what to do if someone puts a poisonous product in his or her mouth. **What should you do in an emergency?** Call 911 and tell an adult.

Life Skills

Communicate Provide a play phone and have children show how they would dial the emergency number. Have children practice what they would say, including their name, the address, and the nature of the emergency.

3 Wrap Up

Give each child a sheet of construction paper. Have children fold the sheets in half lengthwise. Glue the label *safe* at the top of one column and *unsafe* at the top of the other. Have children cut pictures out of magazines and paste them under the appropriate headings.

ASSESSMENT TIP This activity can be used for performance assessment. See Performance Assessment Summary Sheet, TR page 53.

HEALTH BACKGROUND

Preventing Poisonings Children are at special risk of poisoning due to their small size and tendency to put things in their mouths. The best way to prevent poisonings is to keep all hazardous items out of reach in high cupboards, on tall shelves in closets, or in locked cabinets. Designating such an area in bathrooms, kitchens, basements, garden sheds, and garages can help prevent most poisonings.

Other things to do!

Math Activity

Poisons at Home Graph Make a bar graph using the data collected as children indicated whether or not each poison was in their homes.

- List the products across the bottom of the chart, either by name or by using pictures cut from magazines.
- Fill in a square for each child who has each common household item in the home.
- Have children count the items in each column and record the totals.

Science Activity

Safe and Unsafe Leaves Gather leaves from several houseplants and landscaping plants common in your area. Show children some lettuce leaves or other edible leaves. Point out that some things can be eaten (lettuce) but other leaves (those from houseplants and landscaping plants) could be poison. Emphasize that children should never eat the leaves or berries of any plant. They should eat only things that are specifically served to them as food.

Using the Activity Book, page 32

Children draw international NO signs through pictures of poisons.

Say NO to Poisons

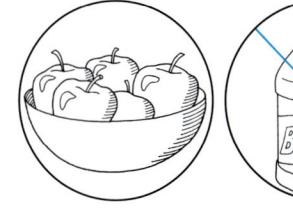

LESSON

OBJECTIVES
- Recognize how fires start.
- Identify ways to prevent fires.
- Describe a fire safety plan.

VOCABULARY
- prevent
- fire
- 911
- escape

PROGRAM RESOURCES
- Teaching Chart 33
- Pattern 12, TR p. 102
- Activity Book, p. 33

MATERIALS
- smoke detector

Teaching Chart 33

Daily Safety Tip

Children playing with matches is a major cause of fires. Children are fascinated with the flame and with how matches light. Emphasize that children should never touch matches or try to light them. Encourage children to tell an adult if they find matches on the street or around the home.

1 Motivate

Show children the smoke detector. **What is this for?** The smoke detector lets you know if there's dangerous smoke. Tell children the smoke detector helps to keep them safe from fires. If you have a fire alarm in your classroom, point to it and ask: **What is the fire alarm for?** to warn that a fire has started Explain that smoke, heat, and flickering light can be signs that something is on fire.

2 Teach

Ask children to tell places where they have seen fires or flames. Explain that *fire* is the burning of materials. Work together to make a list of classroom materials that will burn. The list might include things such as books, papers, desks, and walls.

Learn from Pictures

Show children Teaching Chart 33. Explain that the pictures show things that can start fires. Have children identify each item shown, and talk about where they might have seen each item. Ask for suggestions on how to use the things in the pictures safely. Explain that when they follow the rules, they help to *prevent* fires, or stop them from happening.

- **Candles** Always put candles on a surface that cannot catch fire and far away from blowing curtains or other materials.
- **Fireworks** Only adults should use fireworks, and only in places where they are legal. Children should stay well away from any fireworks displays.
- **Matches and Lighters** Only adults should touch matches and lighters. If children find these objects, they should give them to an adult.
- **Stoves** Never put papers near a hot stove; children should not use stoves unless an adult is there to supervise.

When children understand that they can help prevent fires by avoiding all the things shown on Teaching Chart 33, invite children to trace the path to fire safety with their fingers. Explain that the bird is congratulating them for getting past all the potential fire starters by saying, "You are fire safe."

Activity

Fire Escape Plan Remind children that fires are unexpected events. That's why at school, people practice escaping from a fire by having fire drills. Explain to children that they should know two ways out of every room. Have them help you identify the different exits from your classroom, and describe how they would move from each of these exits to the exterior of the building. Remind children that these same steps should be followed at home. Go over these safety rules for what to do once you exit your home.

- Tell an adult.
- Go to the family meeting place.
- Go to a neighbor's house.
- Call 911 or the fire department.

3 Wrap Up

Make a copy of Pattern 12 for each child. Write the telephone number of your local fire department on the board and have children copy it onto the hat. Have children use the fire hats as they take turns telling what to do to avoid the dangerous things on the path to fire safety.

ASSESSMENT TIP Children should be able to identify things they can do to help prevent fires, such as not playing with matches and keeping flammable materials away from sources of fire.

TEACHER TIP

Appropriate Behavior During an Emergency Drill Review with children the steps of emergency drills such as fire, earthquake, and tornado drills. Discuss the importance of appropriate conduct during such drills. Standing in line, walking in a quick but orderly fashion, staying with the class, and reporting to the right location outside are all very important for the child's safety during a fire drill. Emphasize that though the drill may seem strange or funny, it is important practice for what to do if there is a real emergency.

Other things to do!

Art Activity

Fire Prevention Posters Encourage children to make fire prevention posters. Have them draw pictures of how a fire might start. They might choose something shown on Teaching Chart 33, or another hazard. When their pictures are complete, have them use red markers to put international NO signs over their pictures. Help children label their posters with titles such as "Don't Play with Matches" or "Stay Away from the Stove."

Social Studies Activity

Calling 911 Discuss when it is appropriate to use 911. Emphasize that this number is for extreme emergencies, such as when there is a fire or a serious accident or illness. Remind children that it is inappropriate to call 911 when they break a toy or scrape a knee. Give children a variety of situations, and have them role play a 911 call.

Using the Activity Book, page 33

Children cross out the unsafe fire practices and color the safe fire practices.

Don't Let Fires Start

LESSON 5

OBJECTIVE
- Demonstrate how to stay low when escaping from a fire.
- Demonstrate how to stop, drop, and roll in case of fire.

VOCABULARY
- stop, drop, and roll

PROGRAM RESOURCES
- Teaching Chart 34

Teaching Transparency 11

- Activity Book, p. 34

MATERIALS
- candle, standing upright in a jar with a lid

Teaching Chart 34

Daily Safety Tip
Review the procedures you've developed in case of a classroom or school fire. Remind children to keep their eyes on the teacher when any emergency arises.

1 Motivate

Have children run in place for a minute or two until they are breathing deeply. **What is going in and out of your nose and mouth?** air

- Show children the candle in the jar. Ask them to imagine that the candle is lit. Explain that the candle could burn because air could get into the jar through the open lid. Put the lid on the jar, and explain that the candle would go out once all the air in the jar was used up. Explain that fire needs air, just as people do.

2 Teach

Discuss

Talk about the signs of a fire. The smell of smoke is a sign, as well as the sight of smoke or flames, and the crackling sound of a fire.

Discuss with children that if they see, smell, or hear signs of a fire, they need to follow these rules:

- Get as close to the floor as possible. Smoke rises, so stay low to get the best air.
- Hold a cloth in front of your mouth to help filter out smoke. A wet cloth is best, but a dry cloth is better than nothing.
- Crawl to an exit. If you get to a closed door, feel it to see if it is hot. If it is hot, don't open it.
- If you have to, go out a window.

Learn from Pictures

Show children Teaching Chart 34. Direct attention to the first picture. **What's wrong here?** Child's clothing is on fire.

- Have children look at the second picture. Read the word and have children repeat it. Explain what's going on in the picture: the child has dropped to the ground.
- Have children look at the final picture. Read the word and have children repeat it. Tell children that the child is rolling on the ground to take the air away from the fire so that the fire will go out.
- Put the process together. Point to the words and have children quickly repeat them so they form a sentence: Stop, drop, and roll.

Teaching Transparencies

Teaching Transparency 11 also shows the three steps shown on Teaching Chart 34, and can be used to present this information.

Discuss

Talk with the children about what to do if their clothing catches on fire, just like the child's in the picture: Stop, drop, and roll.

- Ask if anyone knows why they should stop, drop, and roll. Help children understand that fire needs air to keep burning. Running gives the fire more air making it burn faster. Stopping, dropping, and rolling on the ground keeps the fire from getting air and makes it go out.

Activity

Stay Low and Crawl, and Stop, Drop, and Roll Have children spread out and practice the stay low and crawl and the stop, drop, and roll techniques.

3 Wrap Up

Have children run around the room. **Is this what you should do if your clothes ever catch fire?** no Have children show you what they should do. Stop, drop, and roll.

ASSESSMENT TIP Children should be able to demonstrate how to stop, drop, and roll and to explain that this technique is to be used if their clothes are on fire.

TEACHER TIP

Review Fire Safety This lesson provides a good opportunity to review ways to stay safe from fire, such as sleeping in fire-safe pajamas, not playing with matches, and keeping papers away from open flames or hot surfaces such as stove tops. Again show Teaching Chart 33, and review the items children should stay away from in order to be fire safe. Have children role-play what they should do in each of the following situations:

- Some children played with matches. A fire started in the curtains. What should the children do? Stop, drop, and roll, or stay low and crawl away from the fire?
- A little girl reached across her birthday cake. A birthday candle started her dress on fire. What should the girl do? Stop, drop, and roll, or stay low and crawl away from the fire?

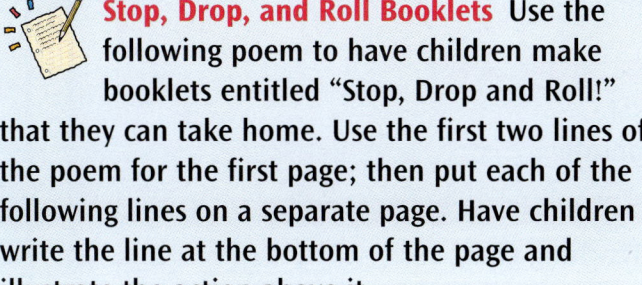

Language Arts Activity

Stop, Drop, and Roll Booklets Use the following poem to have children make booklets entitled "Stop, Drop and Roll!" that they can take home. Use the first two lines of the poem for the first page; then put each of the following lines on a separate page. Have children write the line at the bottom of the page and illustrate the action above it.

If my clothes catch on fire
I know just what to do
I S-T-O-P Stop
I D-R-O-P Drop
I R-O-L-L Roll
That's just what I will do!

Using the Activity Book, page 34

Children trace the words *Stop*, *Drop*, and *Roll* and color the pictures.

Stop, Drop, and Roll

125

OBJECTIVE
- Describe safe ways to behave near or in water.

VOCABULARY
- safe
- unsafe

PROGRAM RESOURCES
- Teaching Chart 35
- Activity Book, p. 35

MATERIALS
- picture of a swimming pool
- magazines to cut up
- poster board
- scissors
- paste

Teaching Chart 35

Daily Safety Tip

Most children drown because they are not properly supervised in or around a swimming pool or bathtub. Therefore, children should never be left unattended near or in water, even with safety devices such as swim floats. Emphasize that children should swim only with an adult. Remind children that in an emergency, they should call 911. Encourage children to review water safety rules with an adult at home.

1 Motivate

Show children a picture of a swimming pool. Tell them they are going to take an imaginary trip to the pool. Ask them to get ready by pretending to pack what they will need to take and by pretending to put on the appropriate clothing. Discuss water activities they would like to do. Ask children if they think these activities are safe. Why or why not? Possible answers: yes, because there is an adult present; no, because some children do not know how to swim.

2 Teach

Learn from Pictures

Show children Teaching Chart 35. Together go over the ways to stay safe near or in water. Explain that the picture shows ways to stay safe.

- Learn to swim. The best thing anyone can do to stay safe near or in water is learn to swim.
- Follow all posted rules and swim where it is allowed only.
- Never swim alone. Swim with a buddy in a proper swimming place.
- Pay attention to the weather. (Discuss lightning and strong wind precautions.)
- Wear a life jacket. Everyone in a boat should wear a life jacket whether able to swim or not. Life jackets must also be worn while jet skiing, windsurfing, tubing, rafting, and water skiing.
- In an emergency, call 911. Notice what is happening, and be prepared for an emergency. Have a cell phone with you.

Discuss

Explain to children that *safe* means "out of danger" and *unsafe* means "in danger." Discuss important swimming pool rules. Tell children that rules keep people safe.

- Swim where the lifeguard can see you.
- Avoid rough play and pushing.
- Never run around the pool.
- Do not dive into shallow water.

3 Wrap Up

Activity

Water Safety Collage Encourage children to make a water safety collage. Have them cut out magazine pictures of people being safe near or in water. Remind them to look at Teaching Chart 35 to make sure the pictures they cut out show safe things to do. When they have finished cutting, have children paste pictures to a piece of poster board to form a collage.

ASSESSMENT TIP Children should be able to identify safe and unsafe ways to behave near or in water.

TEACHER TIP

Ocean Safety Include a discussion about ocean safety. Swimming in the ocean can be dangerous due to currents. Explain that sometimes currents can be too strong to swim in. Tell children not to try to swim against a current if they get caught in one. They should swim across it until they are out of it and then swim to shore. Role-play swimming out of an ocean current. Also remind children that water plants and animals may be dangerous. Avoid plants and leave animals alone.

MEET INDIVIDUAL NEEDS

Kinesthetic Learner Discuss the importance of wearing a life jacket. Show children a real life jacket, and talk about how it is worn and how it works to help keep people safe. Allow children to practice putting on a life jacket in the dramatic play center.

Other things to do!

Math Activity

Favorite Water Activities Graph Discuss with children some of their favorite water activities. Then make a class bar graph.

- List the water activities across the bottom of the chart using words or magazine pictures.
- Have each child write his/her name on a sticky note. Then ask children to place their name above their favorite water activity.
- Have children count the names in each column.
- Discuss the graph as a class.

Language Arts Activity

Journal Writing Reintroduce the words *safe* and *unsafe*. Tell children they are opposites. Tell children you are going to describe some unsafe situations and you want them to tell you the opposite safe situation. Start out by describing a car with two children and an adult in it. The children are standing up in the backseat while the adult is driving. Ask children to tell you the opposite safe situation involving the same car scene. (The adult is driving and the two children are sitting down in the backseat. Everyone has seatbelts on.) Continue describing other unsafe situations. Then have children draw an unsafe picture in their journals and label it with the word *unsafe*. Also have them draw the opposite safe picture and label it with the word *safe*.

Using the Activity Book, page 35

Children color happy faces yellow under pictures of safe water activities. They color sad faces blue under pictures of unsafe water activities.

I Know About Water Safety

LESSON 7

OBJECTIVE
- Explain why it is not safe to pick up anything lying on the street or sidewalk.

VOCABULARY
- dangerous

PROGRAM RESOURCES
- Teaching Chart 36
- Activity Book, p. 36

MATERIALS
- several snack-sized candy bars

Teaching Chart 36

Daily Safety Tip

Most children love animals, but many animals children encounter, especially dogs, can be dangerous. Remind children that they should never approach or reach out to touch a dog, even dogs that are with their owners. When approached by a dog, they should stand still and not make sudden movements or loud noises.

1 Motivate

Ahead of time, put some snack-sized candy bars on the floor. Leave some of the wrappers intact, partially open some, and take small bites out of one or two others. Take the children for a walk around the classroom. Observe what children do as they discover the candies. Bring the class back together and gather up the candy bars.

2 Teach

Learn from Pictures

Show children Teaching Chart 36. Together, identify the objects in each picture. Tell children there are two words that tell about these pictures—dangerous things.

Discuss

Candy Point out the candy on Teaching Chart 36, and the pile of candy children found around the room. **Why might candy be dangerous?** It could be open and thus dirty. Remind children of the lesson on germs. Germs cannot be seen. Even if something such as candy looks safe, it may not be safe because it may contain germs they cannot see. Explain that sometimes people do things to candy that makes it unsafe. Emphasize that candy, even if the wrapper is intact, is not safe to eat if found.

Broken Glass Broken glass can easily cut a person handling it. Explain to children that they should not attempt to clean up broken glass. They should get an adult to help sweep up the glass safely.

Trash Explain that trash can contain germs, as well as sharp objects and broken glass. Children should not play near dumpsters or trash cans, and should not pick up trash unless supervised by an adult and wearing gloves.

Guns, Knives, Rusty Objects, and Needles Explain to children that these are the most dangerous objects they might encounter on the street. All of these objects could harm them or make them ill. If they find *any* of these objects, they should follow these rules:

- Don't touch.
- Tell an adult.

Activity

Should You Touch? Scenarios Suggest a number of scenarios in which children must decide whether or not to pick up an object they find on the street. Some suggestions follow.

- You see a brand new candy bar lying on the street; you see some nails in an empty lot; you see some fireworks that have never been used lying on the grass near your home. For each scenario, the children should respond, "NO! Don't pick it up!"

3 Wrap Up

Remind children of the story of *Benjamin Rabbit and Stranger Danger*. **What did Benjamin Rabbit learn?** Strangers can be dangerous. Ask children some questions about strangers. **Should you talk to a stranger who needs help finding a pet?** Have children respond "No, never!" to each question.

- Point at and name each object on the Teaching Chart again. **Should you touch this?** Have children respond: "No, never!"
- Help children understand that not talking to or going with strangers is one way to keep safe, and not touching dangerous things in the street is another way to keep safe.

ASSESSMENT TIP Children should answer *no* to questions about dangerous objects in the street. They should realize that it is not safe to pick up anything off the street.

TEACHER TIP

Disposing of Dangerous Things Show children pictures of garbage and trash disposal trucks. Discuss the community need for places to dispose of things that are dangerous. Explain that disposal trucks haul away many dangerous things. Emphasize that children should stay away from these trucks.

MEET INDIVIDUAL NEEDS

Visual/Tactile Learners Have children cut pictures of dangerous things from magazines and make a collage. Help them title the collage "Stay Away!"

Other things to do!

Music Activity

Safety Song Have children sing these new words to "If You're Happy and You Know It, Clap Your Hands." Add action to the song by having the children pantomime looking down, seeing something, and then moving away from the imaginary object. Or, beforehand, lay Teaching Chart 36 flat in the middle of the room. Have children sit in a circle, and when they sing the line, "walk on by," have them point to the pictures.

> If you see it on the street,
> walk on by.
>
> If you see it on the street,
> walk on by.
>
> If you see it on the street,
> it could hurt your hands and feet.
>
> If you see it on the street,
> walk on by.

Encourage children to help you make up additional verses, such as

- If you see it on the street, tell your mom . . .
- If you see it on the street, never touch . . .

Using the Activity Book, page 36

Children find five dangerous objects in a park scene and cross them out.

Say NO to Danger

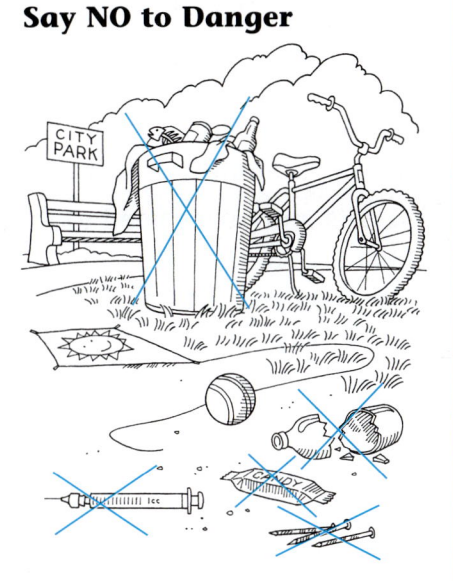

OBJECTIVE
- Explain ways to stay safe when riding in vehicles.

VOCABULARY
- safety
- vehicle

PROGRAM RESOURCES
- Teaching Chart 37
- Activity Book, p. 37

MATERIALS
- classroom rules chart

Teaching Chart 37

Daily Safety Tip

Remind children to look both ways when crossing the street in front of a school bus. Emphasize that they should never cross behind a school bus or wait for the school bus to leave before crossing.

1 Motivate

Direct children's attention to the chart of classroom rules. Read them together. **Why are there rules?** Possible answers: Rules help the class work together; rules keep people from getting hurt; rules keep people safe.

Discuss

Remind children about the rules vehicles follow as they approach intersections, and about rules for crossing streets safely from Lesson 1.

- **Do cars and buses need to follow special rules?** yes **What are some of the rules?** Possible answers: Stop at stop signs and red lights; follow the speed limit. Buses need to stop at railroad crossings; cars need to stop if a school bus stops to let children on or off the bus.

2 Teach

Learn from Pictures

Show children Teaching Chart 37. Talk with the children about car safety rules. **Does your family have car safety rules? What are they?** Possible answers: Sit quietly, buckle your safety belts, children sit in the back seat.

- Talk about the reasons for following safety rules in a car. Remind children that safety belts keep you in your seat if there is a car crash or if the car stops suddenly. Explain that air bags are not safe for small children—they are designed for people of adult size. To be safe, children should always sit in the rear seat of a car.

Discuss

Find out how many of the children in your class ride the bus to school. Have those children suggest some bus safety rules. Make a list of their suggestions on the board. Possible suggestions might include sitting quietly in the seat, facing forward, and not distracting the driver.

- Direct children to the bus side of Teaching Chart 37. Ask for rules for getting on and off the bus. Children should stay back from the road until the bus comes to a complete stop. They should enter quickly, and find a seat immediately. If children must cross the street to get on the bus, they should wait for the bus to stop with its flashers on, and then cross. When exiting the bus, children should cross the street in front of the bus while the lights are flashing and traffic is stopped.

Activity

Bus Stop Place the classroom chairs in a circle for musical chairs. Play or sing the song, "Wheels on the Bus." Tell children that when the music stops, they should all sit as they would on the bus, quietly, straight, and facing forward.

3 Wrap Up

Activity

Bus Stop Arrange the classroom chairs to mimic the seats of a bus. Again use the song "Wheels on the Bus." Have children make the motions that accompany the song, and then make up additional stanzas with suggestions from the children, incorporating safety rules. Some suggestions follow.

- The children cross the street when the lights flash red, lights flash red, lights flash red . . .
- The children in the bus sit in their seats, in their seats, in their seats . . .
- The children in the bus talk quietly, quietly, quietly . . .

When the song is finished, talk to children individually. Ask them to tell you one rule for car or bus safety.

ASSESSMENT TIP Children should be able to identify a variety of rules for car and bus safety, including sitting quietly in the seat and wearing safety belts whenever they are available.

TEACHER TIP

Cars at Home During the discussion of car safety, be sensitive to the fact that some children's families may not have a car, and some family cars may not have air bags or enough seat belts for all passengers. It's important for the children to know the rules anyway.

Other things to do!

Physical Education Activity

Arms that Travel Play and sing the song *Wheels*, page. RA-9. Have children act out the different modes of travel described in the song. They can roll their arms for wagons, bikes, buses and cars; make skating motions for skating; move arms horizontally forward and back for trains. After the song is finished, have children list some rules for staying safe in each mode of travel. Remind children to wear helmets when skating or bike-riding.

Social Studies Activity

Community Travel Create a "Travel in Our Community" display. Have children cut out magazine pictures of different modes of travel available in your community. If possible take a field trip to the local bus transit station or an airport. Ask the staff who work there to tell the children what safety precautions they use, and how passengers can help ensure their own safety while traveling.

Using the Activity Book, page 37

Children circle pictures of safe riders, and draw lines through pictures of children who are acting in unsafe ways.

Riding Safely

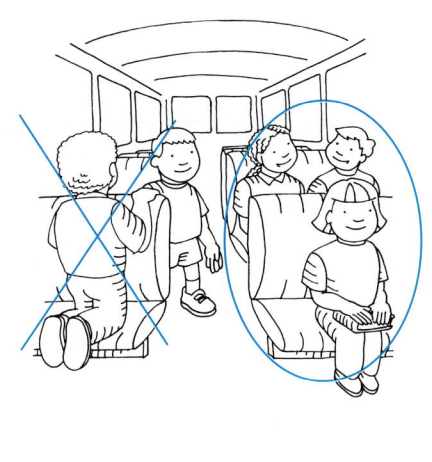

CHAPTER

A Healthy Community

Chapter Organizer

Lesson	Objectives	Vocabulary	Program Resources
Introduce the Chapter pp. 136–137	• Preview the chapter. • Introduce chapter activity center.		• School-Home Connection, TR p. 71 • Take-Home Booklet, TR p. 89–90
Lesson 1 **Community Workers** pp. 138–139 Pacing: 1 class period *1•2•7*	• Define community. • Identify community health and safety workers and their roles.	community safety workers health workers	• Teaching Chart 38 • Activity Book, p. 38
Lesson 2 **Regular Checkups** pp. 140–141 Pacing: 1 class period *1•2•3*	• Explain the importance of regular medical and dental checkups.	checkups preventative care immunization doctor dentist hygienist	• Teaching Chart 39 • Activity Book, p. 39
Lesson 3 **Reuse It!** pp. 142–143 Pacing: 1 class period *1•5•6*	• Recognize that the environment is everything around us. • Identify ways to recycle or reuse a variety of items. • Explain that recycling or reusing items are two ways of reducing the amount of trash.	environment recycle reuse reduce	• Teaching Chart 40 • Poem: "Momma Drives," p. RA-4 • Performance Assessment Summary Sheet, TR p. 54 • Activity Book, p. 40

National Health Education Standards
A complete list of the Standards is provided on the next page.

Key: TR = Teaching Resources

National Health Education Standards

1. Comprehend concepts related to health promotion and disease prevention.
2. Access valid health information and health-promoting products and services.
3. Practice health-enhancing behaviors and reduce health risks.
4. Analyze the influence of culture, media, technology, and other factors on health.
5. Use interpersonal communication skills to enhance health.
6. Use goal-setting and decision-making skills to enhance health.
7. Advocate for personal, family, and community health.

Curriculum Integration

Use these topics to integrate health into your daily planning.

Social Studies
- Visiting and Volunteering, p. 134
- Modeling Our Community, p. 139

Science
- Science Helps Out, p. 134
- Treasure from Trash, p. 134
- Doctor's and Dentist's Visit, p. 141

Physical Education
- Fun with Milk Jugs, p. 143

Math
- Sorting Community Helpers, p. 134

Art
- Our Community Helpers Book, p. 139
- Health Shields, p. 141
- Using 2-L Bottles, p. 143

ASSESSMENT OPTIONS

Portfolio Assessment
Have students select their best work from the following suggestions.
- **Our Community Helpers Book,** p. 139
- **Health Shields,** p. 141
- **My Best Work Portfolio Summary Sheet,** TR p. 42
- **Portfolio Summary Sheet,** TR p. 43

Student Self-Assessment
- **Student Self-Assessment Checklist,** TR p. 38
- **Healthy Habits Checklist,** TR p. 39

Classroom Observation
- **Observation Checklist,** TR p. 36

Performance Assessment
- **Wrap Up,** p. 143
- **Performance Assessment Summary Sheet,** TR p. 54

Daily Assessment
- **Assessment Tips,** pp. 139, 141, 143
- **Activity Book,** pp. 38–40

Cross-Curricular Activities

Science

Science Helps Out
Talk about how scientists have learned how to make useful things from "trash." Discuss products that are made from recycled materials, such as grocery bags, plastic toys, newspaper and many other kinds of paper, and some playground materials.

- Have children assist in setting up recycle boxes for the classroom. Mark one box for white paper, another for colored paper, another for plastics, and a fourth for foil.

- Place different types of paper and other items out, and let children practice putting the items into the correct recycle boxes.

Math

Sorting Community Helpers
Almost everyone knows a community health worker. This activity will help children see that all kinds of people help in their community.

- Have children survey five adults they know (friends, neighbors, relatives) and find out what they do for a living.

- Have children bring their lists to class. Combine the lists into one class list.

- Go through the class list with children, and help them sort the list into people who are community helpers and people who are not community helpers.

- If desired, ask children to draw pictures of the community helpers.

Social Studies

Visiting and Volunteering
Arrange a class visit to a recycling center. Discuss the recycling process. Ask children to bring something from home to turn in at the recycling center.

- Interview the workers at the center. Ask the workers to talk about why their work is important. Find out if any are volunteers. What do they do as volunteers? How can children help?

Science

Treasure from Trash
In this activity children make planters using materials often discarded as trash.

- Cut off the tops of milk cartons or 2-L bottles. Allow children to cover the outside of the planters with construction paper. Once covered, they can be colored or painted.

- Put $\frac{1}{2}$ inch of gravel in the bottom of each planter. Cover with 3 inches of potting soil.

- Have children plant seeds or plants in the soil. Water well, and put in a sunny window. Allow children to take their planters home once the seeds have sprouted or the plants have become established.

Bulletin Board

We Get Regular Checkups
Post a large picture of a doctor and one of a dentist, both in their offices, on the bulletin board.

- Have children draw or cut out pictures of things that happen during a regular checkup, such as a dentist looking at a child's teeth or taking X rays or a doctor using a stethoscope.

- Display children's pictures on the board.

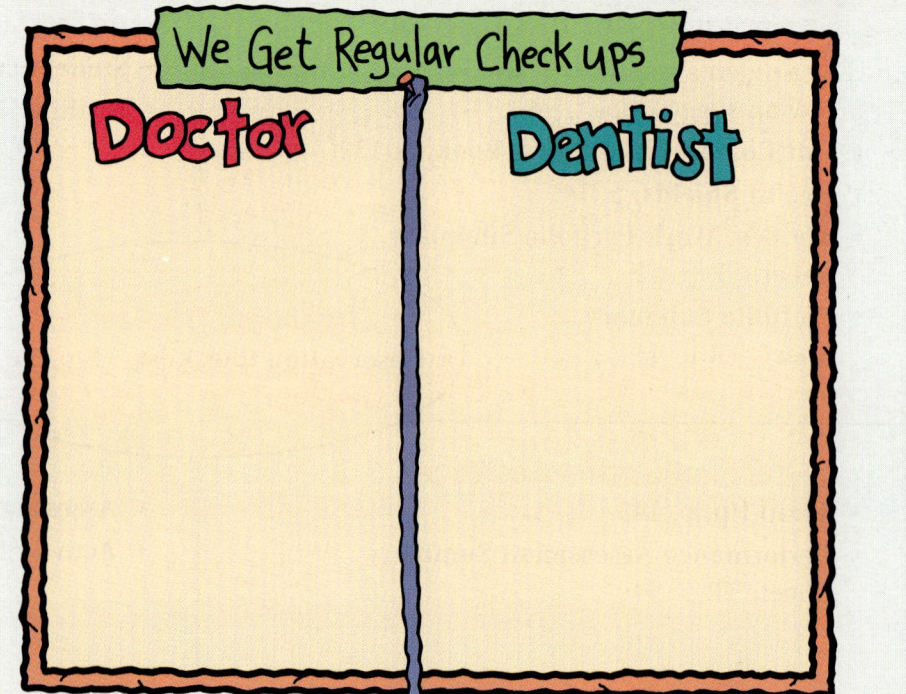

Resources

Books for Children

Read Alouds

Benjamin, Cynthia. *I Am A Doctor.* Barron's Educational Series, 1994. Colorful board book on having a checkup, visiting a friend in the hospital, and playing doctor at home. **EASY**

Halsey, Megan. *3 Pandas Planting.* Turtleback Books, 2000. This fun-filled counting book explains conservation on an elementary level. **AVERAGE**

Kalman, Bobbie. *Community Helpers from A to Z.* Crabtree Publishers, 1997. Alphabet book of community workers, including glossary and index. **ADVANCED**

Books for Teachers and Families

Human Body Encyclopedia of Exposures to Environmental Conditions for Ill Health, Sickness, and Disease Including Various Cancers. 5 Vols. ABBE Publishers Association of Washington, D.C. 1997. This five-volume reference offers valuable health information.

Needleman, Herbert L., M.D. and Philip J. Landigan, M.D. *Raising Children Toxic Free.* Avon Books, 1994. A text in support of toxin-free environments for children.

Videos

Lead Poisoning: What Everyone Needs To Know. AGC Educational Media, 1994. (15 minutes) This video for teachers points to possible areas of lead poisoning and ways to protect children.

My Visit to the Doctor. Kids In Daily Situations, Inc., 1990. (25 minutes) Touches on health concerns, such as hand washing and eating healthful foods.

To the Hospital. Boundary Breakers, 1996. (45 minutes) Children learn about stitches, broken bones, and the emergency room.

Your Health Webliography

The **Webliography** provides links to the Health Background and teaching resources that will support you as you teach the topics in *Your Health.* Simply choose a keyword and you will be taken to a page of links with descriptions of the content you can obtain at each site. The **Webliography** is located on the Teacher Resources page at **www.harcourtschool.com/health** Please review websites before referring your students to them.

Organizations and Agencies

Environmental Protection Agency
Office of Solid Waste
1200 Pennsylvania Ave., NW
Washington, D.C. 20460
800-424-9346
Provides educational information on a variety of environmental issues.

Kids for a Clean Environment
P.O. Box 158254
Nashville, TN 37215
800-952-3223
Focuses on children organizing and implementing ideas to improve the environment.

For more information about health organizations and agencies, please see the *Teaching Resources* book.

Community Health

Your Community Workers A variety of community workplaces would provide appropriate speakers or field trips for this chapter. Suggestions include fire department, police department, and public clinic. Grocery stores also make good field trips to extend this chapter. These stores must deal with many health and safety issues in order to provide safe, fresh food for the community.

Free and Inexpensive Material

Keep America Beautiful
1010 Washington Boulevard
Stamford, CT 06901
203-323-8987
Offers a leaflet that explains why it is important to keep America clean.

The Nature Conservancy
4245 N. Fairfax Drive, Suite 100
Arlington, VA 22203-1606
Works to preserve ecosystems around the world.

Note that information, while correct at time of publication, is subject to change.

Visit **The Harcourt Learning Site** for related links, activities, resources, and the health **Webliography**.
www.harcourtschool.com

CHAPTER 9
Pages 132–143

"I've had a long love affair with the environment. It is my sustenance, my pleasure, my joy."

—Lady Bird Johnson

CHAPTER SUMMARY

In this chapter children
- identify community workers and their roles.
- explain the importance of regular medical and dental checkups.
- describe how the amount of trash can be reduced through reducing, reusing, and recycling.

LIFE SKILLS Children practice *communicating* with health-care professionals and community workers.

A Healthy Community

Health Activity Center

The activities suggested for this chapter's Health Activity Center help children identify community workers and find new uses for items that would be thrown out as trash.

Reduce Trash

This activity helps children visualize how much of what is usually thrown away can be recycled or reused.

Materials Needed (per child)
- trash bag

What to Do Have children bring a trash bag to school and collect their nonfood trash for a week.
- At the end of the week, have children sort through their piles of trash and determine what could be reused or recycled.
- Have them plan ways to reuse the materials.

We Are Helpers

This activity reinforces children's awareness of the roles that community workers play in their lives.

Materials Needed (per child)

- community workers attire and props, such as firefighter hats, police officer hats and badges, lab coats, stethoscopes, prescription pads, paper bags (for trash)

What to Do

- **Option 1** Have children work in small groups to dress up as different community health workers and role-play situations when these workers help.
- **Option 2** Have children dress up as different community workers. When they are all dressed, have them sit in a circle. Go around the circle, allowing each child to stand up and say, "I am a (an) _____, and I help my community by _____."

We Recycle

This activity provides children practical experience in reusing items that are often discarded as trash. It also reinforces sorting and classifying skills.

Materials Needed (per child)

- reusable items, such as broken crayons, scrap paper, toilet paper tubes, margarine tubs
- labeled containers to hold the materials

What to Do Work with the children to make a list of materials that are often thrown away at home but that could be put to other uses in the classroom. These uses could include art materials, planters, and containers. When the list is complete, send a copy of the list home, requesting that parents or guardians send in clean, washed materials for your project.

- Have children work in groups to sort the materials. Be sure to check them beforehand for any sharp edges or packaging that needs to be rinsed.
- Encourage children to make artwork using the sorted materials.

Take-Home Booklet

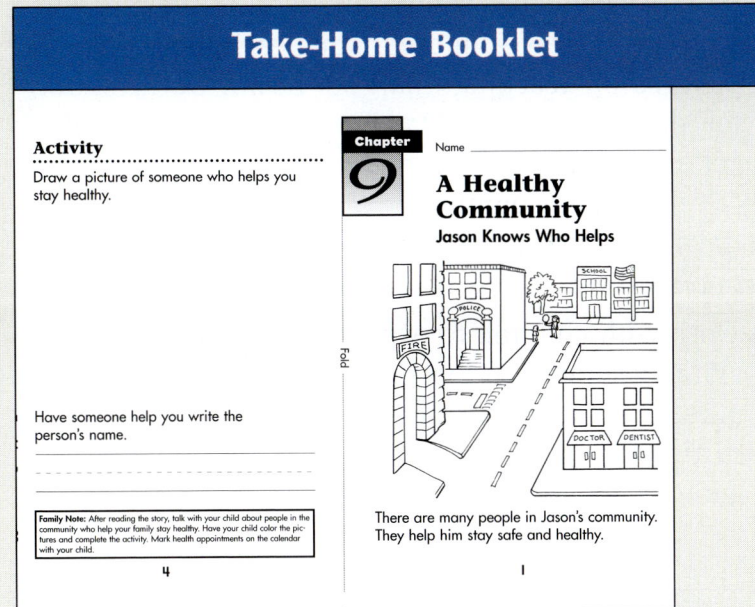

Distribute copies of the Take-Home Booklet, TR pages 89–90. Have children fold the pages to make booklets to share with their families.

School-Home Connection

Distribute copies of the School-Home Connection (in English or Spanish), TR page 71. Have children take the page home to share with their families.

Alternative Use the page for enrichment.

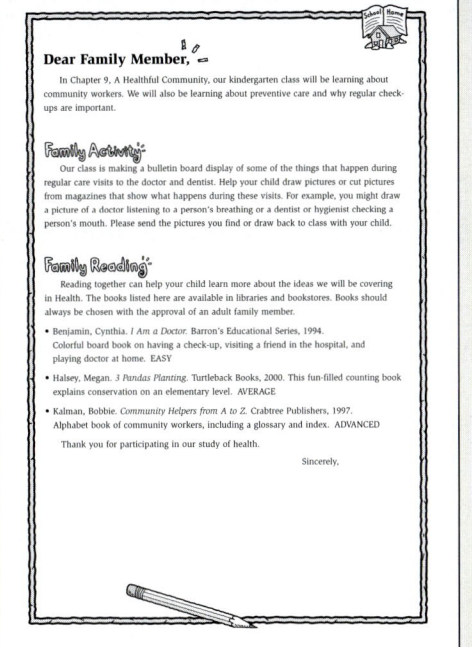

LESSON 1

OBJECTIVES
- Define *community*.
- Identify community health and safety workers and their roles.

VOCABULARY
- community
- safety workers
- health workers

PROGRAM RESOURCES
- Teaching Chart 38
- Activity Book, p. 38

MATERIALS
- bright-colored yarn
- removable tape

Teaching Chart 38

Daily Safety Tip
Remind children of the local emergency number for your area (911 or a local number). Stress that when they need help and can't find an adult to help them, they can get help by calling the emergency number.

1 Motivate

Explain that a community is a place where people live, work, play, and go to school.

- Ask children to tell where they live (address, city or town, state). Write the name of your community on sheets of paper. Explain that communities can be of different sizes but that everyone in a community shares the things in the community.

- Make a class list of all the places they go with their families or by themselves during a week. Children might suggest stores, the library, school, home, doctor or dentist offices, neighbors' homes, parks, hospitals, and adult family members' places of work. When the list is complete, review it with the class. As you read each item on the list, have children raise their hands if they have been to that place in the last week (or month). Reinforce the idea that the community is made up of all these places and the people who make use of them.

2 Teach

Learn from Pictures

Write the terms *safety workers* and *health workers* on the board. Then show children Teaching Chart 38. Have children identify the workers shown. **Why are all of these people on the same page?** They have jobs that help people in the community.

- Direct attention to the terms on the board. Explain that some community workers help keep the community safe. Other community workers help people who are ill. Have children name each type of worker pictured on Teaching Chart 38. health workers: doctor, dentist, nurse, EMT; safety workers: police officer, firefighter, sanitation worker Encourage children to refer to the community workers in a gender-neutral way, such as firefighters, police officers, sanitation workers.

- Work with children to expand the list beyond those workers shown on Teaching Chart 38. Examples of other community workers include librarians, mail carriers, pharmacists, dental hygienists, and crossing guards.

Activity

Community Workers Match Have children come up one at a time and match a community helper to their place of work. You may want to give each child a piece of bright-colored yarn with removable tape on each end so that they can make a line from the person to their place of employment or vehicle. As each child makes a match, he or she should tell the name of the worker, what the worker does for the community, and where he or she works. Some workers may be matched to more than one picture. For example, the EMT works in a vehicle but is also associated with a hospital.

Life Skills

Communicate Community health and safety workers are often the ones children must communicate with in case of an emergency. Remind children of the information they need to tell in case of emergency, including their names, their addresses, and the nature of the problem. Have pairs role-play different situations in which they need to call for help and communicate the problem.

3 Wrap Up

Ask children whom they would call in a variety of situations (a fire, someone ill, a toothache, a dumpster overflowing). Have them point to the picture of the appropriate community health worker.

ASSESSMENT TIP Have children answer the following questions by standing for a *yes* response and sitting in their seats for a *no* response. Add more questions as appropriate to your discussions.

1. Is a firefighter a safety worker? yes
2. Does an EMT take people to the movies? no
3. Does a dentist give you candy? no

MEET INDIVIDUAL NEEDS

Visual Learners Have a volunteer pantomime one of the community worker's jobs. Have others guess the job, who does it, and identify it as a safety or health job.

Other things to do!

Art Activity

Our Community Helpers Book Make a class book titled "Our Community Helpers." Have each child draw a picture of a time when a community helper helped him or her or when he or she saw a community helper help someone else. Encourage children to think about a variety of community helpers and experiences. Children might include crossing guards, people in libraries and stores, and pharmacists as well as the traditional workers shown on Teaching Chart 38. Help each child write a sentence about his or her picture. Gather the pictures into a class book.

Social Studies Activity

Modeling Our Community Provide children with a variety of small boxes, milk cartons, paper towel tubes, paints, and markers, and other art supplies. Have children make models of buildings in their community that everyone shares.

Using the Activity Book, page 38

This activity reinforces who some community health workers are.

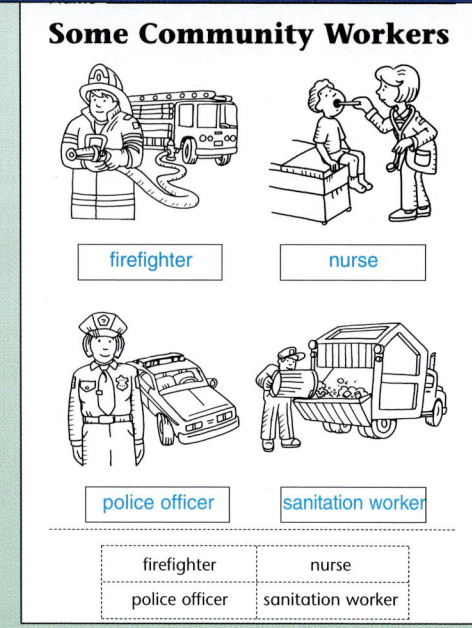

Some Community Workers

139

LESSON 2

OBJECTIVE
- Explain the importance of regular medical and dental checkups.

VOCABULARY
- checkups
- preventative care
- immunization
- doctor
- dentist
- hygienist

PROGRAM RESOURCES
- Teaching Chart 39
- Activity Book, p. 39

MATERIALS
- *The Berenstain Bears Go to the Doctor* by Stan and Jan Berenstain (Random House, 1981)
- toy doctor's kit
- *The Berenstain Bears Visit the Dentist* by Stan and Jan Berenstain (Random House, 1981)

Teaching Chart 39

Daily Safety Tip

Immunizations are essential to prevent serious diseases. Some immunizations confer immunity with one dose; others need to be given in a series or need boosters. Immunization records are important for families to keep. Encourage children to ask their families about their immunization records.

1 Motivate

Read aloud *The Berenstain Bears Go to the Doctor*. When finished, allow children to talk about their experiences with doctors. You may wish to use the following prompts.

- What happens when you go to the doctor?
- What does the doctor do?
- Why do people go to the doctor? Encourage children to talk about times they went to the doctor but were NOT ill. Explain that these visits are called *checkups*. They help the doctor make sure you are growing properly, and that you are healthy.

2 Teach

Discuss

Explain that checkups are also called "preventative care visits" because they help *prevent* a person from becoming ill.

- What happens when you go for a preventative care visit? Possible answers: ears, eyes, nose, heart, lungs are checked.
- Does anything else happen? sometimes injections or shots Remind children that these shots are called *immunizations*. Immunizations keep us from getting some diseases.

Activity

Checkup Ask two volunteers to role-play a doctor and a child getting a checkup. Provide the "doctor" with the toy doctor's kit. Have the volunteers act out portions of a doctor's checkup, such as looking down the throat and listening to the heartbeat. Be sure the checkup includes an immunization. Caution: Do not allow children to use tongue depressors.

Learn from Pictures

Show children Teaching Chart 39, and have them describe what they see. a doctor's examination, a dentist's (or hygienist's) examination, and a calendar

140

Critical Thinking Does a trip to the dentist include preventive care? What kind? A trip to the dentist includes a cleaning by the hygienist. The hygienist is the person who cleans teeth, takes X rays, and does an initial examination for cavities or other problems.

- Have children who have visited a dentist or hygienist talk about their experiences.
- The safety equipment recommended by the American Dental Association can be intimidating to young children. Explain that the face shields, gloves, and masks are to protect both the hygienist and the patient from germs contained in saliva and blood.

Discuss

Redirect attention back to Teaching Chart 39. **Why is there a calendar on the page?** Lead them to understand that doctor and dentist visits need to be scheduled at regular intervals. The immunizations they had as babies were scheduled for specific times in order to keep them safe from disease. Most dentists recommend that teeth be checked twice each year. These regular dental checkups help ensure that teeth grow properly.

3 Wrap Up

Read aloud *The Berenstain Bears Visit the Dentist*. Explain that most times, if people brush and floss regularly, a visit to the dentist is nothing to be worried about.

- Give each child a sheet of construction or drawing paper. Have children fold the papers in half. On one side, have children draw pictures of their doctors. On the other side, have children draw pictures of their dentists. **When should we visit the doctor and the dentist and hygienist?**

ASSESSMENT TIP Children should explain that regular preventive care from both the doctor and the dentist and hygienist helps them stay healthy.

TEACHER TIP

Doctor's and Dentist's Offices Set up an area that can function as a doctor's and dentist's examining room. Brainstorm with the children items to include in the center. Ideas might include X rays, stethoscope, lab coats, pads and pencils for pretend prescriptions, bibs, and safety glasses. You may wish to send home a note to parents or guardians asking for contributions to the center.

Other things to do!

Science Activity

Doctor's and Dentist's Visit Arrange for a doctor or nurse and a dentist or hygienist to visit the class. Encourage the visitors to bring some of the instruments they use in their work, and demonstrate their use on selected volunteers. Ask each health-care professional to explain to children what happens during a checkup. Children may be especially interested in seeing dental X rays of a child's mouth.

Art Activity

Health Shields Have children make shields out of paper plates or sheets of cardboard. Encourage children to decorate their shields with pictures of things that help them stay healthy, such as regular checkups, immunizations, healthful food, and exercise.

Using the Activity Book, page 39

Children label the doctor and the hygienist and color the pictures.

Some Health-Care Workers

dental hygienist

doctor

LESSON 3

OBJECTIVES

- Recognize that the environment is everything around us.
- Identify ways to recycle or reuse a variety of items.
- Explain that recycling or reusing items are two ways of reducing the amount of trash.

VOCABULARY

- environment
- recycle
- reuse
- reduce

PROGRAM RESOURCES

- Teaching Chart 40
- Poem: "Momma Drives," p. RA-4
- Performance Assessment Summary Sheet, TR p. 54
- Activity Book, p. 40

MATERIALS

- reusable items, such as 2-L bottles, fabric scraps, broken crayons, aluminum cans, milk cartons and jugs

Teaching Chart 40

Daily Safety Tip

All items should be thoroughly cleaned before they are reused. Be sure containers such as milk cartons and margarine tubs are completely rinsed before being stored. Provide dish soap for children to clean any reusable items they bring to school.

1 Motivate

Start the lesson by having children take a walk around the classroom and if possible, the schoolyard. When they return to their seats, have them list all the things they saw, both inside and out.

- Explain that all these things make up the *environment*. Explain that the environment is made up of all the living and nonliving things around us. It includes the air we breathe, the food we eat, and the water we drink.

- How can you help keep the school and outdoor environment clean? Help children understand that they can throw things away properly, and not litter. Explain there are other things they can do to help keep the environment clean and reduce trash.

2 Teach

Learn from Pictures

Show children Teaching Chart 40. Have children name the items pictured. Explain that all these items could be considered trash, as they have served their original purpose.

 **Activity**

Reusing Items to Reduce Trash Show children several things that can be reused, such as cloth scraps, milk cartons, buttons, 2-L plastic bottles, broken crayons, clean aluminum cans.

- Tell children that there is no more room in the trash can for items such as these. What can be done? Help children come up with several alternative uses for the materials. Some children may suggest *reusing* the items for projects. Children whose families recycle may suggest recycling some of the items.

142

Discuss

Read the poem "Momma Drives," page RA-4. When finished, have children share their own experiences with recycling. Explain that recycling can be done in several ways. Some areas have trucks that pick up all recyclable materials, just like trash is picked up. In other areas people must separate the different types of recyclables.

- Make a list of the different materials that are recycled. Show children an example of each type of recyclable, such as aluminum cans, glass bottles, newspapers, cardboard, other paper materials, steel cans, and milk cartons. You may wish to collect a variety of plastics that show the different recycling numbers. Explain that the higher the number, the harder it is to recycle.

- Describe a simplified recycling process to children. Materials such as aluminum are shredded, melted, and made into new aluminum cans. Glass items are often sorted by color, melted, and made into new glass products.

Discuss

Redirect attention back to Teaching Chart 40 and the pile of recyclable materials you have shown children. Explain that when you reuse or recycle an item, it makes less, or *reduces,* the amount of trash. **How might reducing the amount of trash help the environment?** Possible answers: less trash will be blowing around (litter), less to carry out to the garbage cans or dumpster.

3 Wrap Up

Make available Teaching Chart 40 and all the recyclable items you brought in. Ask volunteers to come up, pick an item from the pile or point to an item on Teaching Chart 40 and suggest what could be done with the item so that it is not just thrown away. Examples: milk cartons and boxes—planters, pencil holders, scissors holders; broken crayons—melted in a muffin tin to make new multicolored crayons; margarine tubs—paint and glue containers, containers to hold beads or buttons; paper towel and toilet paper tubes—art materials; buttons—art materials. Children may also suggest that some of the items could be recycled.

ASSESSMENT TIP This activity can be used for performance assessment. See Performance Assessment Summary Sheet, TR page 54.

Other things to do!

Art Activity

Using 2-L Bottles Plastic 2-L soda bottles can be used for a variety of purposes. Cut the bottles in half. The tops can be used as funnels. Use the bottoms as planters, or containers for broken crayons or snacks. Be sure to tape over the edges of the plastic to avoid cuts.

Bird Feeders Have each child bring in a clean 2-L bottle. Cut a 3 × 3 inch opening on one side of the bottle, about 2 inches from the bottom. Have children tie rope or twine around the neck of the bottle, fill the bottom inch of the bottles with birdseed, and then take them home.

Physical Education

Fun with Milk Jugs You can use 1-gallon milk jugs for a variety of games.

Ball and Cup Game Cut the front off a jug, leaving the handle and the bottom 3 inches of plastic intact. Place a ball in the toe of one leg of an old pair of pantyhose. Tie the top of the leg around the handle. Children can increase their eye-hand coordination by swinging the ball and trying to catch it in the milk jug.

Milk Jug Toss Cut the front off two jugs, leaving the handles and the bottom 3 inches of plastic intact. Have pairs play catch with tennis balls, trying to catch them in the milk jugs.

Using the Activity Book, page 40

Children use a variety of classroom scraps to make a "Reuse It!" collage.

Reduce Trash—Reuse It!

Glossary

GRADE K

Numbers in parentheses indicate the pages on which the words are defined.

PRONUNCIATION RESPELLING KEY

Sound	As in	Phonetic Respelling	Sound	As in	Phonetic Respelling
a	b<u>a</u>t	(BAT)	oh	<u>o</u>ver	(OH•ver)
ah	l<u>o</u>ck	(LAHK)	oo	p<u>oo</u>l	(POOL)
air	r<u>a</u>re	(RAIR)	ow	<u>ou</u>t	(OWT)
ar	<u>ar</u>gue	(AR•GYOO)	oy	f<u>oi</u>l	(FOYL)
aw	l<u>aw</u>	(LAW)	s	<u>c</u>ell	(SEL)
ay	f<u>a</u>ce	(FAYS)		<u>s</u>it	(SIT)
ch	<u>ch</u>apel	(CHAP•UHL)	sh	<u>sh</u>eep	(SHEEP)
e	t<u>e</u>st	(TEST)	th	<u>th</u>at	(THAT)
	m<u>e</u>tric	(MEH•TRIK)	th	<u>th</u>in	(THIN)
ee	<u>ea</u>t	(EET)	u	p<u>u</u>ll	(PUL)
	f<u>ee</u>t	(FEET)	uh	med<u>a</u>l	(MED•UHL)
	sk<u>i</u>	(SKEE)		tal<u>e</u>nt	(TAL•UHNT)
er	pap<u>er</u>	(PAY•PER)		penc<u>i</u>l	(PEN•SUHL)
	f<u>er</u>n	(FERN)		<u>o</u>ni<u>o</u>n	(UHN•YUHN)
eye	<u>i</u>dea	(EYE•DEE•UH)		playf<u>u</u>l	(PLAY•FUHL)
i	b<u>i</u>t	(BIT)		d<u>u</u>ll	(DUHL)
ing	go<u>ing</u>	(GOH•ING)	y	<u>y</u>es	(YES)
k	<u>c</u>ard	(KARD)		r<u>i</u>pe	(RYP)
	<u>k</u>ite	(KYT)	z	bag<u>s</u>	(BAGZ)
ngk	ba<u>nk</u>	(BANGK)	zh	trea<u>s</u>ure	(TREZH•ER)

911: the telephone number to call when there is an emergency (122)

alcohol (AL•kuh•hawl): the harmful drug in beer, wine, and liquor (106)

arms (ARMZ): the two upper limbs of the body (32)

bite (BYTE): to use the teeth to tear food in order to eat it (48)

body (BAH•DEE): all the parts that make up a person (32)

bones (BOHNZ): the hard parts of the body that support other body parts (34)

brain (BRAYN): the part of the nervous system that directs the way the body works (34)

brush (BRUHSH): to clean the teeth using a toothbrush and toothpaste (50)

144

caffeine (ka•FEEN): the harmful drug in coffee, tea, chocolate, and some soft drinks (106)

calcium (KAL•see•uhm): a mineral found in some foods that helps build strong teeth and bones (52)

checkups (CHEK•ups): periodic visits to the doctor and dentist that help keep a person healthy (140)

chew (CHOO): to use the teeth to grind food in order to swallow it (48)

community (kuh•MYOO•nuh•tee): the place where you live, work, and go to school (138)

conflict (KAHN•flikt): a fight or a disagreement between people (24)

cool-down (KOOL-DOWN): the last part of a physical fitness program in which the body slows down and returns to a resting state. (64)

cooperate (koh•AH•puh•rayt): to work together to accomplish a common goal (22)

cooperation (koh•ah•puh•RAY•shuhn): the act of working together to accomplish a common goal (22)

crosswalk (KRAWS•wahk): a marked place showing where to cross a street safely (116)

dangerous (DAYN•juh•ruhs): not safe (38, 128)

dentist (DEN•tuhst): a person trained to give dental care (140)

disrespectful (dihs•rih•SPEKT•fuhl): being thoughtless in what is said and done (118)

doctor (DAHK•tuhr): a person trained to give health care (140)

drugs (DRUHGZ): things that change the way the body works (106)

energy (EH•ner•jee): the power the body needs to do things (68, 76)

environment (in•VY•ruhn•muhnt): all the living and nonliving things around you (142)

environmental tobacco smoke (in•vy•ruhn•MEN•tuhl tuh•BA•koh SMOHK): tobacco smoke in the air (108)

escape (uh•SKAYP): to get away or get to safety (122)

feelings (FEE•lingz): ways to feel, such as happy, sad, afraid, or excited (18)

fire (FYR): an emergency situation in which something is burning (122)

floss (FLAWS): special thread used to clean between the teeth (50)

food groups (FOOD GROOPZ): the divisions in the food guide pyramid (78)

Food Guide Pyramid (FOOD GYD PIR•uh•mid): picture that shows foods and the groups they belong to as well as how many servings of each group to eat (78)

germs (JERMZ): tiny things that carry disease and can make people ill (82, 92)

growing (GROH•ing): getting bigger and older (32)

gum (GUHM): the pink tissue in the mouth in which the teeth are rooted (48)

happy (HA•pee): feeling pleased about something (18)

head (HED): the part of the body that contains the brain; the part of the body above the trunk (32)

health workers (HELTH WERK•uhrz): nurses, doctors, dentists, and others who work to keep the people in a community healthy (138)

healthful (HELTH•fuhl): good for you (80)

hear (HEER): using the sense of hearing (36)

heart (HART): the part of the body that pumps blood (34)

helmet (HEL•muht): a head covering that protects the skull, brain, and other body parts in the head (116)

hygienist (hy•JEN•uhst): a person trained to clean teeth (140)

I-messages (EYE-MEH•suh•juz): the describing or telling of what you feel about a situation or action (24)

ill (IL): not well (90)

immunization (ih•myuh•nuh•SAY•shuhn): a shot or liquid that gives the body immunity to certain diseases (92, 140)

legs (LEGZ): the two lower limbs of the body (32)

lungs (LUHNGZ): the parts of the body that are used for breathing (34)

mad (MAD): feeling angry (18)

manage stress (MAHN•ihj STRES): apply strategies to deal with the body's reaction to strong feelings (66)

medicines (MEH•duh•suhnz): drugs that are used to help people feel better or stay healthy (102)

mouth (MOWTH): the part of the digestive system that takes in food; a part of the respiratory system that takes in and lets out air (108)

mouth guard (MOWTH GAHRD): a plastic insert placed in the mouth that protects teeth and jaws from injury (52)

muscles (MUHS•uhlz): parts of the body that help the body move (64)

nail clippers (NAYL KLIP•uhrz): device used to trim finger nails and toe nails (60)

nail file (NAYL FY•uhl): device used to shape nails or remove rough or sharp edges from nails (60)

nicotine (NIH•kuh•teen): the harmful drug found in tobacco (108)

password (PAS•werd): a word or phrase known only to family members (118)

pharmacist (FAR•muh•sist): a person trained to prepare medicines (102)

poisons (POY•zuhnz): substances that harm the body if swallowed or absorbed through the skin (120)

posture (PAHS•cher): keeping the body correctly aligned when sitting and standing (62)

prescription (prih•SKRIP•shuhn): order written by a doctor for a medicine (102)

prevent (prih•VENT): to stop or keep from happening (122)

preventative care (prih•VEN•tuh•tivh CAIR): checkups, vaccinations, and other good health habits that help keep a person well (140)

recycle (ree•SY•kuhl): to reuse the materials in an item to make new items (142)

reduce (rih•DOOS): to make less of something, such as trash (142)

refuse (rih•FYOOZ): to say no to someone or something (106)

relax (rih•LAKS): to rest and unwind from the day's activities (68)

respect (rih•SPEKT): being thoughtful in what is said and done (22, 118)

responsible (rih•SPAHNT•suh•buhl): taking care of things that should be done (38)

rest (REHST): quiet time that helps the body grow (68)

reuse (ree•YOOZ): to use things over and over instead of throwing them away (142)

sad (SAD): feeling unhappy (18)

safe (SAYF): out of danger (38, 126)

safety (SAYF•tee) keeping away from danger; not getting hurt (130)

safety gear (SAYF•tee GIR): clothing and equipment, such as a helmet or knee pads, worn to prevent injuries (116)

safety workers (SAYF•tee WERK•uhrz): police officers, fire fighters, and others who work to keep a community safe (138)

scared (SKAIRD): feeling afraid (18)

see (SEE): using the sense of sight (36)

senses (SENT•suhz): ways to use the body to learn, enjoy things, and stay safe; sight, hearing, smell, taste, and touch (36)

shampoo (shahm•POO): a liquid soap used to clean the hair and scalp (60)

siren (SY•rhun): the device that emits a loud warning sound, often found on police cars, fire trucks, and as tornado warning devices (38)

skin (SKIN): the body's covering (34)

sleep (SLEEP): the time each day when the body rests and grows (68)

smell (SMEHL): the sense that enables us to perceive aromas (36)

smoke detector (SMOHK dih•TEKT•uhr): device that emits a loud sound when smoke is present in the air (38)

snack (SNAK): food eaten between meals (80)

special (SPEH•shuhl): different from anyone or anything else (16)

spine (SPYN): the bones of the back and neck (34, 62)

spoil (SPOYL): to go bad (82)

stomach (STUHM•uhk): the part of the body that digests food (34)

stop, drop, and roll: the procedure to follow if one's clothing catches on fire (124)

storage (STOHR•uhdg): putting food away properly to control the growth of germs (82)

straight (STRAYT): in a line (62)

stranger (STRAYN•jer): any person not known well (118)

stress (STRES): the way the body reacts to strong feelings (66)

stretching (STRECH•ing): moving the body in such a way as to extend different muscle groups either before or after an active workout (64)

sunscreen (SUHN•skreen): a lotion or cream that protects the skin from the sun's rays (60)

symptoms (SIMP•tuhmz): the feelings you have when you are ill; sneezing, coughing, sore throats, and so on (90)

taste (TAYST): the sense that enables us to perceive flavors (36)

teeth (TEETH): the parts of the digestive system used to bite and chew food (48)

throat (THROHT): the part of the body that connects the mouth with the stomach and lungs (106)

tobacco (tuh·BA·koh): the plant containing nicotine, with leaves that are dried to make cigarettes, cigars, pipe tobacco, and chewing tobacco (106)

torso (TOHR·soh): the part of the body that contains most of the organs; the part of the body to which the head, arms, and legs are attached; trunk (32)

touch (TUHCH): the sense that enables us to feel objects (36)

traffic (TRA·fik): the vehicles found on streets (116)

trunk (TRUHNK): the part of the body that contains most of the organs; the part of the body to which the head, arms, and legs are attached; torso (32)

trusted adult (TRUHST·uhd uh·DUHLT): an adult who is safe to confide in or who can give a child medicines (104)

unsafe (UHN·SAYF): in danger (126)

vehicle (VEE·huh·kul): a car, truck, or bus (130)

warm-up (WAHRM-UP): the first part of a physical fitness program that prepares the body for vigorous exercise (64)

washcloth (WAHSH·KLAHTH): cloth used to wash the face and body (60)

workout (WERK·owt): the active part of a physical fitness program in which the lungs and heart work at a high capacity (64)

Index

Abduction Prevention, 112, 115, 118–119, 129
Alcohol, 106–107
    effects of, on body, 100
American Academy of Pediatric Dentistry, 45
American Academy of Pediatrics, 13
American Academy of Periodontology, 45
American Automobile Association, 113
American Cancer Society, 99
American Crop Protection Association, 73
American Family Society, 13
American Lung Association, 99
American Optometric Association, 57
American School Health Association, 87
American Skin Association, 57
Anger, dealing with, 15, 21
Asthma and Allergy Foundation of America, 87
Art activities
    about being special, 12
    about breakfast food, 77
    about changes in family, 28
    about community helpers, 139
    about drugs, 107
    about fire prevention, 123
    about food selection, 72
    about health shields, 141
    about medicines, 105
    about responsibility, 41
    about reuse, 143
    about stranger danger, 112
    about teeth, 44, 49, 51
    about traffic lights, 117
    about wellness and illness, 86
Auditory and visual learners, snack choice activity for, 81

Bathing, 60
Blood, 34
Body parts and systems
    blood, 34
    bones, 34
    brain, 34, 108–109
    circulatory system, 109
    digestive system, 74, 77
    ears, 37
    effects of alcohol on, 100
    effects of caffeine on, 107
    effects of drugs on, 100
    effects of exercise on, 30, 66–67, 95
    effects of tobacco on, 108–109
    eyes, 36–37
    heart, 30, 34–35, 95, 109
    identify, 30, 32–35
    lungs, 34, 95, 108–109
    muscle, 34, 64, 95
    nervous system, 108–109
    respiratory system, 108–109, 114, 124
    senses, 30–31, 36–38
    skin, 34, 56, 60–61
    skull, 34
    spine, 34
    stomach, 34
    teeth, 44, 46–53
Bones, 34
Books for students, teachers, and families
    about caring for and losing teeth, 45
    about community and the environment, 135
    about drugs and alcohol, 99
    about families, 29
    about illness and health, 87
    about nutrition, 73
    about personal health and fitness, 57
    about safety, 113
    about self-esteem and feelings, 13
    about the senses, 29
Brain
    effects of tobacco on, 108–109
    protecting from injury, 34
Bread, cultural differences in types of, 81
Breakfast, importance of, 76
Bulletin board activities
    about avoiding spread of germs, 86
    about exercising, 56
    about Food Guide Pyramid, 72
    about getting regular checkups, 134
    about growing up, 28
    about helping at home and at school, 12
    about poisons, 112
    about refusing drugs, 98
    about teeth, 44
Bullies, dealing with, 25

Caffeine, effects of, on body, 107
Calcium and teeth, 44
California Highway Patrol, 113
California Strawberry Commission, 73
Candlelighters Childhood Cancer Foundation, 87
Car safety, 112, 130–131
Checkups, doctor, 140
Chew, proper way to, 48
Child psychologist, 13
Children, differences and similarities among, 16
Circulatory system,
    blood, 34
    effects of tobacco on, 109
    heart, 30, 34–35, 95, 109

effects of tobacco on, 109
exercise and, 30, 95
Clothes, choosing appropriate, for weather, 94–95
Colds, symptoms and treatment of, 91
Communicate
with community health and safety workers, 136, 139
about conflicts, 30, 40
during emergencies, 114, 121, 123, 126
about feelings, 14, 18
about illness, 88, 91
about strangers, 114, 119
about what you sense, 30, 38
resolving conflict through, 24, 30
Community, 138–139
Community workers, 137–139
Conflicts, resolving, 14, 24–25, 40
Cool-down, 64–65
Cooperation, 12, 14, 22–23, 25
Crossing guard, 116
Crossing streets safely, 114, 116–117
Crosswalk, 117

Dental floss, 46
Dental hygienist, 45, 51, 141
Dentist, 45, 51, 134, 140–141
what happens when visit, 140–141
Depression, 19
Digestive system, 74, 77
stomach, 34
Disclosing tablets, 45
Doctor, 134, 140–141
what happens when visit, 140–141
Drama activities
about car safety, 112
about conflict resolution, 25
about disease prevention, 93
about feelings, 12, 23

about growing and changing, 28
about helping out, 23
about managing stress, 56
about need for sleep, 56
about stranger danger, 119
about taking medicines safely, 105
Droppers, using, 101–102
Drugs, 106–107
difference between medicines and, 106

Ears, parts of, 37
Emergencies, what to do in, 38–39
Emergency phone number, 114–115, 121–123, 125, 138
Energy, food as source of, 76–77
Environment, 142–143
Environmental Protection Agency, 135
Environmental tobacco smoke (ETS), 108
Exercise
effects of, on body, 95
effects of, on heartbeat, 30
favorite ways to, 56
managing stress through, 66–67
safe, 64–65
safety equipment for, 32
Eyes
parts of, 37
protecting from sun, 36

Feelings
acting out, 12
changing, 20–21
class booklet about, 14
drawing, 19
identifying, 18–19
interpreting through art, 15
review of, 23

sharing with friends and family, 18
tell adult about scared or sad, 20
turning sad into happy, 15
Fire drills, 38, 123
Fire escape plan, 123
Fire safety, 38–39, 122–125
procedures for, 124–125
in school, 123
stop, drop, and roll procedure for, 124–125
Firefighter, 39
Fire station, 39
Fires, 122–125
dangers of smoking as cause of, 109
Flossing, 46, 50–51
Food
body's need for, 76–77
good for teeth, 46–47, 53
safe handling of, 82–83
storing, 83
Food groups, 78–79,
Food Guide Pyramid, 72, 75, 78–81
Fruits and vegetables
importance of, 78
washing, 80, 82

Germs, 128
avoiding spread of, 50, 88–89, 92–94
Growth, 28, 32–33
Gum of tooth, 48, 53

Health workers, 138–139
Hearing, sense of, 31, 36
Hearing impairments, 37
Heart, 34
effects of tobacco on, 109
exercise and, 30, 95
location of, 34
Helmets, 34, 114, 117

Helping
　at home, 12
　at school, 12
Human growth, 32–33
Hygiene
　bathing, 16
　caring for skin, 60–61
　cleaning nails, 60–61
　rules in school, 16
　washing hair, 60–61
　washing hands, 16, 82, 92–93

"I" messages, 24–25
Illness, symptoms of, 90–91
Immunizations, 92–93, 140–141
International Reading Association, 73
Internet resources
　about dental health, 45
　about disease prevention, 87
　about family activities, 29
　about health and fitness, 57
　about nutrition, 73
　about recycling and reuse, 135
　about safety, 113
　about stress management and health, 13
　about tobacco and drugs, 99

Jack and Jill of America Foundation, Inc., 29

Keep America Beautiful, 135
Kids for a Clean Environment, 135
Kinesthetic learners
　body parts activity for, 35
　cooperation activity for, 23
　digestion activity for, 77
　exercise activity for, 65
　life jacket activity for, 127
　posture activity for, 63
　refusal activity for, 107
Kinesthetic/visual learners
　feelings activity for, 21
　senses activity for, 39

Language activities
　about body parts, 41
　about conflict resolution, 25
　about exercise, 65
　about feelings, 23
　about food choices, 79
　about food safety, 83
　about refusing tobacco, 109
　about responsibility, 41
　about safe and unsafe water activities, 127
　about sense of hearing, 39
　about sense of touch, 37
　about stop, drop, and roll fire safety procedure, 125
　about traffic signs, 117
　about using senses to stay safe, 39
Life skills
　communicate
　　about conflicts, 30, 40
　　about feelings, 14, 18
　　about illness, 88, 91
　　about strangers, 114, 119
　　during emergencies, 114, 121, 126
　　to resolve conflicts, 14, 24
　　what senses tell you, 30, 38–39
　　with community health and safety workers, 136, 139
　make decisions
　　about crossing the street, 114, 116–117
　　about food, 46, 53, 74, 80
　　about medicines, 100, 105
　　about snacks, 74, 80–81
　manage stress, 14, 20, 66–67
　refuse
　　to use drugs, 100, 107
　　to use tobacco, 100, 109
　resolve conflicts, 14, 24
　about chores, 40
Lungs, 34
　effects of smoke on, 114
　effects of tobacco on, 108–109
　exercise and, 95

Make Decisions
　about crossing the street, 114, 116–117
　to escape fires, 124–125
　about food, 74
　about medicines, 105
　to prevent fires, 122–123
Matches, never play with, 122
Math activities
　about caring for teeth, 53
　about community health workers, 134
　about cooperation, 12
　about dangerous items, 112
　about feelings, 19
　about food, 72
　about fruits and vegetables, 81
　about growing, 33
　about illness, 91
　about measuring medicines, 103
　about personal care, 61
　about poisons at home, 121
　about safe and unsafe substances, 98
　about sense of taste, 37
　about similarities and differences among people, 17
　about sleep, 69
　about staying well, 95
　about stress management, 67
　about toothbrushes, 51
　about water safety, 127

153

Medicines, 100–103
　difference between drugs and, 106
　dispensing in school, 103
　flavored, 104
　taking safely, 104–105
Mouth guards, 52–53
Muscles, 34
　exercise and, 64, 95
Music activities
　about avoiding spread of germs, 93
　about body parts, 33
　about body's energy, 77
　about dangerous items, 129
　about drugs, 107
　about feelings, 19, 21
　about food safety, 83
　about posture, 63
　about skin care, 61
　about stress management, 67
　about symptoms of illness, 91
　about teeth, 44

National Association for the Education of Young Children, 57
National Family Partnership, 99
National Grange, 57
National Lead Information Center, 113
National PTA, 13
Nervous system
　brain, 34, 108–109
　effects of tobacco on, 108–109
　senses, 30–31, 36–38
Nicotine, 109
911 [emergency phone number], 114–115, 121, 123

Orthopedist, 29
Over-the-counter medicines, 100–103

Parents' Resource Institute for Drug Education, 99
Pediatric nurse, 87
Pharmacia Corporation, 87, 113
Pharmacist, 99, 102–103
Physical Education activities
　about effects of exercise on heartbeat, 30
　about effects of smoking on body, 109
　about posture, 63
　about reuse, 143
Plants, poisonous, 120
Poisons
　avoiding, 120–121
　plant, 120–121
　say no to, 112
Police officer, 113
Posture
　at computer, 62–63
　developing good, 62–63
Prescription medicines, 100–103
Preventive care, 140–141
Products
　dangerous, 120–121
　safe and unsafe, 115

Recycling, 136–137, 142–143
Refuse
　to use drugs, 100, 107
　to use tobacco, 100, 109
Resolve conflicts, 14
　about chores, 40
Respect, 22–23, 25, 119
Respiratory system
　effects of smoke on, 114
　effects of tobacco on, 108–109
　lungs, 34, 95, 108–109, 114
Responsibility, 40–41
Reuse, 136–137, 142–143
Root of tooth, 48, 53

Sadness, 19
Safety
　around animals, 128
　around dangerous items, 128–129
　around guns, 128–129
　around household appliances, 120
　around strangers, 112, 118–119, 129
　around water, 126–127
　fire, 122–125
　when riding in vehicles, 130–131
　school bus, 130–131
Safety belts, 130
Safety equipment, 32, 34, 52
Safety gear, 117
Safety workers, 138–139
School
　helping at, 16
　hygiene rules in, 16
School bus safety, 130–131
Science activities
　about body sounds, 35
　about calcium and teeth, 44
　about chemical reactions, 98
　about effects of exercise on body, 95
　about food spoilage, 72
　about function of toothpaste, 51
　about functions of teeth in animals, 49
　about poisonous plants, 121
　about recycling, 134
　about reusing trash, 134
　about structure of tooth, 53
　about sunburn, 56
　about taking temperature, 86
　about using the senses, 28
　about visiting doctor and dentist, 141
Secrets, good and bad, 115
Senses
　communicate what you

perceive through, 30
  hearing, 31, 36
  identify, 36–37
  sight, 36
  smell, 31, 36
  taste, 37
  touch, 31, 37
  using to stay safe, 37–38
Shots, 92
Sight, sense of, 36
Signs, traffic, 112, 114, 116–117
Skeletal system
  bones, 34
  skull, 34
  spine, 34
Skin, 34
  protecting and caring for, 56, 60–61
Sleep
  to help avoid illness, 102
  need for, 56, 68–69
Smell, sense of, 31, 36
Smoke, dangers of, 124
Smoke detectors, 38, 122
Snacks, choosing healthful, 74–75, 80–81
Social Studies activities
  about calling 911, 123
  about colds, 86
  about community, 139
  about field trip to exercise facility, 65
  about healthful food choices, 81
  about recycling, 134
  about smoking, 98
  about traffic signs, 112
Special, why each child is, 16–17
Spine, 34
  posture and, 62–63
Stomach, 34
Stop, drop, roll, 124–125
Stranger danger, 112, 115, 118–119, 129
Stress, managing, 20, 56, 66–67
Stretching, 64–65
Sugar Association, Inc., 45
Sunburn, 56, 60
Sunglasses, 36
Sunscreen, 60–61
Symptoms of illness, 90–91

Taste, sense of, 37
Teeth, 44
  caring for, 46–53
  harmful use of, 53
  losing baby, 48–49
  parts of, 48
  protecting from injury, 52
  types and functions of, 46–49
Temperature, body, 88
Tobacco, 106–107
  effects of, on body, 100, 108
  refusal to use, 108–109
Toothbrushing, 44–45, 50–51
Touch, sense of, 31, 37
Touches, disrespectful, 119
Traffic signs and signals, 116–117
Trash, reducing, 136–137, 142–143
Trusted adult, 115, 119

U.S. Department of Agriculture, 73
U.S. Department of Health and Human Services, 29

Video resources
  about alcohol, 99
  about family, 29
  about germs and staying well, 57, 87
  about lead poisoning, doctors, and hospitals, 135
  about nutrition, 73
  about permanent and baby teeth, 45
  about safety, 113
  about senses, 29
  about stress management, feelings, and conflict resolution, 13
Violence, prevention, 24–25, 118–119
Vision impairments, 37
Visual and auditory learners, stress management activity for, 67
Visual and tactile learners, teeth activity for, 49
Visual learners, community activity for, 139

Warm-up, 64–65
Washing fruits and vegetables, 80, 82
Washing hands, 16, 82
  to avoid spread of germs, 92–93
  proper way of, 61
Water Safety, 126–127
  life jackets, 127
  ocean safety, 127
  procedures for, 126
Wellness, 88–89, 94–95
Workout, 64–65

Read-Aloud Anthology

Read-Aloud Anthology

CONTENTS

Poems and Rhymes

New Neighbors, by Aileen Fisher RA-2

Best Friends, by Jeff Moss RA-2

Rhinos Purple, Hippos Green, by Michael Patrick Hearn RA-2

Good Night, by Aileen Fisher RA-2

This Tooth, by Lee Bennett Hopkins RA-2

Ruth Luce and Bruce Booth, by N. M. Bodecker RA-2

Exercises, by Bette Killion RA-3

Nell & Jack Horner, by Father Gander RA-3

Oh my goodness, oh my dear, by Clyde Watson RA-3

Sneeze, by Maxine Kumin RA-3

Rainy Day, by William Wise RA-4

Jellybeans Up Your Nose, by Jeff Moss RA-4

I Did a Nutty Somersault, by Jack Prelutsky RA-4

Momma Drives, by Arnold Adoff RA-4

Stories

The Enormous Turnip, by Alexei Tolstoy RA-5

The Bundle of Sticks, an Aesop Fable RA-5

Body on Strike! an Aesop Fable RA-6

Benjamin Rabbit and Stranger Danger, by Dick and Irene Keller RA-6

Songs

The Sharing Song RA-8

Head and Shoulders, Knees and Toes RA-8

Wheels RA-9

Clap Your Hands RA-9

The Mulberry Bush RA-10

One Finger, One Thumb RA-10

New Neighbors
by Aileen Fisher

When Smiths packed up
and moved away,
and Judy was gone,
I cried all day.

I knew I'd never
like anyone
as much as Judy
or have such fun.

Then Browns moved in
with a silky cat
and a dog with puppies.
Imagine that!

And a girl named Becky . . .
and I forgot
all about missing
Judy a lot.

Best Friends
by Jeff Moss

Kristy says she has a best friend,
And a best best friend,
But she says I'm her best best best friend.
I told her I think people should have just one best friend with one "best."
Otherwise you could have a best best best best best best best best best best best friend
And whoever was just your best best best friend would think you probably didn't like them very much at all.

Rhinos Purple, Hippos Green
by Michael Patrick Hearn

My sister says
I shouldn't color
Rhinos purple,
Hippos green.
She says
I shouldn't be so stupid;
Those are things
She's never seen.
But I don't care
What my sister says,
I don't care
What my sister's seen.
I will color
What I want to—
Rhinos purple,
Hippos green.

This Tooth
by Lee Bennett Hopkins

I jiggled it
    jaggled it
        jerked it.

I pushed
    and pulled
        and poked it.

But—

As soon as I stopped,
and left it alone,
This tooth came out
on its very own!

Good Night
by Aileen Fisher

This day's done.
Tomorrow's another.

Good night, Daddy.
Good night, Mother.

Good night, kitten,
book, and brother . . .

In one dream
and out the other.

Ruth Luce and Bruce Booth
by N. M. Bodecker

Said little Ruth Luce
to little Bruce Booth:
"Lithen," said Ruth
"I've a little looth tooth!"

Said little Bruce Booth:
"Tho what if you do?
that'th nothing thpethial—
I've a looth tooth too!"

EXERCISES
by Bette Killion

Stand tall and stretch,
    reach up, up high;
    pretend you're a tree
    growing right through the sky.

Bend to the floor
    with your knees held straight;
    touch your heels 'til you look
    like the figure eight.

Spread out your arms
    from your waist, turn half round;
    back and forth like a clock
    that is being wound.

Hop, hop on one foot;
    then hop on the other;
    pretend you're a bird
    bobbing after its mother.

Leap up so high
    you could jump in a nest
    then flop down, cross-legged,
    and take your rest.

Sneeze
by Maxine Kumin

There's a
sort of a
tickle
the size of a
nickel,
a bit like the
prickle
of sweet-sour
pickle;

it's a
quivery
shiver
the shape of a
sliver,
like eels in a
river;

a kind of a
wiggle
that starts as a
jiggle
and joggles
its way to a
tease,

which I
cannot
suppress
any longer,
I guess,
so pardon me,
please,
while I
sneeze.

Oh my goodness, oh my dear
by Clyde Watson

Oh my goodness, oh my dear,
Sassafras & ginger beer,
Chocolate cake & apple punch:
I'm too full to eat my lunch.

Nell & Jack Horner
by Father Gander

Little Jack Horner sat in a corner,
Eating his Christmas pie.
He stuck in his thumb and pulled out a plum,
And said, "What a good boy am I!"

Little Nell Horner sat in a corner,
Eating her tarts and jam.
She took a small bite and smiled with delight,
And said, "What a good girl I am!"

And though it is sweet, an occasional treat
Won't make your parents say, "Whoops!"
If you try every day to choose foods the right way
From the basic nutritional groups.

Rainy Day
by William Wise

I do not like a rainy day.
The road is wet, the sky is gray.
They dress me up, from head to toes,
In lots and lots of rubber clothes.
I wish the sun would come and stay.
I do not like a rainy day.

Momma Drives
by Arnold Adoff

Momma Drives
    This
      Pick
        Up
Truck
    Full of
Newspapers
      To
The
    Re
    Cycle
    Center   and I help carry
        The bags inside

    Momma drives and I am along
        To work
And
For the good talk
    This good ride

I Did a Nutty Somersault
by Jack Prelutsky

I did a nutty somersault
and landed with a thump.
I struggled to my feet again
but tumbled on my rump.
I tried to keep my balance
but invariably fell,
and every time I topple
I let out another yell.

Backwards, forward, even sideways,
I fell every sort of way,
as a growing crowd applauded
my theatrical display.
I flopped, I flipped, I skidded,
I performed a barrel roll.
My arms and legs kept flapping,
they were out of my control.

My feet shot out from under me
the moment I arose.
I took a flying header,
nearly damaging my nose.
So I suppose I'm qualified
to offer this advice–
when you try out *your* roller blades,
don't do it on the ice.

Jellybeans Up Your Nose
by Jeff Moss

Johnny stuck jellybeans up his nose,
That's a pretty dumb thing to do.
But the other kids said, "Hey, John's real cool.
Let's put beans up our noses, too!"
Well, a kid can't breathe with beans up his nose
'Cause they get all stuck inside.
So John and the kids, well, I hate to say it,
But they coughed and they choked and they died.

That's a pretty grim tale, I must admit,
And it may not all be true,
Still when somebody cool does something dumb
You don't have to do it, too.

So don't be one of those
With jellybeans up your nose.

The Enormous Turnip

A Russian Tale by Alexei Tolstoy

Once upon a time an old man planted a little turnip and said: "Grow, grow, little turnip, grow sweet! Grow, grow, little turnip, grow strong!"

And the turnip grew up sweet and strong and big and enormous.

Then, one day, the old man went to pull it up. He pulled and pulled again, but he could not pull it up.

He called the old woman.
The old woman pulled the old man,
The old man pulled the turnip.

And they pulled and pulled again, but they could not pull it up.

So the old woman called her granddaughter.
The granddaughter pulled the old woman,
The old woman pulled the old man,
The old man pulled the turnip.

And they pulled and pulled again, but they could not pull it up.

The granddaughter called the black dog.
The black dog pulled the granddaughter,
The granddaughter pulled the old woman,
The old woman pulled the old man,
The old man pulled the turnip.

And they pulled and pulled again, but they could not pull it up.

The black dog called the cat.
The cat pulled the dog,
The dog pulled the granddaughter,
The granddaughter pulled the old woman,
The old woman pulled the old man,
The old man pulled the turnip.

And they pulled and pulled again, but still they could not pull it up.

The cat called the mouse.
The mouse pulled the cat,
The cat pulled the dog,
The dog pulled the granddaughter,
The granddaughter pulled the old woman,
The old woman pulled the old man,
The old man pulled the turnip.

And they pulled and pulled again, and up came the turnip at last.

The Bundle of Sticks

A farmer and his wife had four children, two girls and two boys. They should have been very happy, but they weren't. Instead they were sad, because the children could not get along together.

"Stop it! Stop it!," shouted the farmer when his children quarreled.

"No more fighting!" screamed the farmer, covering his ears.

But the fighting just went on and on. Each child played alone, and each child did chores alone. Each child stood alone against all the other children.

The farmer's wife didn't yell. She didn't cover her ears. The farmer's wife had a different idea. She collected a pile of sticks and tied them together to make a bundle. The next time the children quarreled, she showed them the bundle of sticks.

"Go ahead," said the farmer's wife. "Try to break it in half."

Each child tried, but not one could break the bundle. So the farmer's wife untied the bundle and gave a stick to each child. "Now try," she said. And each child easily broke a stick in half.

"Let this be a lesson to you," the farmer's wife told the children. "The sticks are strong when they are together. They are weak when they stand alone. Families are stronger when the members stick together, too."

And from that day on, the children stopped quarreling and stuck together.

Body on Strike!

One day, Mouth, Hands, and Teeth held a meeting.

"Have you noticed," said Mouth, "that we do all the work, but Tummy gets all the food?"

"That's right," signed Hands. "Why should we work so hard to get food for Tummy? Let's go on strike. We will not work until Tummy does something nice for us."

Teeth said nothing.

So for two days Hands did not take any food, Mouth did not open, Teeth had nothing to do at all, and Tummy just growled and growled.

On the third day, Mouth spoke weakly. "This is not working out the way I thought it would," Mouth whispered.

"No, it is not," Hands signed slowly. "I can hardly move. None of us seem to be working right."

So Hands took some food, Mouth opened to receive it, and Teeth crunched and crunched. All the body parts felt much better right away. Even Tummy stopped growling.

"I guess Tummy does earn its food after all," said Mouth as soon as it could speak again.

"I agree," signed Hands. "From now on we'll take good care of Tummy."

And Teeth showed themselves in a wide smile.

Benjamin Rabbit and Stranger Danger

by Dick and Irene Keller

Benjamin Rabbit hopped across the puddles on his way to school. Small as he was, Benjamin was a first-rate puddle jumper. And, young as he was, Benjamin knew a lot.

For one thing, Benjamin knew his full name. His first name—Benjamin—and his last name—Rabbit. And he knew his mother's name—Maud—and his father's name—Claude.

Benjamin also knew his phone number <u>and</u> his area code—TEN numbers! He knew them by heart.

And he knew his address—46 Green Street in the town of Meadowbank in the state of Ohio.

His teacher said it was important to know the name of the town and the name of the state where you live.

Benjamin liked his teacher a lot. She helped him learn to read and write. And sometimes she invited other people to come to school and talk to the students. Special people—like fire fighters and police officers.

That very morning, when Benjamin got to school, a police officer named Sergeant Strong came in to talk to Benjamin and his classmates.

Sergeant Strong began by saying that he had some very bad news. He told the class that Katy Cottontail had disappeared! And she was last seen talking to a stranger.

Benjamin could hardly believe it. He was very upset. He felt like crying.

"I know it's sad," said Sergeant Strong. "And I know it's scary. But we're going to talk about Stranger Danger—bad strangers. You need to know how you can make sure it won't happen to <u>you</u>."

Benjamin sat up straight and paid attention.

"First," said Sergeant Strong, "does everyone know what a stranger is?"

"I do," said Benjamin. "A stranger is a grown-up you don't know."

"Right," said Sergeant Strong. "But how can we tell a good stranger from a bad stranger?"

"I guess we can't," said Benjamin.

"Right," said Sergeant Strong. "That's why we have to be careful of <u>all</u> strangers. Bad strangers and good strangers can look alike.

"Now I'm going to give you a list of Stranger Danger Dos and Don'ts. We will read it out loud."

Stranger Danger DOs and DON'Ts

1. **DON'T** talk to strangers.
2. **DON'T** go near a stranger's car.
3. **DON'T** take candy or money or anything else from a stranger.

If a stranger follows you by car or on foot,

4. **DO** yell "Help!" as loud as you can.
5. **DO** run to the nearest place where there are other people.
6. **DON'T** run to a lonely place.

If you are home alone,

7. **DON'T** open the door for anyone.
8. **DON'T** tell anyone on the phone that you are home alone.

"Now," said Sergeant Strong, "let's pretend for a moment. I want you to imagine that you are out shopping in a store and all of a sudden you don't see your mother anywhere. You're lost! OK?"

Benjamin nodded, "OK."

"What would you do?" asked Sergeant Strong. "Would you ask a stranger to help you find your mother?"

"No!" yelled the class.

"Would you go to the parking lot to look for your mother?"

"No!" yelled the class.

"Would you go to the nearest check-out counter and ask the check-out person to help you find your mother?"

"Yes!" yelled the class.

"Right," said Sergeant Strong. "If you are lost in a store or a shopping mall, you go to the nearest check-out counter and ask the clerk to help you."

"I can do that," said Benjamin.

"Of course you can," said Sergeant Strong. "Now let's pretend again. Imagine you're home alone. Your mother is not home."

Benjamin nodded.

"Suppose the doorbell rings or someone knocks on the door," said Sergeant Strong. "Would you open the door?"

"No!" yelled the class.

"Right," said Sergeant Strong. "Never open the door to anyone when you are home alone.

"But what if the phone rings and someone asks to speak to your mother. Do you say, 'My mother's not home?'"

"No!" yelled the class.

"Right," said Sergeant Strong. "But what would you say if someone on the phone asks to speak to your mother?"

"I know," said Benjamin. "I'd say, 'My mother's busy and she can't come to the phone.' And then I'd hang up right away."

"Very good," said Sergeant Strong. "Never tell anyone on the phone that you're home alone."

"I see you know a lot," the sergeant went on. "And now I'm going to tell you some Stranger Danger tricks. You've all been taught to be kind and helpful to other people, right?"

"Right," said Benjamin.

"So what do you do if a stranger asks for your help?"

Benjamin Rabbit didn't know.

"What if you are out playing," said Sergeant Strong, "and a stranger says, 'I hurt my arm. Will you help me carry this package?'"

"Or suppose a stranger says, 'Help me open my car door. It's stuck. You're so strong, I bet you could open it.'"

"Would you help that stranger?"

"No!" yelled the class.

"Right," said Sergeant Strong. "Good strangers don't ask youngsters to help them. They ask other grown-ups. NEVER talk to strangers! And if a stranger talks to you, ignore it. Pretend you don't hear it and walk away."

"I can do that," said Benjamin.

Benjamin hurried home from school that day to tell his mother all he had learned. He had hopped about halfway home—with a lot of lovely puddles still to cross—when he suddenly noticed that a car was coasting along beside him, very slowly, next to the curb.

"Hi!" he heard a voice say. "You're getting wet. Hop in. I'll give you a ride."

Benjamin pretended not to hear. He hopped a little faster.

"Your mother sent me to get you," said the stranger. "She's sick and she sent me to bring you home."

Benjamin knew that was a Stranger Danger trick. His mother would never send a stranger to get him. He hopped as far from the curb as he could get.

"OK, pal," said the stranger. "I bet you don't know so much. I bet you don't even know the way to Main Street."

"I bet I do know," said Benjamin. "It's two blocks over."

"What? What did you say?" said the stranger, opening the car door. "I can't hear you. Come a little closer."

Benjamin started to move toward the car and then—just in time—he remembered the Stranger Danger Dos and Don'ts. DON'T GO NEAR A STRANGER'S CAR!

Benjamin ran like the wind, yelling, "Help!" as loud as he could. When he got to the corner, he told the crossing guard about the bad stranger.

When he got home, he told his mother.

"You did the right things, Benjamin," said his mother, giving him an extra-big hug. "I'm so glad you know the Stranger Danger Dos and Don'ts. Always remember them."

Benjamin put the list on his wall where he would see it every day. And Benjamin Rabbit always remembered.

Yes, Benjamin Rabbit knew a lot.

The Sharing Song

Head and Shoulders, Knees and Toes

Wheels
Sylvia Worth Van Clief and Florence Parry Heide

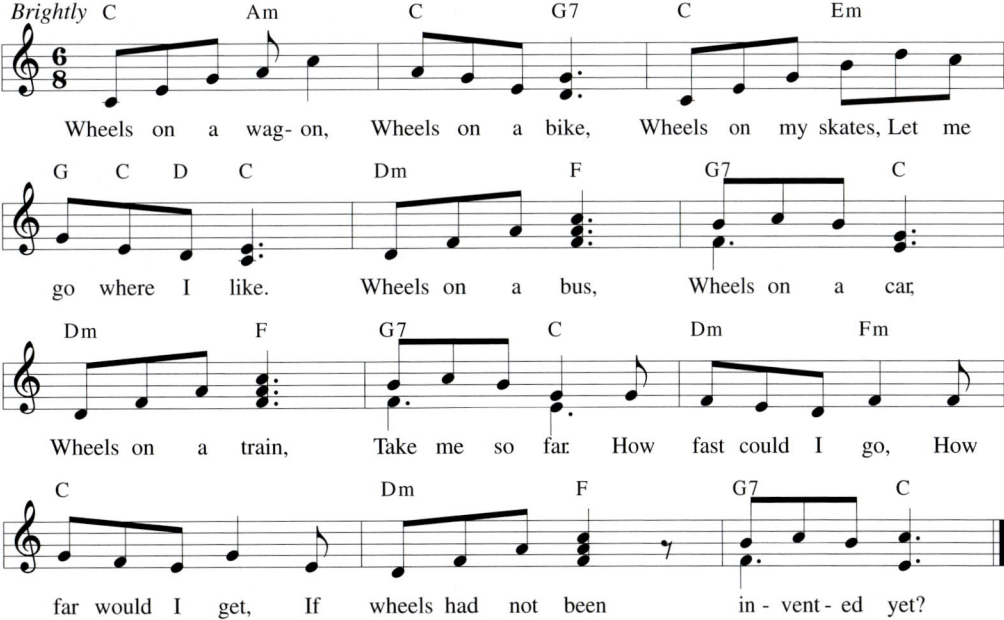

Wheels on a wagon, Wheels on a bike, Wheels on my skates, Let me go where I like. Wheels on a bus, Wheels on a car, Wheels on a train, Take me so far. How fast could I go, How far would I get, If wheels had not been in-vent-ed yet?

Clap Your Hands

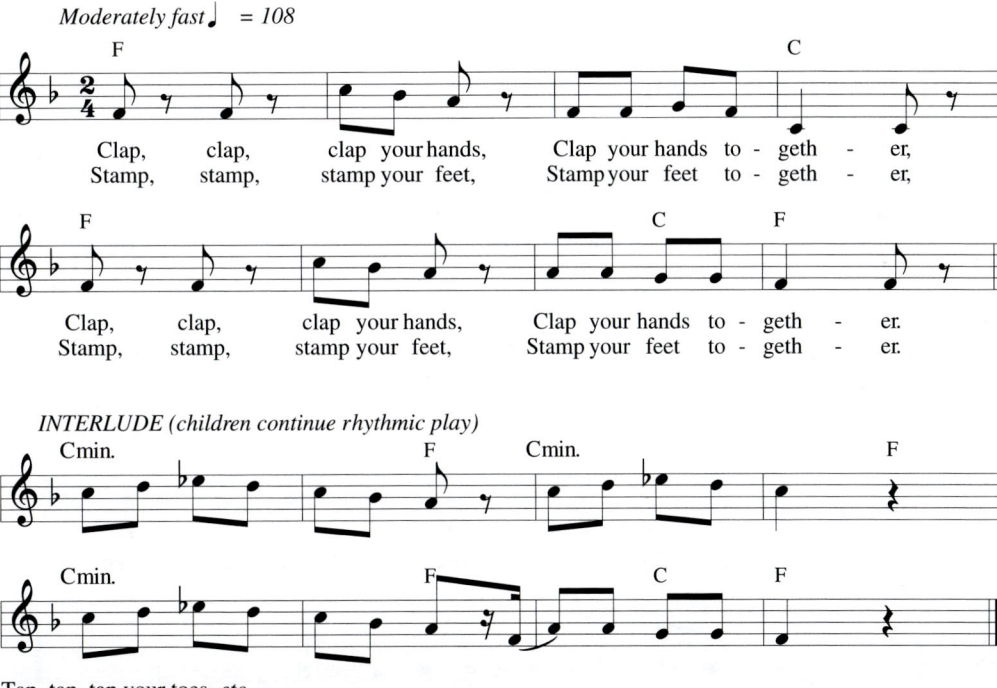

Clap, clap, clap your hands, Clap your hands to-geth-er,
Stamp, stamp, stamp your feet, Stamp your feet to-geth-er,
Clap, clap, clap your hands, Clap your hands to-geth-er.
Stamp, stamp, stamp your feet, Stamp your feet to-geth-er.

Tap, tap, tap your toes, *etc.*
Nod, nod, nod your head, *etc.*
Shake, shake, shake your hands, *etc.*
Stretch, stretch, stretch up high, *etc.*

The Mulberry Bush

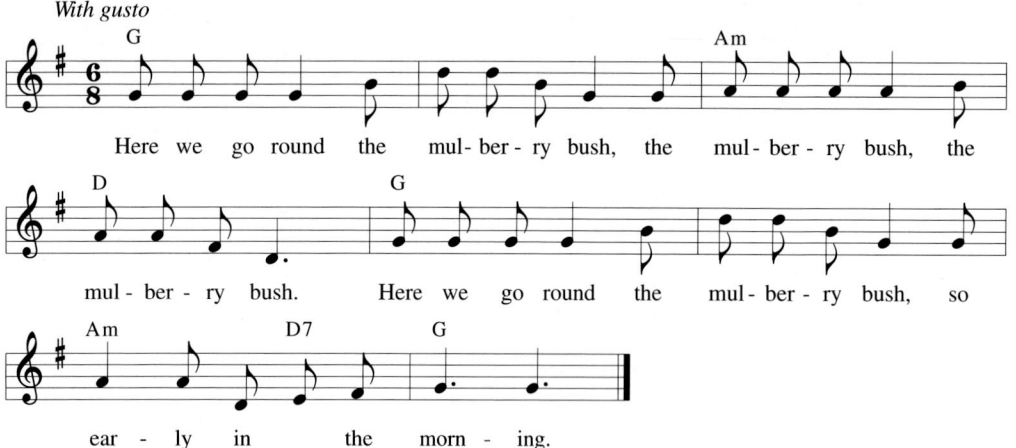

This is the way we wash our clothes, *etc.*
So early Monday morning.

This is the way we iron our clothes, *etc.*
So early Tuesday morning.

This is the way we mend our clothes, *etc.*
So early Wednesday morning.

This is the way we scrub the floor, *etc.*
So early Thursday morning.

This is the way we sweep the house, *etc.*
So early Friday morning.

This is the way we bake our bread, *etc.*
So early Saturday morning.

This is the way we go for a walk, *etc.*
So early Sunday morning.

One Finger, One Thumb

2. One finger, one thumb, one hand, two hands,
   Keep moving.
   One finger, one thumb, one hand, two hands,
   Keep moving.
   One finger, one thumb, one hand, two hands,
   Keep moving.
   And we'll all be happy and gay.

Add in turn:
3. One arm, *etc.*
4. Two arms, *etc.*
5. One leg, *etc.*
6. Two legs, *etc.*
7. Stand up—sit down, *etc.*
8. Turn around, *etc.*

Teacher Reference Section

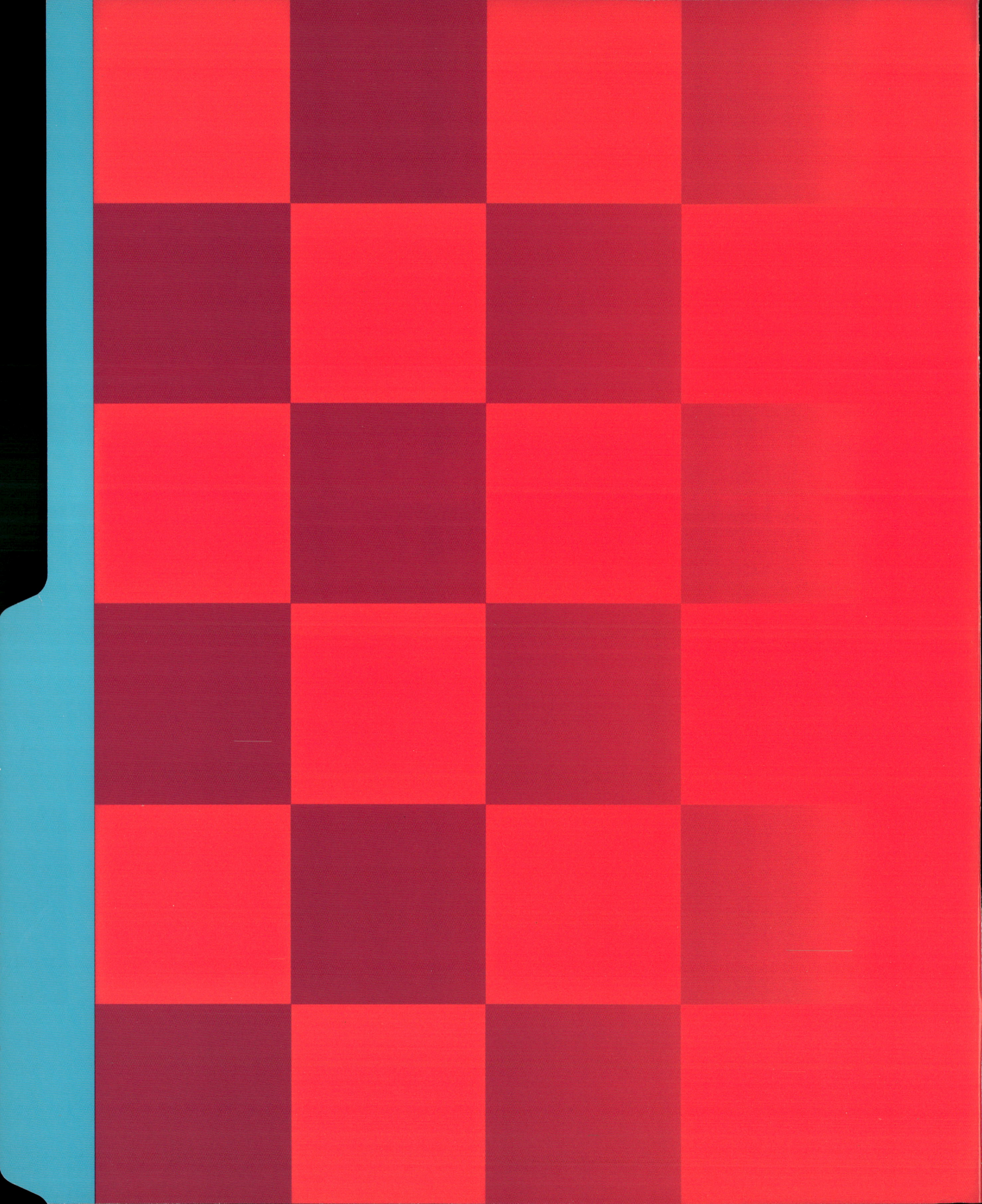

Teacher Reference

Author Articles

Injury Prevention Is a Partnership
by Jan Marie Ozias, Ph.D. R.N. **TR-2**

Preventing Drug Use
by Kathleen Middleton **TR-4**

Nutrition Behaviors for Children
by Carl A. Stockton, Ph.D. **TR-6**

Becoming Physically Active
by Charlie Gibbons, Ed.D. **TR-8**

Scope and Sequence, Grades K–2

Your Health–Program Organization **TR-10**

Emotional, Intellectual, and Social Health **TR-12**

Family Life, Growth, and Development **TR-13**

Personal Health and Physical Fitness **TR-14**

Nutrition **TR-16**

Disease Prevention and Control **TR-17**

Drug Use Prevention **TR-18**

Injury Prevention **TR-20**

Community and Environmental Health **TR-21**

Author Articles

Injury Prevention Is a Partnership
Jan Marie Ozias, Ph.D., R.N.

Why are injury prevention and control of concern to schools?
- Injuries are the leading killer of children and youth in the United States and a major cause of hospital care and long-term disability. Of the 22 million injuries to children that occur yearly in the United States, it is estimated that 10 to 25 percent occur in and around schools and school events.
- Schools are not only where students learn about safety practices but also where students spend many hours daily. The community expects schools to teach students knowledge and skills for safe, responsible lifestyles. Parents want to trust that school buildings, the ways to and from schools, and school activities are safe—all the time.
- Schools are work sites for many adults in every community. The people who staff schools need protection from unnecessary risks and need to take responsibility for injury prevention practices.

Why don't we use the term accidents anymore?

The U.S. Centers for Disease Control and Prevention analyzed "accidents" using the concept of epidemiology (the study of diseases that affect people) and determined that most accidents are not random occurrences. They are predictable and preventable.

Let us examine a fatal car collision caused by a teenage driver who was drinking, showing off, and driving on a rain-slick road without using a seat belt. None of these factors is a random occurrence, that is, a true accident. The event and the injuries that resulted follow a predictable pattern. Epidemiology examines the relationship among three elements:
- **Host**—a person who could become ill or injured due to his or her own resistance, skills, or state of mind
- **Agent**—a direct cause of illness, such as a virus, or of harm, such as a car
- **Environment**—such as rules, weather conditions, and cleanliness

If we can alter any one of the three epidemiological elements, we can break the chain of events that lead to a high risk of illness or harm. For example, immunizing a child breaks the chain of events leading to disease if the child is later exposed to a virus. Here is a home safety example:
Host: Curious 5-year-old child
Agent: Cigarette lighter
Environment: unsupervised garage with flammable materials

Changing any of the three elements breaks the link between the host and the agent. If you teach young students the skill of self-discipline and the risks of fire, add adult supervision to the environment, or keep lighters out of reach, no fire!

In order to help students and staff identify what can and cannot be controlled, we use *unintended injury* to refer to burns, crashes, and falls. (These were previously called *accidents*.) We distinguish unintended injuries from deliberate or *intended injuries*, injuries caused by violence, assault, and self-harm.

Do children think injuries are preventable?

Children can tell us about injury prevention—they know it's not just about "accidents" or "kids being kids." In a study of 12 elementary schools, students were asked about their playground injuries. Almost a third of the injured students thought they could have prevented their injuries. When they were asked how, the most common replies were *not going so fast, watching, being more careful, not fighting,* and *avoiding the situation.* About half the same injured students thought someone else or something in the environment had influenced the injury. The most frequent reasons were *actions of another student* or *an object,* such as a rock or playground equipment. Developmentally, students can learn to use their senses to recognize hazards like these, connect them to unsafe situations, and then act to prevent injuries.

What do we know about students' injuries?

Detailed reports about student injuries come from the National Pediatric Trauma Registry study of school-age children (5- to 18-year-olds) seen in 74 emergency rooms between 1988 and 1995. Here are some results from that study:
- More injuries (49 percent) occurred in recreational areas than in any other school area.
- Falls were the most common cause of injury (46 percent), followed by sports activities (30 percent).
- Assaults or intended injury caused 10 percent of the injuries.
- Students with disabilities were more likely to be hurt; 17 percent of the injured students already had a disability or chronic illness.
- Forty-six percent of the injuries occurred among 10- to 14-year-olds.
- Almost 40 percent of the cases involved head injuries.

Do schools handle injuries properly?

The same hospital emergency room study also found that 16 percent of the children received no or inadequate first aid; they were sent home rather than sent to receive care. How prepared is your school to handle injuries? Does it have a registered nurse and staff trained in first aid? Who fills in for the nurse if he or she is unavailable?

Where do violence and abuse fit in injury prevention?

Assault injuries to students seen in emergency rooms included beatings (more than 50 percent of the assaults), stabbings (14 percent), gunshot wounds (10 percent), or being deliberately hit by an object. Although violence receives much more media attention and causes staff to worry, most of the students injured at school—in a ratio of 9 to 1—are injured *un*intentionally. Regardless, conflict resolution as a life skill can reduce aggression and intended injuries, especially when it is taught in elementary school and applied in the home, community, and workplace. The Children's Safety Network identified over 40 curricula that include violence prevention, but few were well evaluated for effectiveness. One reference for developing age-appropriate violence prevention curriculum is *Promoting Social and Emotional Learning: Guidelines for Educators.* Alexandria, VA: Association for Supervision and Curriculum Development (1997).

"Stranger" danger addresses community concerns for children when they are unsupervised. Many children also may be at risk in the presence of a neighbor, a family acquaintance, or even a relative. Teachers should work with approved school resources to include opportunities for students to learn how to handle uncomfortable situations involving touch, secrets, or pressure by an older person to do something that children feel is wrong or unsafe.

Are school buses safe?

While much attention is being given to installing seat belts (safety belts) in school buses—primarily to reinforce the habit of using them in cars and to prevent disruptive behavior—school buses are quite safe. Considering the number of passenger miles they travel, school buses are 37 times safer than cars. Even so, an average of 11 children die annually in school bus crashes. Another 30 pedestrians die getting on or off a bus, or are hit by a bus or a passing vehicle. Half of these pedestrians are children between the ages of five and seven!

What needs to happen in schools?

In addition to quality student instruction, the Centers for Disease Control and Prevention (2001) recommends that schools

- establish a safety council that includes parents and students as part of a school health program advisory committee. The safety council would identify and correct safety hazards and establish safety policies.
- develop reporting methods so that school staff can analyze unintended and intended injuries and target the most common or most serious situations and develop better prevention strategies.
- develop and implement emergency plans to properly assess, manage and refer injured students.

What are safety education priorities for elementary grades?

Among elementary-school children, common unintended injuries are related to the following:

- traffic
- playgrounds
- bicycles
- fire
- water
- personal trauma (falls, cuts)

Appropriate education goals for elementary grades are to develop in students **habits** of safety that will guide **behaviors** and prepare students for the risk-taking years of middle school. We must convey more than just knowledge of safety risks and rules, we must focus on habits and behaviors (*what to do*) and skills (*how to perform the behaviors*). Positive role models at school and at home, guided practice, and social reinforcement of emerging skills are appropriate strategies to build these habits and behaviors.

Preventing Drug Use
Kathleen Middleton

Education to prevent drug use is most effective when it is included as part of a comprehensive health education program that begins in elementary school and continues through high school. Such an education starts in kindergarten with basic messages about safe behavior around unknown substances and about appropriate use of medicines, and continues with developmentally appropriate instruction throughout the school years.

Effective education to prevent drug use must include more than facts about the effects of drugs. Knowledge alone about the effects of drugs is not enough to prevent drug use; children must develop the skills they need to be able to remain drug-free. To effectively resist the pressures toward drug use that permeate our society, children must learn they have the ability to *refuse* to use drugs. Research over the past several years has indicated success in programs in which children practice life skills, including refusals, decision making, goal setting, conflict resolution, communication, and stress management.

Before they reach adolescence, most children report that they are strongly opposed to drug use. But with the onset of adolescence comes the desire to experiment, coupled with the need to assert one's independence. This stage of growth and development makes children much more susceptible to pressures to experiment with drug use.

In primary grades, children can be taught facts about dangerous substances and can begin to practice the skills they need to say *no* to pressures and to protect themselves in dangerous situations. By the time they are in sixth grade, many children will have been approached to try tobacco, alcohol, or other drugs, as well as to participate in other unsafe behaviors. By this time children must already have had the reinforcement of repeated practice in saying *no*. They also need the confidence to withstand peer pressure, make safe decisions, communicate effectively, manage stress, and set goals for the future.

Drug Use Statistics

In the 1980s, the U.S. Centers for Disease Control and Prevention began conducting national school-based surveys to measure the prevalence of health-risk behaviors among students in grades 9 through 12. In 1999, the Youth Risk Behavior Survey (YRBS) reported the following drug use behaviors:

- More than 47 percent of the students surveyed had used marijuana during their lifetimes.
- Over 8 percent had used a form of cocaine at some point, and at least 4 percent had used it within the last month.
- More than 3 percent had used steroids without a doctor's prescription.

- Nearly 2 percent had injected illegal drugs.
- Over 14 percent reported inhalant use; or sniffing intoxicating substances and just over 4 percent had used inhalants within the last month.

Perhaps not surprisingly, the drugs most commonly used were the drugs that are legal for adult use—tobacco and alcohol. The YRBS survey reported the following statistics:

- More than 80 percent of the students surveyed had had at least one drink of alcohol during their lifetimes, and more than 50 percent had had a drink in the last 30 days.
- More than 70 percent had tried cigarette smoking, and 34 percent had smoked during the last month.
- Almost 8 percent of the students surveyed had used smokeless tobacco during the last 30 days.

Although these statistics reflect high-school drug use, the behaviors are an outgrowth of what has been learned in earlier grades. Many researchers feel that by the time students are in high school, it's almost too late to prevent drug use. The foundation for drug-use prevention must be laid during childhood.

Healthy People 2010

Healthy People 2010: Understanding and Improving Health includes objectives for youths 12 to 17 years old to reduce the prevalence of personal health risks. The goal of Objectives 27-4a, 26-9a, and 26-9b is to "increase the average age of first use" of tobacco products, alcohol and marijuana by adolescents and young adults aged 12 through 17 by 2, 3, and 4 years respectively. Baseline data from 1997–1998 indicated an average age of first use for cigarettes to be 12 years; for alcohol, 13.1 years; and for marijuana, 13.7 years. A 1999 review of trends indicated that little progress had been made in the attempt to reduce the initiation of cigarette smoking by children and youth. Downward trends in alcohol and marijuana use among students 12 to 17 years old were reversed in 1995.

Young adults are unlikely to develop problems of alcohol and drug use if the age of first use can be delayed beyond childhood and adolescence. The U.S. Department of Health and Human Services review indicated a consensus that children are never too young to be reached with consistent messages about the health effects of alcohol and other drugs.

Effective Education

Evaluation of drug-use prevention programs has identified some key elements of success. Programs that work include not only information but activities to help build students' personal social skills. Essential skills include the following:

- communication
- stress management
- decision making and goal setting
- refusing

The first three skills provide the basis for the skills of refusing. Communication skills help students clearly communicate their feelings and thoughts. Stress-management skills help students handle their stress without turning to drug use. Decision-making and goal-setting skills help students consider consequences and look to the future. Effective refusals incorporate all these skills.

Finally, students need to feel confident in order to remain drug-free. Research has shown that students who practice skills in an education setting not only develop the skills but also develop a feeling of empowerment and the belief that they can use the skills. This feeling of confidence is considered a key aspect of adolescent success in remaining drug-free. When we provide children opportunities to practice these skills throughout the elementary grades, we offer them the foundation they need to protect themselves in adolescence.

Nutrition Behaviors for Children
Carl A. Stockton, Ph.D.

As I think about promoting positive dietary behaviors in children, I have to look at my three-year-old's current eating habits. Her eating practices are being molded at this early stage in her life. Children learn at a young age what kinds of food adults around them eat. In trying to teach her about positive nutritional choices, I find myself selecting healthful foods for her, such as green beans, apples, oranges, and other fruits and vegetables, that are part of my own diet. Nutritional eating practices are learned behaviors, and it is important that we start molding these behaviors early in a child's life.

Poor Health Habits

Our society has been extremely negligent in promoting positive eating behaviors in our children. Many studies have shown that poor diets and lack of physical activity together account for more than 300,000 premature deaths among adults each year. These poor health habits begin in our children. According to the U.S. Centers for Disease Control and Prevention, the percentage of children who are overweight has more than doubled in the past 30 years, and more than 5.3 million children (13 percent) are seriously overweight. Studies have shown that obese children are more likely to become obese adults. As adults, they are at increased risk for many premature diseases.

Eating habits of children and young people in the United States are poor. Children make poor nutritional choices that put them at risk for health problems. Contrary to common misconceptions, children do not instinctively select the nutrients that they need for proper growth and development. If I allowed my three-year-old daughter to select food instinctively, she would have a diet of candy, soda, and cookies—hardly a healthful diet.

Another common misconception is that children can handle a poor diet when they are young because they will burn off the Calories; this is a dangerous misconception. Although it is true that children are able to metabolize the extra Calories because of increased activity, the poor eating habits they develop in childhood will continue into adulthood and can be detrimental. Establishing good nutritional habits during childhood is critical because changing poor eating behaviors in adulthood is difficult. Think about your own nutritional habits. I challenge you to choose one nutritional habit that you would like to change and to spend one week trying to change that habit. You can probably guess that trying to change the habit would be difficult. Now consider that if you had developed a more positive eating pattern as a child, you would most likely not need to make this behavior change as an adult.

Poor Diets

Children would get the proper amount of nutrients if they could only learn proper eating habits. Contrary to common beliefs, children do not need vitamin and mineral supplements. Unless there is a medical reason for vitamin and mineral supplements, children receive all the nutrients they need through a balanced diet. Taking vitamin pills only seems to be an easy solution for making up the nutrients missed in a child's dietary intake.

On another note, did you know that pound per pound children need to consume more water than do adults? Children lose a greater percent of water through evaporation than adults. Therefore, children need to consume more water per pound of body weight than adults need to consume.

Even though adults have shown some improvement in their dietary patterns, our children's eating habits remain poor. According to the U.S. Department of Health and Human Services, more than 84 percent of children eat too much fat. Children on average consume about 40 percent of their calories from fat. Children are not consuming enough fruits and vegetables in their diet. The National Cancer Institute recommends that children consume five servings of fruits and vegetables per day. Only 20 percent of our children actually meet this recommendation. Did you know that 51 percent of our children eat less than one serving of fruit a day? Furthermore, fried potatoes account for a large proportion of the vegetables eaten by children.

Did you know that one in five students skips breakfast on a regular basis? Several research studies have found that not eating breakfast can affect children's intellectual performance in school. Even moderate malnutrition can have a long-term effect on how well a child performs in school. Several studies have reported that undernourished children become sick, miss school, and score lower on tests than do children who receive the proper amount of nourishment. Therefore, it is important for children to eat properly and not skip meals.

Promoting Good Nutrition

What can we do as teachers to encourage our students to become better eaters? The opportunity to promote better eating habits is in front of us. We have a captive audience to whom to promote good nutrition and also positive health behaviors. We as teachers need to develop a comprehensive scope and sequence for nutrition education. It is important to keep reinforcing positive eating behaviors at every grade level. Nutrition education involves more than just educating students about healthful eating. We need to help children learn skills, not just facts about nutrition. The USDA's *Nutrition and Your Health: Dietary Guidelines For Americans, 2000* is a good source for learning diet and lifestyle skills. In this document, you can find healthful activities and practices that students can actually put into practice.

Give children repeated opportunities to practice healthful eating. Practicing a positive health behavior enough times will usually make that behavior the norm for children, not the exception. Teaching children about nutrition is no different from teaching children math skills. If we want our children to excel in mathematics, we give them multiple opportunities to practice math problems. The same holds true for developing positive eating practices. Practice, practice, practice!

Practicing Good Nutrition

What types of activities can teachers do to promote positive nutritional practices in children? First of all, request healthful snacks for class parties. This will create a positive atmosphere for eating these kinds of foods. Give students many chances to taste foods low in fat, sodium, and added sugar and foods high in vitamins, minerals, and fiber. Also teach children how to make healthful choices in the school cafeteria or when packing their lunches. This promotes positive behaviors and keeps children involved in learning about nutrition. Emphasize the positive aspects of healthful eating rather than the harmful effects of unhealthful eating.

Finally, make nutrition education activities fun. Be creative with your activities, and try to show your students that learning can be fun. Nutrition education curricula resources exist and are readily available, often for free. Many nutrition-based materials can be obtained from volunteer agencies and governmental offices. Use them!

I would be remiss if I failed to mention the use of computers and technology in the classroom. If you are fortunate enough to have computers in your classroom, integrate the use of these learning tools with nutrition education. Surf the nutrition information highway, search CD-ROMs, and experience nutrition multimedia along with your students. Who knows, even your own nutritional habits may improve!

Becoming Physically Active
Charlie Gibbons, Ed.D.

Children have always enjoyed the opportunity to play outdoors and rarely refuse to take advantage of an opportunity to run and have fun. However, in recent years not as many children are outdoors playing. Some studies have shown that children are less active and that childhood obesity is on the rise. How true is this? Are children in the United States becoming less active and more overweight? If they are, what are the influencing factors?

Physical activity and fitness have become such a national health concern that several national documents from the U.S. Department of Health and Human Services have emphasized the importance of physical activity and fitness. *Healthy People 2010*, the national initiative that established health objectives for the first decade of this century, includes objectives to increase levels of moderate and vigorous physical activity among adolescents, to increase the proportion of trips made by walking and bicycling, and to decrease the amount of time young people spend watching television. *Physical Activity and Health: A Report of the Surgeon General* emphasizes that regular participation in moderate physical activity is an essential component of a healthy lifestyle.

How physically active are children and adolescents?

Numerous national studies (First and Second National Children and Youth Fitness Study, The President's Council on Physical Fitness and Sports School Population Fitness Study, Youth Fitness Behavior Surveillance System, and *Healthy People 2010*) have been conducted to determine the physical activity levels of children and adolescents in the United States. The general finding is that children and youth in the United States are less active and physically fit than is recommended for optimal protection against future chronic diseases.

In addition to studies conducted on fitness levels of children and adolescents, a number of studies have been conducted to determine the prevalence of childhood obesity in the United States. The general finding is that children and youth are getting more overweight.

Why are children and adolescents less physically active and fit?

If children and adolescents are less active and are becoming more overweight, there must be some influencing factors. Researchers have emphasized the influencing role of television watching on sedentary (inactive) behavior and obesity. Television watching is a popular childhood leisure activity. The majority of children spend more time watching television than they spend in school. During television watching, physical activity ceases and metabolism slows down. As television watching increases among children and adolescents, physical activity decreases. As physical activity decreases among children and adolescents, obesity increases. According to the U.S. Centers for Disease Control and Prevention (CDC), the percentage of young people who are overweight has more than doubled in the past 30 years, and the number of deaths due to inactivity and poor diet is at least 300,000 a year for all ages.

In recent years there also has been an explosion in the use of computers, computer games, and video games by children and adolescents. These advances in technology also may help to promote sedentary behavior among children and adolescents and to increase the likelihood of obesity and the development of chronic diseases.

Television is a very powerful medium that has a pervasive influence on the health knowledge, attitudes, and behavior of children, adolescents, and adults. Researchers have suggested another avenue in which television watching influences obesity. Television watching may influence obesity among children and adolescents by increasing the number of nutritional messages to which they are exposed. Much too often foods in commercials and the foods shown in television programs are high in Calories and low in nutritional value.

What health problems are associated with inactivity?

Researchers have found obesity in childhood and adolescence to be associated with developmental risk factors for cardiovascular diseases, hypertension, high blood cholesterol, and diabetes. These problems become more pronounced in adulthood. Obese children are at an increased risk of obesity as adults. Recent studies have shown that the problems of obesity and physical inactivity among young adults are increasing at alarming rates. As the prevalence of adult obesity increases, morbidity and mortality increase.

At the same time, children and adolescents today are being bombarded with societal messages that emphasize thinness. These social pressures for thinness increase the health risk for overweight youth suffering from eating disorders.

What are the benefits of regular physical activity?

According to the *Report of the Surgeon General*, regular physical activity that is performed on an almost daily basis reduces the risk of developing or dying from some of the leading causes of illness and death in the United States.

Regular physical activity improves health in the following ways:
- It reduces the risk of dying prematurely from heart disease.
- It reduces the risk of developing high blood pressure.
- It reduces feelings of depression and anxiety.
- It helps control weight.
- It reduces the risk of developing diabetes.
- It helps build and maintain healthy bones, muscles, and joints.
- It promotes psychological well-being.
- It helps alleviate stress.

What is physical activity and fitness?

Have you ever gone for a walk? Have you ever done any gardening? If your answer is *yes* for these activities, or for any activities of this energy level or higher, you have been involved in physical activity. And if you have engaged in these types of activities for at least 30 minutes per day, you have been improving your fitness. You have been engaging in physical activity that will help ensure Calories are expended and health benefits will be conferred. Children and adolescents should engage in
- aerobic activities that will help improve and maintain the cardio–respiratory system,
- physically challenging activities that will improve and maintain the muscular system, and
- stretching activities that will improve and maintain flexibility and help prevent injuries.

Children should learn the importance of warm-up activities, which prepare the body for physical activity and prevent injuries, and of cool-down activities, which allow for continual blood return from the lower extremities of the body to prevent blood from pooling in the legs.

How can teachers help?

It is important to remember that children and adolescents are less likely to engage in physical activity and will choose inactivity if they are not enjoying the physical activity. A healthy level of physical activity requires regular participation in activities that increase energy expenditure above resting levels. An active child participates in physical education classes, plays sports, performs regular household chores, spends recreational time outdoors, and regularly travels by foot, bicycle, or roller blades. Opportunities for physical activity should be fun, increase confidence in participation in physical activity, and involve friends and peers. Positive role models for physical activity include parents and teachers.

If children and adolescents are supposed to be able to carry out only everyday tasks with vigor and alertness and without undue fatigue, then for too many of them there is no need for physical activity because their everyday tasks do not require much energy. With the increase in television watching, computer use, and playing computer and video games, more and more children and adolescents are engaging in more sedentary practices. The lack of participation in physical activity by the youth of the United States is a national concern. It is imperative that this concern be addressed by the families, schools, and communities in the United States.

As a teacher, you can help alleviate this problem with your students by modeling a physically active lifestyle, helping them understand the importance of being physically active, and encouraging them to participate every day in physical activity that they enjoy.

Program Organization

Content Areas	Kindergarten	Grade 1	Grade 2
Emotional, Intellectual, and Social Health	1 All About Me	1 Me and My Feelings	1 My Feelings
Family Life, Growth, and Development	2 Growing and Learning	2 My Senses Help Me Grow	2 My Family
Personal Health and Physical Fitness	3 Caring For My Teeth 4 Staying Fit and Healthy	3 My Teeth 4 Taking Care of My Body	3 Caring for My Teeth 4 Keeping Fit and Healthy
Nutrition	5 Food for Health	5 Wonderful Food	5 Food for Fitness
Disease Prevention and Control	6 Staying Well	6 Staying Well	6 Staying Well
Drug Use Prevention	7 Medicines Help– Drugs Hurt	7 About Medicines and Drugs	7 Medicines and Drugs
Injury Prevention	8 Keeping Safe	8 Being Safe	8 Staying Safe
Community and Environmental Health	9 A Healthy Community	9 Keeping My Neighborhood Healthy	9 Caring for My Neighborhood

Integrated content areas: human body systems, consumer health

Grade 3	Grade 4	Grade 5	Grade 6
1 About Myself and Others	1 Your Needs and Feelings	1 Dealing with Feelings	1 Setting Goals
2 Me and My Family	2 Living and Growing	2 Growth and Development	2 Patterns of Growth
3 Keeping My Body Fit	3 Your Health and Fitness	3 Keeping Fit and Healthy	3 Health and Fitness
4 Food for a Healthy Body	4 Food and Your Health	4 Foods for Good Nutrition	4 Preparing Healthful Foods
5 Preventing Disease	5 Guarding Against Disease	5 Learning About Disease	5 Controlling Disease
6 Medicines and Other Drugs	6 Medicines, Drugs, and Your Health	6 Legal and Illegal Drugs	6 Drugs and Health
7 Avoiding Alcohol and Tobacco	7 Harmful Effects of Alcohol and Tobacco	7 About Tobacco and Alcohol	7 Tobacco and Alcohol
8 Keeping Safe	8 Staying Safe	8 Planning for Safety	8 Safety and First Aid
9 Health in the Community	9 Living in a Healthful Community	9 Working for a Healthful Community	9 Community Health

Scope and Sequence

Emotional, Intellectual, and Social Health

Grade K	Grade 1	Grade 2	Grade 3
• Identify what makes each child special and unique. • Identify feelings. • Recognize that everyone has feelings. • Recognize that feelings can change and that people have ways of changing how they feel. • Demonstrate ways to cooperate with and respect each other. • Explain how to resolve and avoid conflicts.	• Recognize what it means to be special. • Identify some ways people are special. • Recognize that all people have feelings. • Identify different kinds of feelings. • Recognize that feelings may be expressed without words. • Identify ways to show feelings. • Recognize that all people feel angry sometimes. • Identify ways to feel better when angry. • Identify ways to cope with and manage stress. • Apply stress management skills to new situations. • Recognize the importance of respect in getting along with others. • Discuss ways to show respect in speech, touch, and actions. • Recognize the value of having friends. • Identify ways to be a friend and to make new friends.	• Recognize that each person is unique. • Identify qualities that make people special. • Recognize that everyone experiences many different feelings. • Practice ways to deal with angry feelings. • Recognize that everyone feels worried or afraid at times. • Recognize the need to communicate feelings of worry or fear to someone who can help. • Identify ways to cope with or manage stress. • Apply stress management skills to a personal situation. • Differentiate between mistakes and deliberate wrong actions. • Recognize the importance of learning from mistakes and apologizing when harm, even unintentional, is caused. • Explain what it means to show respect and to be polite. • Identify ways to show respect in actions, words, and touch. • Recognize the importance of having friends. • Identify ways to make new friends.	• Recognize the importance of respecting and taking care of oneself. • Describe ways to exhibit responsible behavior. • Recognize that feelings are expressed by words, actions, and body language. • Identify effective ways to change or cope with unpleasant feelings. • List situations involving fear that require immediate help from a trusted adult. • Identify effective strategies for dealing with fear, stress, anger, and grief. • Identify ways to manage stress. • Apply stress-management skills to situations at school. • Describe practical methods for establishing and building healthful relationships. • Recognize the importance of standing up for personal values when faced with negative peer pressure. • Recognize that effective communication skills include both speaking and listening skills. • Realize the importance of compassion, kindness, apology, and forgiveness. • Identify strategies for resolving conflicts. • Use negotiation to resolve conflicts with friends and peers.

Family Life, Growth, and Development

Grade K	Grade 1	Grade 2	Grade 3
• Describe how the body changes as you grow. • Identify major external body parts. • Identify spine, lungs, stomach, brain, heart, and bones, and tell what each organ does. • Identify the five senses and tell what they do. • Identify ways to keep the senses safe. • Identify how the senses help keep people safe. • Describe what it means to be responsible. • Identify ways to be responsible.	• Explain the difference between living and nonliving things. • Classify things as living or nonliving. • Identify the five senses (sight, hearing, smell, taste, touch). • Identify the body parts that gather information from each sense. • Describe ways in which people use their senses. • Recognize that living things grow. • Describe ways in which people grow. • Recognize what a family is. • Identify ways family members show love for other family members. • Identify polite actions. • Recognize the importance of being polite to family members. • Identify skills for resolving conflicts. • Apply conflict resolution skills to family situations. • Name things families can do together.	• Recognize that all people grow physically. • Identify stages of human growth. • Identify the five senses. • Recognize the role of the senses in growth, learning, and safety. • Recognize that learning is another way of growing. • Determine what it means to be responsible. • Recognize that people have families. • Identify ways families help people grow. • Recognize that every family member is responsible for helping other family members. • Identify ways to help at home. • Identify ways to get along with family members. • Recognize ways of showing love for family members. • Identify skills to resolve conflicts. • Apply conflict-resolution skills to family situations. • Recognize that family members teach one another. • Recognize that each family has its own rules and customs.	• Describe different kinds of families and the basic needs that families of all kinds attempt to meet. • Describe ways family members can work and play together. • Describe some of the big changes that can affect the members of a family. • Identify ways that family members can help each other when big changes happen. • Identify communication skills. • Use communication skills to get along with family members. • Describe each stage of the human life cycle. • Compare the four stages of the human life cycle. • Describe how growth occurs. • Compare kinds of cells and how they are designed to do special jobs. • Describe one kind of growth in addition to physical growth and the changes that occur as a result. • Identify ways to care for your body.

Scope and Sequence Continued

Personal Health and Physical Fitness

Grade K	Grade 1	Grade 2	Grade 3
• Describe two different types of teeth and explain their functions. • Demonstrate the proper way to brush teeth. • Explain how to floss teeth. • Describe situations that are safe or harmful for teeth. • Identify foods that are healthful or unhealthful for teeth.	• Describe the basic functions of teeth. • Differentiate between teeth used for biting and teeth used for chewing. • Explain that people have two sets of teeth during their lives. • Recognize the process of losing baby teeth. • Recognize the importance of keeping teeth clean to maintain dental health. • Demonstrate awareness of proper brushing technique. • Recognize the importance of flossing to maintain dental health. • Demonstrate awareness of proper flossing techniques (with adult assistance). • Review the proper function of teeth. • Explain safe alternatives to behaviors that are unsafe and damaging to teeth. • Identify steps for making decisions. • Apply the decision-making process to choices about caring for teeth. • Recognize the importance of regular dental care. • Identify what a dentist does. • Identify what a dental hygienist does. • Identify the parts, functions, and purpose of the eye, ear, skeleton, and digestive, circulatory, respiratory, muscular, and nervous systems.	• Identify the parts of the tooth. • Explain why children lose teeth. • Differentiate between primary and permanent teeth. • Recognize the importance of brushing and flossing. • Demonstrate proper brushing and flossing techniques. • Describe foods that build strong teeth—or keep teeth healthy. • Identify decision-making steps. • Use decision-making skills to make decisions about tooth care. • Identify the services provided by dentists and dental hygienists. • Explain how cavities are formed and repaired. • Identify the parts, functions, and purpose of the eye and ear and of the skeletal, digestive, circulatory, respiratory, muscular, and nervous systems. • Recognize that germs cause illness. • Identify ways to fight germs by keeping clean. • Explain that the sun's rays can cause sunburn. • Identify how to protect the skin from sunburn. • Recognize the value of the sense of sight. • Identify ways to care for and protect the eyes.	• Identify the parts and functions of the body's sense organs, skeletal, muscular, digestive, circulatory, respiratory, and nervous systems. • Explain how and why to keep skin clean. • Explain how and why to protect skin and eyes from the sun. • Explain how plaque can lead to cavities and loss of teeth. • Describe and demonstrate how to brush and floss correctly. • Explain how to protect teeth from injury. • Explain how the parts of the ear function. • Describe how to take good care of the ears and the nose. • Describe different ways exercise helps the body. • Explain how and why to get aerobic exercise. • Explain why sleep is helpful. • Identify goal-setting steps. • Practice goal-setting steps to get enough rest. • Explain how to use safety gear, warm-ups, cool-downs, and water to stay safe during exercise. • Describe what to do in case of injury.

Personal Health and Physical Fitness

Grade K	Grade 1	Grade 2	Grade 3
	• Explain how staying clean helps fight germs. • List five ways to stay clean. • Identify sunburn. • List ways to protect the skin from sunburn. • Identify benefits of good posture. • Demonstrate good posture when standing, walking, and sitting. • List three things exercise does for the body. • Recognize daily activities as forms of exercise. • Identify exercise as a way to manage stress. • Apply stress management skills. • Identify ways to stay safe during play and exercise. • Explain the importance of stretching before and after exercise. • List four things sleep does for the body.	• Recognize the importance of the sense of hearing. • Identify ways to care for and protect the ears. • Explain the effects of exercise on the body. • Identify ways to exercise. • Identify ways to exercise safely. • Identify exercise as a way to manage stress. • Apply stress-management skills in stressful situations. • Explain the effects of sleep on the body.	

Scope and Sequence Continued

Nutrition

Grade K	Grade 1	Grade 2	Grade 3
• Identify ways to protect and care for skin. • Explain why cleanliness is important. • Describe good posture. • Explain why good posture is important. • Describe what it means to exercise safely. • Identify a warm-up, workout, and cool-down. • Describe how stress feels. • Identify ways to manage stress. • Identify signs of sleepiness. • Recognize that sleep and rest are necessary for good health.	• List three ways the body uses food. • Define energy and give examples of ways the body uses energy. • Identify the food groups on the Food Guide Pyramid. • Compare how much of the pyramid each group takes up. • Name examples of foods from each food group. • Identify a preferred food from each food group. • Discuss the advantages of trying a variety of foods. • Consider how the senses are involved in making food choices. • Identify breakfast, lunch, and dinner as meals many people eat each day. • Recognize the importance of eating breakfast to start the day. • Identify the steps in the decision-making process. • Apply the decision-making process to making healthful food choices. • Identify healthful snacks. • Explain that healthful snacks are low in fat, salt, and sugar. • Discuss the purpose of television food advertisements. • Evaluate the claims of food advertisements.	• Define energy. • Identify ways the body uses energy from food. • Identify the food groups on the Food Guide Pyramid. • Compare recommended servings for the food groups. • Recognize that the body needs water as well as food to stay healthy. • Identify ways to get the necessary amount of water each day. • Identify healthful choices for lunch. • Identify foods high in fat, salt, or sugar as those to be eaten sparingly. • Identify food shopping as a time to make healthful choices. • Explain how to check the ingredients list for nutritional content. • Identify steps for making decisions. • Use decision-making steps to choose healthful snacks. • Identify ways to avoid taking germs into the body at mealtimes.	• Identify healthful food choices. • Explain why eating healthful foods is important to good health. • Describe where food comes from. • Explain how to use the Food Guide Pyramid to plan a healthful diet. • Describe how people get the water they need to stay healthy. • Explain why food is needed at regular intervals. • Describe how to choose healthful snacks. • Identify steps for making decisions. • Use the decision-making steps to make healthful snacks choices. • Define ingredients and tell how to use labels to choose foods with the most nutritious ingredients. • Explain why a food's price varies. • Explain why it is important to store foods properly. • Describe ways to handle foods safely.

Disease Prevention and Control

Grade K	Grade 1	Grade 2	Grade 3
• Recognize that the body needs food for energy. • Identify food groups. • Explain why the food groups are arranged in a pyramid. • Identify healthful snacks. • Demonstrate ways to be safe when eating. • Identify ways to handle food safely. • Describe what it feels like to be ill. • Identify symptoms of illness. • Describe ways to keep disease from spreading. • Describe ways to stay well.	• Explain what it means to be ill. • Develop awareness of signs of illness. • Identify steps for communicating. • Apply communication skills in times of illness. • Identify germs as a cause of disease. • List ways to limit the spread of germs. • Identify colds as a common childhood illness. • Demonstrate awareness of the signs of a cold. • Explain what vaccines are. • Recognize the importance of vaccines in preventing disease. • Identify what an allergy is. • Recognize common allergens and allergy symptoms. • Identify ways to stay healthy.	• Define illness and disease. • Describe signs of illness. • Identify communication skills. • Apply communication skills to talking about illness. • Name ways to avoid spreading germs and illness. • Identify two diseases spread by germs. • Define vaccines and explain their purpose. • Identify diseases that can be prevented by vaccines. • Describe symptoms of head lice. • Identify ways to prevent transmission of head lice. • Define asthma and allergies. • Distinguish between asthma or an allergic reaction and the presence of a communicable disease. • Name people who help you stay well. • Identify habits and practices that help you stay well.	• Define symptom and disease, and list some common symptoms of disease. • Explain what a disability is, and discuss how to treat a person with a disability. • Define infectious disease. • Compare and contrast bacteria and viruses. • List some infectious diseases and their symptoms. • Explain two ways a person can become immune to a disease. • Define medicine, and explain the importance of taking all medicines only as directed. • Define noninfectious diseases, and list three examples. • Compare and contrast allergies and asthma. • Explain what happens to sugar in a person with diabetes. • Explain how a healthful lifestyle reduces a person's chances of getting certain diseases. • Identify ways to manage stress. • Apply stress-management skills to help control disease.

Scope and Sequence Continued

Drug Use Prevention

Grade K	Grade 1	Grade 2	Grade 3
• Describe why medicines are used. • Identify different forms of medicines. • Describe how to take medicines safely. • Use refusal skills to say no to drugs. • Recognize that tobacco and tobacco smoke harm the body. • Use refusal skills to say no to tobacco products.	• Explain what medicines are. • Recognize when medicines are given. • Explain why children should never take medicines on their own. • Identify people who can help children with medicine. • Identify some common drugs. • Recognize that some drugs are legal for adults but are still unsafe for children and unhealthful for everyone. • Explain the harmful effects of caffeine. • Identify the harmful effects of tobacco and tobacco smoke. • Recognize that tobacco use is habit-forming. • Identify the harmful effects of alcohol. • Distinguish between medicinal use of alcohol and drinking alcohol. • Explain what it means to refuse. • Demonstrate techniques for refusing and avoiding drugs. • Identify skills for refusal. • Apply refusal skills to say no to unsafe use of medicines and use of drugs.	• Explain what medicines are. • Tell what medicines do. • Explain how medicines can be used safely. • Recognize that children should never use medicines on their own. • Identify drugs as substances that change how the body works. • Distinguish between medicines and other drugs. • Describe the effects of caffeine on the body. • Identify foods and drinks that contain caffeine. • Recognize that tobacco products contain nicotine. • Explain how tobacco use and exposure to tobacco smoke harm the body. • Identify the harmful effects of alcohol on the body. • Recognize that drinking and driving is dangerous and illegal. • Recognize the need to practice refusing drugs. • Name other strategies for avoiding drugs. • Identify ways to make refusals. • Use refusal skills to refuse alcohol and tobacco.	• Explain what drugs are. • Distinguish between drugs that help the body and drugs that harm the body. • Differentiate between OTC medicines and prescription medicines. • Describe ways medicines can help people and how medicines are taken or applied. • Understand that medicines can be helpful only if they are used correctly. • List the rules for using medicines safely. • Explain what caffeine is and what it does to the body. • Suggest ways to avoid foods and drinks with caffeine. • List the dangerous physical effects of using inhalants, marijuana, or cocaine, and tell why these drugs should be avoided. • Describe how to avoid breathing inhalants. • Emphasize the importance of saying no to drugs. • Suggest ways to avoid dangerous drugs. • Identify refusal skills. • Use refusal skills to say no to drug use. • Describe the harmful effects of nicotine and alcohol on the body. • Identify products that contain tobacco or alcohol.

Drug Use Prevention

Grade K	Grade 1	Grade 2	Grade 3
			• Identify the effects of tobacco on specific human body parts. • Describe the hazards of environmental tobacco smoke. • Describe some effects of alcohol on specific body organs and on behavior. • Identify safety risks associated with alcohol use. • Describe some laws regarding the sale, use, and packaging of alcohol and tobacco products. • Explain reasons for refusing and demonstrate ways to refuse tobacco and alcohol. • Identify skills for refusals. • Use refusal skills to say no to alcohol and tobacco.

Scope and Sequence Continued

Injury Prevention

Grade K	Grade 1	Grade 2	Grade 3
• Identify ways to stay safe when crossing streets or playing. • Identify steps to stay safe. • Explain how to use steps to stay safe. • Explain the dangers of poisons. • Recognize that anything may be a poison if used unsafely. • Recognize how fires start. • Identify ways to prevent fires. • Describe a fire safety plan. • Demonstrate how to stop, drop, and roll in case of fire. • Demonstrate how to stay low when escaping from a fire. • Describe safe ways to behave near or in water. • Explain why it is not safe to pick up anything lying on the street or sidewalk. • Explain ways to stay safe when riding in vehicles.	• Explain safe techniques for crossing streets. • Recognize the importance of wearing safety belts. • Explain safe practices for riding in a car. • Identify common household hazards. • Explain techniques for recognizing and responding to an emergency. • Identify common fire hazards. • Explain how to react in a fire emergency. • Review skills for refusal. • Apply refusal skills to maintain personal safety. • Identify common safety problems at school. • Explain safe techniques for using playground equipment. • Explain what it means to take responsibility for safety. • Explain safe techniques for riding a bus. • Describe what a stranger is. • Explain techniques for avoiding danger when dealing with strangers.	• Explain the importance of being prepared for emergencies. • Identify steps in home fire-preparedness. • Demonstrate the stop, drop, and roll procedure. • Identify strangers. • Explain steps for avoiding danger with strangers. • Recognize the role of rules in maintaining safety. • Identify rules for staying safe in school and on the playground. • Identify ways to resolve conflicts. • Apply conflict-resolution skills to reduce risk of injury. • Explain how to cross streets safely. • Recognize responsibility for safety in a car. • Identify ways to stay safe while riding in a car. • Identify ways to stay safe while riding a bike. • Recognize the importance of wearing safety gear. • Identify ways to stay safe while skating, skateboarding, or riding a scooter. • Identify ways to stay safe around animals. • Explain the appropriate steps in treating an animal bite. • Define first aid and tell when it is needed. • Identify first-aid measures for a cut.	• Recognize that there are people who are responsible for keeping children safe. • Practice safety rules on the way to and from school and at school. • Describe how to stay safe around strangers. • Explain how to avoid conflicts and get along with bullies. • Identify steps to resolve conflicts. • Use negotiation to handle conflicts with friends. • Make a home fire escape plan. • Describe how to safely escape a home fire. • List safety rules for using electricity and household products. • Identify safety gear. • Explain safety rules for bicycling. • Know what features to look for when purchasing a helmet. • Identify steps to make decisions. • Use decision-making steps to stay safe. • Learn how to get emergency assistance when someone has been injured or accidentally poisoned. • Describe first aid for cuts, scrapes, insect bites, and stings.

Community and Environmental Health

Grade K	Grade 1	Grade 2	Grade 3
• Define community. • Identify community health and safety workers and their roles. • Explain the importance of regular medical and dental checkups. • Recognize that the environment is everything around us. • Identify ways to recycle or reuse a variety of items. • Explain that recycling or reusing items are two ways of reducing the amount of trash.	• Explain the meaning of community. • Discuss the roles of various community health and safety workers. • Explain what nurses do. • Identify places where nurses work, with emphasis on clinics and schools. • Explain the work of a doctor. • Distinguish between general practitioners and specialists. • Recognize that garbage poses a health risk to a community. • Identify the role of sanitation workers in maintaining public health. • Define litter. • Identify responsible ways to dispose of trash and avoid litter. • Identify steps for making decisions. • Apply the decision-making steps to choices about disposing of trash. • Recognize the benefits of recycling. • Demonstrate how ordinary objects can be reused.	• Explain how a hospital serves a community. • Describe what happens when you stay in a hospital. • Identify some of the people who work in a community hospital. • Describe how trash is collected. • Explain that communities dispose of trash in landfills or by burning. • Recognize that trash can pose health problems for a community. • Explain recycling. • Identify ways to reduce trash by reusing and recycling. • Review steps of making decisions. • Apply decision-making skills to responsible use of resources. • Explain why clean water is necessary for life and health. • Explain ways that people can fight water pollution. • Explain why clean air is necessary for life and health. • Identify ways that people can fight air pollution.	• Define community. • Explain some of the responsibilities of people who work to promote public health. • Compare and contrast hospitals and clinics. • Define pollution. • List several sources of air pollution. • Explain how noise pollution can be harmful to humans. • List several sources of water pollution. • Describe how water is treated so that it is safe for human consumption. • Explain how groundwater becomes polluted. • Identify steps in the goal-setting process. • Use goal-setting skills to protect the environment. • Discuss how to prevent litter from becoming an unsightly part of the community. • List ways to reduce, reuse, and recycle.